By Faith
ISAAC

ELSA HENDERSON

Copyright © 2023 Elsa Henderson.
Second Edition

All rights reserved. No part of this book may be reproduced, stored, or transmitted by any means—whether auditory, graphic, mechanical, or electronic—without written permission of both publisher and author, except in the case of brief excerpts used in critical articles and reviews. Unauthorized reproduction of any part of this work is illegal and is punishable by law.

"Scripture quotations taken from the Amplified® Bible, Copyright © 1954, 1958, 1962, 1964, 1965, 1987 by The Lockman Foundation Used by permission." (www.Lockman.org)

All Scriptures taken from NIV unless otherwise noted. THE HOLY BIBLE, NEW INTERNATIONAL VERSION®, NIV® Copyright © 1973, 1978, 1984, 2011 by Biblica, Inc.® Used by permission. All rights reserved worldwide.

ISBN: 979-8-89031-803-9 (sc)
ISBN: 979-8-89031-804-6 (hc)
ISBN: 979-8-89031-805-3 (e)

Because of the dynamic nature of the Internet, any web addresses or links contained in this book may have changed since publication and may no longer be valid. The views expressed in this work are solely those of the author and do not necessarily reflect the views of the publisher, and the publisher hereby disclaims any responsibility for them.

One Galleria Blvd., Suite 1900, Metairie, LA 70001
(504) 702-6708

To my grandchildren

Jaseff, Aaron and Nathan
Joel and Tyler
Isaac, Bethany and Graeme
Becky and Richelle

I have prayed
that I will leave you
a spiritual legacy.

Contents

Endorsements vii
Acknowledgements ix
Preface xi
Faith Hall of Fame xiii
God's Faith Hall of Fame xv

Part One
Abraham's Faith Journey

Chapter 1   Abram Hears God's Voice 3
Chapter 2   Abram Leaves Haran 27
Chapter 3   Detour to Egypt 41
Chapter 4   Abram Separates from Lot 54
Chapter 5   Abram Rescues Lot 66
Chapter 6   The Covenant Promise 81
Chapter 7   "Helping Yahweh" 91
Chapter 8   The Covenant Sign 101
Chapter 9   Sarah Laughs in Unbelief 109
Chapter 10   Bold Enough to Bargain 113
Chapter 11   Another Faith Detour 117
Chapter 12   Living Water 131
Chapter 13   Child of Promise 137
Chapter 14   Ishmael Has To Go 140
Chapter 15   Abimelech and Beersheba 148
Chapter 16   Planting a Faith Garden 156

Part Two
Isaac's Faith Journey

Chapter 17 Son of the Commandment 167
Chapter 18 The Death of Sarah 182
Chapter 19 Lot Pays a Visit 189
Chapter 20 Lessons from Lot 211
Chapter 21 A Wife for Isaac 218
Chapter 22 Yahweh Speaks to Rebekah....................................... 240
Chapter 23 Twins!... 247
Chapter 24 The Death of Abraham... 254
Chapter 25 Friction Over the Firstborn 260
Chapter 26 Signs of Rebellion 266
Chapter 27 Jacob Buys the Birthright.. 278
Chapter 28 Isaac Hears God's Voice 284
Chapter 29 Isaac's Failure of Faith... 288
Chapter 30 The Rebel 297
Chapter 31 Esau Shows His True Colors 302
Chapter 32 By Faith Isaac 312
Chapter 33 The Fear of Isaac 319
Chapter 34 Jacob Leaves Home... 324
Chapter 35 Esau Takes a Third Wife 328
Chapter 36 Faith That Fears 333
Chapter 37 Faith That Rests 339

Study Guide... 341
Bibliography... 357

Endorsements

"By Faith Isaac is an intriguing and riveting novel which portrays the dynamic Old Testament story of the patriarch Isaac, his walk of faith, and his relationship with Yahweh his GOD. Was this reason enough for GOD to include him in the Bible's Great Hall of Fame recorded in Hebrews? Elsa Henderson's amazing innovative and creative competence will keep you turning pages until you discover why."

—Dr Jean Barsness,
missions consultant and professor of global studies
conference speaker and author

"It is one thing to know the facts of a scenario, it is quite another to read a creative and imaginative interpretation of those facts. Elsa Henderson has brought the account of Abraham and Isaac to life in a way that is fresh, scintillating, and captivating. The reader will never view these two biblical giants the same way again. I strongly endorse this unique book."

—Gordon Elhard
founding member, Centre Street Church, Calgary, Canada
retired school principal and superintendent

Acknowledgements

To my mother, Elsie McElheran Bromley, a master storyteller, who taught me to love the Bible before I could read by telling its stories so vividly. To this very day my favorite books are biblical novels.

To my father, Percy Bromley, who taught by example the discipline of research and the importance of accuracy. From him I learned to pick up New Testament clues to Old Testament stories.

To my husband, Roy Henderson, the first editor of everything I write.

To my aunt Pearl McElheran, who gives me much-needed criticism. At times we agree to disagree.

To Jack Scrivens, a new old friend, who has encouraged me along the way.

Above all, to my heavenly Father, who instilled in me a love of puzzles. I love finding little bits and pieces scattered throughout the Bible that shed light on a story I am studying. I love putting the pieces together. If there be any glory or any praise, let it all be to Him.

Preface

"I will not let you go unless you bless me."

Those were the words that came to me as I stood at the front of the church.

It was February 2006. I was attending a Blackaby conference at Centre Street Church in which Richard Blackaby and his father Henry had challenged us to spend quality time in God's Word. When Richard Blackaby gave the altar call, I wanted to go forward, but none of the reasons he listed applied to me. Finally he said, "Some of you want to go forward, but you don't know why."

That was me! I went.

"I will not let you go unless you bless me," I told the Lord. That was my heart's desire—to hang onto God until He blessed me. I resolved to spend quality time in God's Word.

The next morning I awoke an hour and a half earlier than usual and got up to study God's Word before breakfast, a pattern I have followed ever since.

I began my study with the story of Jacob wrestling with God in Genesis 32, taking notes as I studied. And God blessed me. I learned so much! In time my notes began to come out in story form.

What is this? I wondered. *If God is teaching me this way, I will pursue it.*

My study led me to Hebrews 11:20: "By faith Isaac blessed Jacob and Esau in regard to their future." What?! Isaac made it into the Bible's great Faith Hall of Fame for merely speaking a blessing? How much faith does it take to do that? How does blessing his sons rank with Noah's building the ark or Abraham's leaving his country?!

By Faith Isaac became the title of my story even before I knew the answer to the questions.

In May 2006 I jumped at the opportunity to travel to Israel with a tour group led by Pastor Henry Schorr. Being in Israel gave me a visual perspective for the story of Abraham, Isaac and Jacob, and enabled me to fill in details of the Bible story I was writing.

After the Israel trip I went back to writing *By Faith Isaac*. Some days I surrounded myself with reference books—Bible, concordance, Bible dictionary, commentary. Sometimes I just sat at the computer with my Bible open and typed as I imagined the story unfolding. Sometimes I had to stop writing the story in order to research something on the internet.

Through the whole writing process God blessed me.

I would like you to share those blessings by reading my book. I would also challenge you to spend quality time in God's Word. I challenge you also to hang on to God with a vice-like grip as Jacob did, and say, "I will not let you go unless you bless me."

And He will. Believe me, He will.

Elsa Henderson
July 2013

Faith Hall of Fame

"Without faith," the Bible says, "it is impossible to please God, because anyone who comes to him must believe that he exists and that he rewards those who earnestly seek him" (Hebrews 11:6).

Hebrews chapter 11 names outstanding members of the great Faith Hall of Fame and cites them for the acts in their lives which required the greatest leap of faith.

The first one mentioned is Abel. What was his great leap of faith?

Abel was the first man born into a sin-cursed world to offer a blood sacrifice for his sins. His brother Cain did it his own way rather than God's way, and God did not look favorably on his offering. Why is Abel mentioned first, and not Adam?

Abel was the first person born by human conception rather than direct creation. Whereas Adam at first lived in the Garden of Eden, Abel was not born into a perfect environment. We can argue that Adam was different from us in some ways. Abel was not. Furthermore, Adam did not make the first blood sacrifice—God did. (Adam must have made many such sacrifices subsequently.)

The second name in the Faith Hall of Fame is Enoch. His entire life was such a consistent walk of faith that God decided to skip the physical death process and take him directly to Heaven.

Third, Noah's great faith act was building the ark. He believed God's prophecy that judgment was coming in the form of a flood.

Fourth, Abraham was cited for no less than four acts of faith.

By faith Abraham launched out into the unknown. He obeyed God's call to leave his country, his people and his father's household and go to a land God would show him. And Abraham went, even though he did not know where he was going.

By faith Abraham lived with insecurity. He lived like a stranger in a foreign country, and he lived in tents, moving from place to place.

By faith Abraham believed God for the impossible—that he and Sarah could become parents even though he at 99 was past age, and Sarah at 89 was, and always had been, barren.

Abraham's greatest leap of faith was to believe God in the face of contradiction. God had promised, "It is through Isaac that your offspring will be reckoned," yet God asked Abraham to sacrifice Isaac! Abraham reasoned something no human being up to that time had ever experienced or witnessed—that God could raise Isaac from the dead. Science fiction before its time!

Next in the Faith Hall of Fame is Isaac. "By faith Isaac blessed Jacob and Esau in regard to their future."

Merely speaking a blessing?! How does this act rate alongside Noah's building the ark and Abraham's great acts of faith?

"And thereby," as Shakespeare would say, "hangs a tale."[1]

---

[1] William Shakespeare, *As You Like It*, 1600. xiv

God's Faith Hall of Fame

Hebrews 11

Name	Believed God for:	Act of Faith
Abel	Salvation	Offered a blood sacrifice for sin.
Enoch	Daily living	Walked with God.
Noah	Coming judgment	Built the ark.
Abraham	Facing the unknown	Left Ur, not knowing where he was going.
Abraham	Living with insecurity	Lived like a stranger, in tents, moving from place to place.
Abraham & Sarah	The impossible	Believed God for a child in spite of barrenness and old age.
Abraham	Contradiction (God's command and His promise seemed mutually exclusive) Isaac	Sacrificed Isaac, the son of promise.
Isaac	??? Why is faith needed to speak a blessing?	Blessed Jacob and Esau in regard to their future.

PART ONE

Abraham's Faith Journey

1

Abram Hears God's Voice

"Tell me, please, Father," Isaac pleaded, "tell me again about hearing the voice of Yahweh. When was the first time you heard his voice?"

Thirteen-year-old Isaac had heard the story many times before, but he never tired of hearing it, and Abraham never tired of telling it.

"I was living in Ur in the province of Chaldea. My brother Haran had died, my father was planning to go to Canaan so I thought I would never see him again, and the physician had just confirmed that my wife was barren. I was grieving and depressed when something amazing happened to me."

"What happened?" asked Isaac as if he was hearing the story for the first time.

"The God of glory appeared to me."

"What do you mean, 'the God of glory'?"

"I don't know how else to describe him," Abraham said. "I knew it was Yahweh, the one my forefathers had told me about. Yahweh had walked and talked with Adam and Eve in the Garden of Eden. Later he had walked with Enoch and talked with Noah. It couldn't be the moon god of Ur. He never walked or talked with anybody. He never did anything.

"Then one evening I was sitting alone on the roof of my house watching the sun set and the darkness close in and thinking about Yahweh. Suddenly I was aware of a bright light. At first I thought I had fallen asleep and it was morning. But I was still facing west, not the rising sun.

"As I watched, the light began to move, and I became aware of a presence inside the light. I watched in wonder at the beauty of the sight. Instinctively I was aware of Yahweh's rank, high above all the nations he had made. My heart welled up with praise, and I began to whisper his name in awe.

"Then he spoke."

"What did he sound like?" Isaac asked.

"His voice was rich and powerful—more compelling than any voice I had ever heard."

"And you knew it was Yahweh."

"Yes. It had to be. It had to be the voice Noah had heard. No one had heard Yahweh's voice for hundreds of years," Abraham continued, "at least not that I knew about."

"What did he say?"

"'Leave your country and your people,' God said, 'and go to the land I will show you.'"[2]

Isaac's eyes were shining. "Yahweh spoke to you. Wow!"

Isaac paused to grasp the wonder of it.

"Did he say anything else?"

"No. That was all. Then the light faded."

"Didn't he tell you to leave your father's household and promise to make you a great nation and promise to bless you?" Isaac asked.

"Not the first time he spoke," Abraham replied. "He said that later, when I was in Haran. This time I was still in Ur."

"Was it hard to obey Yahweh?" Isaac asked.

"Yes and no."

Isaac waited for his father to elaborate. He knew he couldn't rush the storyteller.

---

[2] Acts 7:3

"Leaving my country was the easy part. As you know, I was born in Ur in Chaldea, the country south and west of the Euphrates River near where it joins the Tigris before it flows into the Persian Gulf."

Isaac mentally followed a map his father had once drawn for him.

"My father Terah was a wanderer."

Abraham paused. "I suppose his parents suspected he would be a wanderer when they named him. Yahweh must have whispered into their hearts."

"Why do you say that, Father?"

"Because of the name they gave him. Terah means 'wandering'."

"Grandfather certainly lived up to his name," Isaac interjected.

"Yes, he certainly did," Abraham agreed. "He was born in northern Mesopotamia, the land between the two great rivers, Tigris and Euphrates. He was born northwest of Nineveh and directly north of Haran in the land of his forefathers Eber and Peleg. The Hittites, who were equal in power to the Babylonians, had a trade route through the land of Eber that ran east-west between the centre of the Hittite empire and Nineveh. From Nineveh they could continue on to Asshur, Babylon, Ur, the Persian Gulf and the ends of the earth. Father Terah wanted to see all the places he heard about.

"As a young lad he loved to visit Haran, the closest city on a major caravan route. Terah was fascinated with all things new and different. When he was old enough to leave home, he explored other places, other cultures, even other religions. His father Nahor—your great grandfather, not your uncle Nahor—wanted him to get married and settle down. But my father Terah never stayed in one place long enough to get married. With each trip he wandered farther away.

"Eventually he ended up in Ur, the sister city to Haran, and a city outstanding for its trade, wealth and culture. It was also famous as the centre of worship of the moon goddess, whose temple was atop an enormous step pyramid called a ziggurat.

"In many ways Ur was like Haran. It was on several trade routes, the major one being between the Persian Gulf and Babylon. Its culture was much like Haran's, and its people even worshipped the same moon god, though they called it by a different name.

"With all the connections he had made during his travels, Terah did well financially by establishing himself in trade and commerce. His business enabled him to pursue his interest in travel. In new places he found new and different goods which he could bring back and sell in Ur. The wealth he accumulated enabled him to build warehouses for his goods and to live in a large mansion with many servants. His traveling necessitated having soldiers or guards to watch over his warehouses in his absence.

"After living in Ur for a while, Terah announced that he was preparing to make a trip all the way to Canaan."

"I didn't know Grandfather ever was in Canaan."

"He wasn't. He had traveled mostly east of Haran. Now he wanted to see the western world. But he never got there."

"What happened?"

"Terah married my mother—your grandmother."

"And that ended his dream of going to Canaan?"

"Yes. Mother was no wanderer. She had no interest in travel. She insisted that Father stay in Ur and live in the big house he currently owned. He was well enough known now that traders sought him out. He didn't have to travel as much. Besides, it was not long until Mother was pregnant. They named their son Haran.

"Of all the places Father had visited on his travels, Haran was his favorite. He loved the city of Haran and the surrounding fertile plains between the Euphrates River and another large tributary. He still dreamed of traveling, but the best he could do for the time being was name his son after a city of his travels.

"Terah was a wanderer in another way, too. Not only did he wander the earth. He also wandered from Yahweh. His father Nahor had taught him about Yahweh, but Terah was only mildly interested—at least in his early life.

"Terah's curiosity about other religions developed into a hobby. In Haran he bought a couple of teraphim for himself and began acquiring other idols from other places. Gradually Terah himself became an idol worshipper. His interest in idols became a religion and then a vocation. He set up a workshop in his house and started making and selling idols.

His business was so lucrative that he expanded it and employed skilled artisans to make idols of wood, stone, silver and gold. Eventually he had so many idols, that he had to build a grand house to keep them in.

"The Chaldeans loved to worship idols—the more the better. Terah's wealth had made him a prominent citizen, but his house of idols brought him even more prestige and social rank. Terah's prestige and influence increased even more when he installed two giant idols of Ur's moon god Nannar and his consort Ningal. He declared twelve of the idols to be chief gods, one for each month of the year.

"Soon people from all over Ur and the surrounding area were flocking to Terah's house of idols to gaze at his amazing display of idols and to worship them. Terah obliged by officiating as high priest. He also sold incense, flowers, rice and other things to those who wanted to worship the idols and sacrifice to them, which added to his wealth.

"Eventually Terah forgot about Yahweh."

"Had Grandfather Terah ever heard Yahweh's voice?"

"No."

"Then how could he be expected to believe in Yahweh?"

"The same way you do, son. By learning from those who do believe.

"Terah's father Nahor knew Noah," Abraham continued.

"The one who built the ark?" Isaac asked.

"Yes. Noah knew Methuselah and Methuselah knew Adam. Their lives overlapped by more than a hundred years each. Noah was my grandfather's great, great, seven-times-great grandfather—the father of everybody on earth. Noah was well over nine hundred years old at the time and in surprisingly good condition for an old man. Though his body was weak, his voice was strong, like a man in his prime. Grandfather Nahor marveled at that. Noah's voice was strongest when he was talking about Yahweh. Nahor loved to visit Noah and learn about Yahweh. Noah died when Nahor was 27."

"How old was Noah?" Isaac asked.

"He was 950 years old."

"Wow," said Isaac. "I can't imagine that. Nobody lives to that age now."

"No," Abraham said. "And that will become part of my story about Terah. But first let me return to my grandfather Nahor. His father taught him about Yahweh, as had his father before him. Nahor loved to hear the stories about Yahweh and the Great Flood—stories passed down from those who had experienced it first hand.

"Nahor also spent a lot of time with Eber, his great-great grandfather. Eber was a young man when people in Babylon decided to make a name for themselves by building a tower. The people had learned to make bricks, which were far easier to build with than stone. Stone had to be cut into uniform blocks in order to be usable for tall buildings. That was tedious, backbreaking work. The builders also discovered that tar made a better seal than mortar.

"If they could build their cities upward rather than outward, they would not be scattered over the face of the whole earth—or so they thought. They would build a tower that would reach to the heavens.

"But Yahweh had other plans. He didn't want evil doers concentrated in one place and collaborating together to practice increasingly more evil deeds."

"I know what he did," Isaac interjected. "He confused their language."

Abraham smiled approvingly at his son.

"Yes." Abraham paused. "Come to think of it, there may have been a second reason for confusing their languages. Yahweh doesn't even want all the *good* people concentrated in one place. He wants them scattered throughout the earth. Like salt. To preserve the world from evil."

"So that's why he told you to leave your country?" Isaac asked.

"Quite likely, son. So I could be salt, and so he could teach me to live by faith. But that's another story.

"Suddenly the architects and planners of the tower in Babylon couldn't convey their instructions to the foremen. The foremen couldn't convey their instructions to the laborers. The builders couldn't understand the people working next to them. The project had to be abandoned. Babylon became known as Babel.

"Our forefather Eber was a young man when all this happened. His wife had just given birth to a son. They called him Peleg, 'division', because Yahweh divided the earth into countless language groups. Each language group wandered off in a different direction.

"Which brings me back to another wanderer—my father Terah. His chief interest was travel, and learning about other places and people and cultures. As I said earlier, other religions were fascinating to him. Though Terah lived in Ur far from his original home, he kept in touch with his relatives in the land of Eber by sending messages with the caravans that passed through Ur. When followers of Yahweh visited him, he went through the motions of following Yahweh. But mostly he worshiped the idols in his house of idols in Ur.

"Then something changed his thinking. People began to die 'young'—what people of those days considered young. Before the Great Flood most people lived to be 900 years old. Arphaxad, the first of Terah's ancestors born after the Flood died at the age of 465. Peleg, the first of our forefathers to be born after Yahweh confused people's languages at Babel, died at the age of 239—roughly half the age of Arphaxad. Then Terah's own father Nahor died at the age of 148. What was happening? Arphaxad at 465, Peleg at 239, and Nahor at 148 had all died of old age, not of disease or accidental causes.

"When death came to Terah's own family, he started looking for answers. He looked for the oldest and wisest person he could find. Upon making some enquiries, Terah discovered that the oldest person alive lived only a few days' journey east of Ur. Shem, Noah's son, lived in Susa in the land settled by Shem's son Elam.

"Terah went to visit Shem. He wanted to talk about death. 'How could my father Nahor die so young?' Terah asked.

"Shem didn't seem surprised. Before the Great Flood, he explained, men had routinely lived nine hundred years or more. Noah's own grandfather Methuselah lived to be 969 years old and died of old age a week before the flood. At the same time that Yahweh decided to send the flood, he also decided to limit man's days to 120 years."[3]

---

[3] See Genesis 6:3

"'A hundred and twenty years!' Terah said to Shem in surprise, 'I'll be 120 on my next birthday, and I'm in the prime of life!'

"'I know,' Shem said to Terah. 'Yahweh has not cut everybody off at the age of 120. I am 570 years old and not yet on my deathbed. But we are seeing the beginning of a shorter life span. Mark my words. You will soon see people dying of old age when they are only 120 years old.'"

"Shem was right, wasn't he, Father?" Isaac said.

"Yes, son," Abraham said. "The earlier people were born, the longer they lived.

Shem, who was born before the Flood, outlived many of his descendants. A few who were born before the dispersion are still alive—such as Eber and his father Shelah. But those born since have aged much more quickly. Most of them are fortunate if they live long enough to see their great grandchildren. Your own grandfather Terah did not live long enough to see you born."

"I hope you don't die at the age of 120, Father," Isaac said. "You are already 113."

"I have a feeling Yahweh will give me many more good years," Abraham replied.

"Yahweh once told me, 'Go, walk through the length and breadth of the land, for I am giving it to you.'[4] That's what I am doing, and I still have lots of walking to do."

"That's part of the Promise, isn't it, Father?" Isaac said.

"Yes, son. That's part of the Promise. But a promise does you no good unless you act on it. That's what faith is—acting on Yahweh's promise."

"I want to walk the land with you, Father."

"You will, son. We will walk it together. And as you walk, remember. Claim Yahweh's promise with every step. Walk in faith."

"I will, Father. I will."

"But we have wandered off topic," Abraham said. "Where were we?"

Isaac had to think for a minute.

"We got onto the topic of age because people started dying."

---

[4] Genesis 13:17

"Oh, yes." Abraham picked up his story. "After grandfather Nahor died, Terah visited Shem more regularly. Terah wanted to compare life after the flood with Shem's memories of life before the flood. But Shem kept coming back to the same topic—Yahweh. Shem talked as if he knew him personally. Terah listened politely and went through the motions of worshiping Yahweh when he was with Shem, but he didn't follow Yahweh with his heart.

"Within a year of grandfather Nahor's death, Terah had a second son. This time they named him closer to home—Nahor—after the grandfather he would never know.

"By the time Nahor was born, Haran was married and the father of a son. The baby was so tiny that they called him Lot. 'Pebble'. He reminded Haran of the little pebbles his friends used in casting lots. Haran himself never admitted to gambling!

"Ten years after brother Nahor, I was born. Father was 130, Mother was 90 and my brother Haran was 60. Haran's children, a son and two daughters, were more like my siblings than my nephew and nieces. When Mother died three years after I was born, Terah went back to Shem to ask for an explanation and took my brother Nahor and me with him.

"'Yahweh didn't guarantee that we would live to be 120,' Shem told Terah. 'He just set 120 as a rough maximum.'

"For the remainder of Shem's life, Terah visited him as often as he could. Father Terah almost always took me along. I was fascinated to learn details about the Flood from someone who had helped build the ark and had survived the Flood. From Shem I had pretty direct information about everything that happened since Creation! Soon I learned to love Yahweh the way Shem did, but Father still worshipped idols."

Abraham paused to remember the thread of their conversation.

"People were dying," Isaac prompted him.

"Oh, yes," Abraham remembered. "Mother had died when I was three and Nahor was 13. With two young sons to raise, Father Terah married again. My stepmother looked after us as if we were her own. When I was ten years old, my half sister was born."

"Father named her Sarai, meaning 'Yahweh is prince.' All Father's conversations with Shem had convinced him that Yahweh was in many ways superior to other gods. Father was willing to concede that Yahweh was a prince among gods, but not that he was the supreme God. Nor was he willing to acknowledge that Yahweh was the only true God. He believed some things that Shem and others had taught him about Yahweh, but he was still wandering spiritually. He still maintained his house of idols."

"I know that your half sister Sarai is now my mother Sarah," Isaac said. "How did that come about?"

Abraham paused, remembering.

"Growing up, I saw Sarai only as my sister. But when she began blossoming into a young woman, I began to see her differently. I had always been proud of her good looks as a child, but now she was a stunning beauty. I was attracted to her in more ways than one. But . . . ."

Abraham's voice trailed off.

"But you were concerned that she was too close a relative," guessed Isaac.

"Yes. Father noticed the attraction developing between us, and called me aside for a talk. 'I see the way you look at Sarai, Son,' he said. I knew what he was driving at.

"'But she's my *sister*,' I said."

"'Correction,' Father replied. 'She's your *half* sister. Almost everybody marries their first or second cousin. That assures that they have the same beliefs and values, and usually makes for a stronger marriage than marrying someone out of your culture. If you are concerned about too-close blood lines, remember that Sarai's mother was no blood relation to me whatsoever. That would make your blood ties to her no closer than if, as society expects, you married a cousin.'"

"That set me at ease," Abraham said to Isaac, "and we were married right away. 'You two don't need a betrothal period because you have known each other all your lives,' Father said. 'And seeing you already live under the same roof, the sooner you marry the better.' Sarai and I were married within the week. She was seventeen and I was 27."

Isaac changed the subject.

"You said Yahweh told you to name me Isaac?"

"Yes. Your name means 'laughter'. I laughed with delight at Yahweh's sense of humor. He loves to do the impossible. At an age when all fertile women are long barren, he made your mother, who had always been barren, fertile! She was eighty nine when Yahweh predicted your birth, and ninety when you were born!"

Isaac laughed together with his father.

"Your mother laughed, too, at Yahweh's prediction. She overheard the conversation between me and the three heavenly visitors, but she laughed in disbelief. When confronted, she tried to deny it, but Yahweh knows and sees everything. Such denial was pointless.

"But we both laughed with joy when we discovered she was pregnant. And we have laughed together many times since you were born. We laughed at your stumbling efforts to walk. Laughed at your funny ways of expressing yourself when you were learning to talk. Laughed with pleasure at watching you grow and develop. No parents enjoyed their child more than the two of us.

"And everyone who hears the story of your birth laughs with us. No one loves telling the story more than Sarah. 'Who would have said to Abraham,' she loves to say, 'that Sarah would nurse children? Yet I have borne him a son in his old age.'[5] *His* old age, she says, and everybody laughs, knowing that *hers* is the greater miracle!"

"So you are the only one of us not named by Yahweh," Isaac concluded.

"Oh, no. In my lifetime I have been known by three different names. My father named me Aram, meaning 'exalted'. I guess he had great expectations for me. After an incident in Ur, I became known as Abram. 'Exalted father'. But at the same time as Yahweh renamed Sarah, he gave me the name Abraham. 'Father of many' or 'father of a multitude.' The name change was part of Yahweh's Covenant with me."

"Why was your name changed in Ur?" Isaac asked.

"Changing a person's name is not uncommon," Abraham explained. "A name change indicates a significant happening in a person's life.

---

[5] Genesis 21:7

A man may rename his wife at the time of their marriage. Or a man may assume the title Abu when he becomes the father of his first son. Remember when our neighbor Nadal became Abu Nadal?"

Isaac nodded. "When his son was born. After having six girls!"

"Sometimes people assign the title as an expression of respect," Abraham continued. "That's what happened to me. Even as a child I knew that it was silly to worship the sun or the moon. I knew there had to be a God greater than the sun and the moon, who had created them and the whole world. By visiting my ancestor Shem, I learned that His name was Yahweh.

"It was even sillier to worship idols, which were created by man. I saw them being fashioned in my father's workshop! I hated Father's house of idols, and tried to convince him to abandon his idolatry. I hated it even more when Father put me in charge of his house of idols, to dust and polish and generally keep it in order. I hated the uselessness of caring for dead stone and wood. I shouldn't be doing this, I thought. I wanted to worship Yahweh. I talked to as many of the worshippers at Father's house of idols as I could and tried to convince them that their belief in idols was false and foolish. When they weren't convinced and when I thought I could get away with it, I chased Father's customers away.

"When Father decided to appoint me as salesman and groom me to take over his idol business, I could stand it no longer. In my frustration I took a big stick and swung all around me, knocking gods off their pedestals and breaking arms and heads. I whacked away at the largest idols, the moon god Nannar and his consort Ningal, but they were too big for my stick to make any impression. I dropped my stick and pounded away at Nannar with my fists, tears running down my face.

"Having vented my anger and frustration, I surveyed the damage and started to wonder how I could explain my actions to my father. Then I had an idea.

"Putting the stick in the hand of Ur's moon god, I ran to my father, crying: 'Abba, Abba, come quick! The gods are fighting among themselves!'

"Father came running. Surveying the chaos, he demanded, 'What happened?'

"I was ready with my answer. 'That big bully of a god took that stick and suddenly began hitting the smaller gods, saying they weren't doing what he told them. When other gods tried to stop him, he hit them too. What can I do?'

"'That's all a pack of lies,' Father replied angrily. 'Those gods are all dead, just wood and stone. They can't fight among themselves.'

"'Then, Abba,'" I said, 'why do you worship them and spend so much money sacrificing to them?'

"Father had no answer.[6] His anger faded. He smiled, than laughed out loud. I joined him in his laughter."

"What happened to the house of idols?" Isaac asked.

"It had to be closed for repairs. When I saw that Father had plans to re-open it, I began to argue with him. I think that is where Yahweh developed my powers of persuasion. If I could convince my father to abandon the worship of idols, I could convince almost anybody."

"I presume you won the argument," Isaac concluded.

"Yes," Abraham replied. "Terah the wanderer had finally stopped wandering spiritually. Father's house of gods never did re-open, and eventually it was torn down."

"How did the people of Ur react—the ones who worshiped at Grandfather's house of gods?" Isaac asked.

"When they came and found the idol house locked, and later demolished, they asked questions about what happened. That gave me great opportunities to try to convince them to abandon idol worship and worship the living God, Yahweh.

"I told them that there was only one God, the Creator of the universe, and that other gods were powerless to contribute anything to the happiness of men. Just as the idols have no power of their own to help others or even to defend themselves against attacks such as

---

[6] Author's note: This story was told to me by my father, Percy L. Bromley, who heard it long ago from a man who claimed his source was Josephus, the Jewish historian. More recently I discovered that this story exists with minor variations in the traditions of both Judaism and Islam.

mine, so the sun and moon and heavenly bodies have no power of their own. They are subservient to a Greater Power, who regulates their movements. The Creator—the One who commands the sun, moon and stars—is the One to whom alone we ought justly to offer honor and our thanksgiving."

"How did the citizens of Ur respond?" Isaac asked.

"On several occasions they raised a tumult against me, but many of them respected me, and some were convinced to follow Yahweh. They were the ones who changed my name. They respected me for standing up against the surrounding culture of idolatry. Out of respect they started calling me Ab Aram instead of Aram—'exalted father' instead of 'exalted'. That was soon shortened to Abram."

Isaac interrupted his father's story. "But your current name, Abraham, 'father of a multitude', doesn't fit. You are the biological father of only one. Two, if you count Ishmael."

"Yahweh wasn't wrong in renaming me," Abraham responded patiently. "He renamed me prophetically. The story isn't finished yet. *You* are the heir of Yahweh's promise. I have faith that Yahweh will do what he promised—make me a great nation, and do it through *you*. I may not see the Covenant fulfilled in my lifetime, but you will see the beginning of it. And if not you, then your children, or your children's children. You too must have faith, Isaac. You must have faith that Yahweh will make of *you* a great nation."

"I do, Father. At least I think I do."

There was a pause in the conversation.

"How did we get onto this topic?" Abraham asked his son. "What were we talking about?"

"We were talking about Yahweh's voice," said Isaac. "I asked you if it was hard to obey Yahweh's voice, and you said, 'Yes and no.' We were also talking about death."

Abraham picked up his story.

"Death, as you will see, played a big part in my father Terah's story, and in mine too. Nine generations of his forefathers were alive when he was born. For the first half of his life, death was a foreign concept to him. Noah had died two years before he was born, but all his other forefathers were alive.

"Then, beginning when Terah was 115, death fell like a hammer every few years, starting with Noah's grandson Arphaxad. When Shem died at the age of 600, even I felt the loss. He had been so instrumental in teaching me about Yahweh. When death claimed Terah's grandfather, his second wife, and most unexpected of all, his firstborn son Haran, Father Terah was devastated. How could Haran be dead? Haran was not yet a hundred. Father went into a deep depression.

"Before Haran was born, Father's dreams of traveling had died, and now his son too was dead. One day he started talking about traveling again. Dreaming the old dream of going to Canaan seemed to lift his spirits. Father began to get itchy feet.

"With Haran dead and no wife to veto the trip, Father felt there was nothing left to hold him in Ur. Besides, his prestige in Ur had slipped somewhat after he closed his house of idols. By this time my brother Nahor had married Haran's daughter Milcah and had settled down to raise a family. Father had also found a husband for Haran's other daughter Iscah. Haran's son Lot, though not yet married, was old enough to take care of himself. The whole family was preparing to say farewell to Father.

"At the time, I was struggling with my own grief. My brother Haran had died. Now my father was talking of going all the way to Canaan, which seemed like death to me. And Sarai and I had a more private grief.

"For years we had wanted children. Finally after twelve years of marriage, Sarai went to see a physician. He confirmed what we had suspected. Sarai was barren. We were both devastated.

"You see, Father wasn't the only one with dreams. I dreamed of a family. Somehow with my name Abram, 'exalted father', I had always pictured my future as being surrounded with family members who looked up to me. If Sarai was barren, I would have to rethink that dream.

"Besides, Sarai and I were tired of the useless and crime-breeding idolatry all around us. Where was there a city free of idolatry, a city of purity and beauty where the True and Living God alone was served and worshiped? Into this restless longing, God spoke."

"What did he say?" Isaac asked.

"The God of glory appeared to me, as I already told you, and said, 'Leave your country and your people, and go to the land I will show you.'"[7]

"What did you do?"

"I immediately got up and went into the tent to tell Sarai. We talked long into the night. Yahweh had a city prepared for us—just like the city we longed for! We must go and find it. We might not find it in this life, but we must spend all our time and energy looking for it.

"We both recognized that this would be not just a physical journey, but a spiritual one as well. Gladly we responded and prepared to go. Though Yahweh had not specifically said so, we felt the first step of the journey was to set out with father Terah. We had no idea whether we would get as far as Canaan or whether we would go even further. We didn't even know how long we would travel together with Terah. But we knew Yahweh would show us when to take a separate path. Our faith journey began that night."

"How did Grandfather react when you told him?"

"He was surprised and delighted. When he first decided to go to Canaan, he planned on going alone. He had planned on leaving his business in the charge of Lot, Nahor and me, but now he had a better idea. We would all go. He would sell his business, house and warehouses, and re-invest in something more suitable for the long journey. Cattle and sheep could be driven from place to place and would provide us with food—meat, milk and cheese. Along the way, livestock could be traded in exchange for other food and supplies.

"The more Father talked, the more excited he got. Ideas kept coming, one after another. He could hire a few Bedouins to teach him and his servants the basics of the nomadic lifestyle and raising livestock. We would need a few camels as pack animals. And tents. Even Father's

---

[7] Acts 7:3

warehouse guards would come in useful. They could be trained to fight off cattle and sheep rustlers.

"Father welcomed the thought of having family members as traveling companions. Lot could join us. He had no ties to Ur. His father Haran had died, and his sisters, being married, were no longer his responsibility. We would be nomads! The whole family! Even Nahor!

"But Nahor put his foot down. He was married and his wife had just announced that she was pregnant. They weren't going anywhere, thank you very much!

"Sarai and I didn't have any particular ties to Ur. We soon caught the excitement of the prospect of travel to new lands. That excitement dulled the pain of confirming that Sarai was barren. We immediately started preparing to leave Ur."

"So you left your country," said Isaac.

"Yes."

"And your people."

"Yes. I left my brother Nahor and his family behind, as well as the Eberite people who lived in Ur. During the hundred years that Terah had lived there, many Eberites influenced by him had left their land north of Haran and settled in Ur. We all spoke Eber's language, but only a handful of us claimed to follow his God, Yahweh. Shem and Eber, and Noah before them, had always done their best to dissuade people from following other gods, but few would listen. Most of the godly Eberites had stayed in the land of Eber. Most of my people who lived in Ur and Chaldea preferred to worship a god who was more 'tangible', like the city god of Ur, the moon god Nannar.

"Nannar had never appealed to me, but after seeing the God of glory, I had absolutely no desire to worship stone-cold idols. And Yahweh was no longer intangible.

"I can see why Yahweh called me to leave my country and my people," Abraham said to Isaac. "So few of them followed Yahweh. Some of those who did tried to worship both Yahweh and Nannar. I don't think I would ever have been drawn into idol worship. But I was always going against the grain of my culture. It was a struggle to continuously try to persuade others to follow Yahweh exclusively of other gods, and to convince them that many of their practices were evil.

"I looked forward to the nomadic lifestyle. The contemplative life. I had heard Yahweh's voice once. I hoped I would soon hear it again."

Isaac switched topics.

"Grandfather Terah set out for Canaan, but he never got there, did he?"

"No."

"What happened?"

"Father was a wanderer by nature," Abraham explained, "but he was getting older and he tired more easily. All that travel finally caught up to him. When we reached the western edge of Babylonia, we stopped in Haran.[8] 'Just for a while,' Father said.

"Haran was a beautiful place in the plains of Paddan Aram between the Euphrates River and one of its tributaries. It was well watered, and had plenty of easy grazing for our herds and flocks. Besides, Haran was very well located on the busy caravan road connecting with Nineveh, Asshur and Babylon in Mesopotamia, and with Damascus, Tyre and Egyptian cities in the west and south. The camels stopped for water, and the caravan drivers needed food, so we could purchase anything in the world we wanted in exchange for our livestock.

"When I saw Haran, I understood why Father had fallen in love with the place and named his son after it. Father soon found business acquaintances, and the situation was pleasant, so we settled down for a while. The place seemed to comfort Father and to lessen his grief over losing his son.

"Living in Haran, we were not far from the land of Eber, where Father was born. He took me to see my relatives and get acquainted with my family roots.

"Only two of Terah's forefathers remained alive—Eber and his father Shelah. Both of them had been born before the Dispersion, before people moved away because they couldn't understand the languages spoken around them. While we were visiting them, Father mentioned

---

[8] See Genesis 11:31

his desire to travel to Canaan. Father and I were both surprised at the reaction.

"Shelah and Eber looked at each other. You know that kind of look. The look that speaks volumes. Except Father and I couldn't hear what they were saying to each other. All we heard was silence.

"'What?' Terah asked. 'Did I say something wrong? Is there something wrong about wanting to go to Canaan?'

"'No,' said Eber, 'there's nothing wrong with going to Canaan.' And again he gave Shelah 'the look'.

"Finally Eber spoke. 'Is it alright if we tell them?'

"'I suppose,' said Shelah.

"'The family has always been reluctant to speak of that day,' Eber began. Then he told us the story, beginning with a question.

"'If I asked you Noah's occupation, what would you say?' Eber asked us.

"'I would say he was a carpenter,' Terah replied.

"'That's what most people think,' said Eber. 'People automatically think of his building the ark and assume he was a carpenter.'"

Isaac interrupted Abraham's story. "That's what I would assume, too."

"But Eber informed us differently, son," Abraham said. "Noah was a farmer. A man of the soil.[9] He built the ark at Yahweh's command, but his first love was making things grow. And for the first few decades after the Flood, things grew exceptionally well."

"Because of all the silt washed down by the Great Flood?"

"Yes, son. Noah developed wonderful gardens and orchards which produced an abundance of vegetables and fruit. But his pride and joy was his vineyard. Noah made wonderful wine. One year, for some reason which Noah did not fully understand, the wine turned out much stronger than usual. Noah was never a drunkard. He was regarded by everybody as blameless. Even those who never met him would tell you he was a righteous man.[10] But one day he got drunk."

I can't imagine that," said Isaac.

---

[9] See Genesis 9:20
[10] See Genesis 6:9

"Nor can I. Maybe he drank the strong wine on an empty stomach, which always exaggerates the effect of alcohol, but he got drunk. The first one to notice was Noah's youngest son Ham. He had gone into Noah's tent to ask him something, and he found Noah passed out on the floor with his private parts uncovered."

Isaac gasped.

"Ham thought it was hilarious," Abraham continued. "He found his two brothers, Shem and Japheth, just outside the tent, and laughingly told them about Noah and urged them to come and see.

"Shem was horrified at the thought of his father drunk, but even more horrified at Ham's reaction. Ham's son Canaan was nearby, heard the commotion, and wanted to gawk at his grandfather. Shem stopped him from going inside and realized something had to be done quickly or their father would be a matter of gossip for the whole community. Shem and his brother Japheth devised a plan whereby they could cover their father without looking on his nakedness. Together he and Japheth took a garment and laid it across their shoulders; then, with their faces turned away from their father, they walked in backwards and covered him up.[11] They left without turning around.

"A short while later Shem spotted Canaan sneaking out of his grandfather's tent. He hadn't seen him enter. Had Canaan been there before they covered Noah up?

"Shem asked Canaan what he had been doing, but he ran off without waiting for the scolding he knew he would get from his uncle. At the time Shem and Japheth thought no more of it.

"When Noah awoke from his drunken stupor, Shem and Japheth told him what had happened and what Ham had done."

"What did Noah do when he realized that he had been drunk?" asked Isaac.

"Of course, he was mortified to discover that he had gotten drunk, but he knew he had not done it intentionally. It was an accident of circumstances. But he was very angry at Ham. It was a righteous anger. In fact he felt the power of Yahweh upon him and opened his mouth to let Yahweh speak through him.

---

[11] See Genesis 9:23

"What did he say?" Isaac asked.
"He said,

> 'Cursed be Canaan!
> The lowest of slaves
> will he be to his brothers.'"[12]

"He spoke in poetry!" Isaac exclaimed.
"Yes. Yahweh put the words in his mouth."
"But why did Noah curse *Canaan* and not Ham?"
"I don't know. And neither did Noah or Shem or Japheth. They all thought Ham was the wrong doer. But Yahweh knows our hearts. He sees beyond what we see, and he must have deemed that what Canaan did in secret or even in his heart was worse than what Ham did outwardly."
"Maybe Canaan had something to do with getting Noah drunk," Isaac speculated.
"That could be," Abraham agreed, "but I doubt that Yahweh would have cursed him merely for getting someone drunk. I think it must have been more serious than that. Maybe it was a combination of getting Noah drunk with the purpose of gazing at his naked body."
"Did Noah say anything else?" Isaac asked.
"Yes. And that was why Shelah and Eber reacted the way they did to Terah's desire to go to the land of Canaan."
"What did he say?"
"He said,

> 'Blessed be Yahweh, the God of Shem!
> May Canaan be the slave of Shem.
> May God extend the territory of Japheth;
> may Japheth live in the tents of Shem,
> and may Canaan be his slave.'"[13]

"Yahweh spoke through Noah again?"

---

[12] Genesis 9:25
[13] Genesis 9:26-27

"Yes, son. It was a prophecy. God repeated it for emphasis—that Canaan would be a slave to Shem. More than three centuries had passed since that prophecy, and no one had seen a hint of its fulfillment. Shem and Canaan never had any dealings with each other, in fact Canaan seemed to avoid Shem. Then Ham and his sons moved away.

"After the dispersion and the confusion of languages, Shem couldn't even converse with Ham. Ham and his descendants moved even further away and established themselves in their territories by their clans and nations, each with its own language. One of those territories is Canaan.

"For the rest of his life, Shem had wondered how it would be possible that Canaan could ever be a slave to him. Shem and Noah wondered why Yahweh had singled out Canaan to be cursed, but they never had the opportunity to question him further."

"When Eber finished his story," Abraham continued, "my father Terah spoke up. He had recently been in the marketplace when a caravan came through. The travelers had been through a variety of countries, including Canaan. When questioned about the Canaanites, the chief camel driver spoke up. The Canaanites had a whole pantheon of gods, he said, and their worship practices were lewd and immoral even by pagan standards. From what the camel driver could gather, the Canaanite god El was a bloody tyrant who dethroned his own father, murdered his favorite son and decapitated his own daughter. In spite of that, the Canaanites revered El as head of the pantheon and father of another god Baal. Prostitution and sexual perversion are a big part of Canaanite worship."

"Do you think they got their religion and ideas of worship from their ancestor Canaan?" Isaac asked.

"That's what my father Terah theorized," said Abraham. "If the seeds of sexual immorality were growing in Canaan's heart, it is no wonder Yahweh cursed him."

"Before the Flood Yahweh saw how great man's wickedness on the earth had become and that every inclination of the thoughts of his heart was only evil all the time.[14] So he sent the Great Flood. But the Flood

---

[14] Genesis 6:5

didn't change man's heart. After the Flood, Yahweh said virtually the same thing. 'Every inclination of man's heart is evil from childhood.'[15] That sounds like a description of Canaan.

"Since Yahweh promised never again to destroy all living creatures by a flood, some people took that as license to do what they pleased. After Yahweh confused people's languages, they spread out across the face of the earth. But there are still pockets of evil in many places. And Canaan is one of them."

"Didn't knowing about the Canaanites and their open immorality discourage Grandfather from going to Canaan?" asked Isaac.

"Yes. It certainly made him hesitate about going. But Shelah and Eber immediately felt that Terah's desire to go to the land of Canaan was of God. Terah was a descendant of Shem. Maybe this was the beginning of the fulfillment of the prophecy that Canaan would be the slave of Shem. They urged Terah to follow his heart and go. That was when I spoke up and told them about hearing the voice of Yahweh in Ur.

"'Did Yahweh tell you to go to Canaan?' Eber asked.

"'No,' I told him. 'He just said leave your country and your people and go to the land I will show you. I've come as far as Haran, but haven't heard from Yahweh since.'

"But you did hear Yahweh's voice in Haran, didn't you, Father," Isaac said.

"Yes, son. A few years later."

"But Grandfather Terah never did get to Canaan. What happened to his dream?" Isaac asked.

"Originally he intended to move on," Abraham explained. "But year after year went by, and he always planned to go 'next year'. Eventually he got too old to move on. Then my brother Nahor moved from Ur to Haran to be close to Father in his last years. As the oldest remaining son, he was officially responsible to look after Father in his old age. Father finally died at the age of 205, having outlived most of his peers."

"Do you miss living in Haran or Ur?" Isaac asked.

"No. I prefer to look forward, not backward."

---

[15] Genesis 8:21

"When people ask you where you are from, what do you say? Ur, or Haran, or Babylonia?"

"None of those places," Abraham replied. "Yahweh broke my attachment to country when I left Ur. When I started to feel attached to Haran, Yahweh moved me away again. Since leaving Haran, I have felt no attachment to any country. Since coming to Canaan, I haven't been in any place long enough to put down roots. When people ask, I simply say I am an alien."

Abraham paused. There was a faraway look in his eyes.

"Every few days or weeks I roll up my tent and move on. I look forward to the day when I live in a place with foundations. I suspect I will never feel at home until I reach the City with unshakeable foundations whose architect and builder is God.[16] Then I can roll up my tent forever. I will be home."

Just then Sarah came in.

"Time to wash up for dinner," she said.

---

[16] See Hebrews 11:10

2

Abram Leaves Haran

"Father," Isaac asked, "when did Yahweh tell you to leave your father's household, and where were you at the time?"

It was the Sabbath, and Isaac was looking forward to a good, long conversation with his father. On work days their discussions were often interrupted.

"I was thoroughly settled in Haran," Abraham began, "in Aram Naharaim, the country between two rivers—the Habur River and the great Euphrates River. I was 75 years old. Father was 205. Nahor and Lot lived nearby and kept an eye on him. We had lived in Haran for about 35 years by then. Aram Naharaim had become our country.

"One day while I was tending a flock of sheep, I heard a voice saying, 'Leave your country, your people and your father's household and go to the land I will show you.'"[17]

"How did you know he was speaking to *you*?" Isaac asked.

"No one else was in sight. Usually I have lots of people around me—my servants asking for instructions, or merchants trying to sell me something, or your mother wanting to show off her latest outfit or jewelry purchase, or asking about preparations to receive an important guest. But this day was unusually quiet."

---

[17] Genesis 12:1

Abraham paused thoughtfully.

"Until *he* spoke."

"What did he sound like?"

"His voice was rich, powerful, and compelling—I felt loved when I heard it."

"And you knew it was Yahweh," Isaac said.

"Yes. I had heard that voice once before. I could never forget it."

"What else did he say, Father?"

Isaac knew the answer, but he asked anyway.

"I will make you into a great nation," Abraham began. Then Isaac joined him in reciting the poem.

> "I will make you into a great nation
>   and I will bless you;
> I will make your name great,
>   and you will be a blessing.
> I will bless those who bless you,
>   and whoever curses you
> I will curse; and all peoples on earth
>   will be blessed through you."[18]

"The Covenant," Isaac said. "I love hearing it in Hebrew. It sounds so much better than when you say it in the language of your Amorite friends when you are talking with them."

"Poetry always loses something in translation, Son. This promise wasn't the actual Covenant. That came later. This promise and its accompanying command were the precursor to the Covenant."

"Didn't Yahweh say the same thing when you were in Ur?"

"No. When I was back in Ur, he said only, 'Leave *your country and your people*, and go to the land I will show you.'[19] He didn't mention my father or his household or make any promises."

"Why would he ask you to leave your father and his household?"

---

[18] Genesis 12:2-3
[19] Acts 7:3, italics added

"I didn't understand at the time, but in retrospect, there are lessons I learned that I never would have learned if I hadn't been alone and fully dependent upon God. Being alone built my faith. With no family around to turn to for advice, I had to get my directions straight from Yahweh. I know that if I had traveled to Canaan with my father, he, being the wanderer that he was, would have made the decisions as to when to move and where to go. I think Yahweh also wanted to get me away from those who might worship Yahweh half-heartedly. That is more dangerous than outright paganism."

"Didn't all your family—Grandfather Terah, Uncle Nahor and cousin Lot—all love and worship Yahweh?" Isaac asked.

"Of my family members, Lot was the most ardent follower of Yahweh," Abraham replied. "But I sometimes wondered about my father and my brother."

"Are you suggesting that Grandfather Terah was not true to Yahweh?" Isaac was shocked by his father's suggestion. "Didn't he listen to Shem, just as you did?"

"Yes, he did. Between Shem's stories and my arguments, we convinced Terah to follow Yahweh, from anything that I could see. And Father certainly seemed to be blessed by my encounter with the God of glory. At times I felt that the command from Yahweh to leave our country and our people was for both of us. But after settling in Haran, Father's interest in Yahweh slowly faded. First I noticed that he often made excuses when Sarai and I invited him to join us in celebrating the Sabbath. Lot was always happy to join us, though Nahor was sometimes indifferent. Then one day I saw a pair of teraphim on display in Father's home."

"What are teraphim?" Isaac asked.

"Teraphim are household gods. When I confronted Father about them, he said they were just some figurines that someone in the marketplace had talked him into buying. Sometimes teraphim are very vile. Father's weren't lewd. They appeared innocent enough, but they were definitely teraphim."

"Do people worship teraphim?" Isaac asked.

"People don't make offerings of food and flowers to them like they do to traditional gods, and they don't pray or burn incense to them on a daily basis. But they do consult them from time to time in the same way they consult a spirit medium. Many people believe their teraphim are the source of their prosperity."

"How can that be?" Isaac asked.

"Fathers pass them along, usually to their firstborn sons, when they feel it is time to make decisions concerning their estate. The teraphim are treated like a legal document. The owner of the teraphim becomes head of the family. He is responsible for his parents until they die, and with the responsibility comes a double portion of the inheritance."

"If the parents linger on in their old age, wouldn't that decrease the value of the double portion?" Isaac asked.

"No," his father replied. "Caring for the parents does not decrease the inherited portion of the firstborn because the estate is divided only after the father's death. For a daughter the teraphim are particularly important. Usually the inheritance is divided amongst the sons, and the daughters inherit nothing. Their husbands are expected to take care of them. If the teraphim are given to a daughter, her husband is assured of inheriting property from his wife's father. The woman's brothers receive proportionately less of their father's estate."

"Did Grandfather Terah believe this?" asked Isaac incredulously.

"At first I didn't think so," Abraham said. "I didn't want to believe so. But when he started talking about giving his teraphim away, I knew they were more than decorative figurines.

"Father used me as a sounding board for his deliberations. Should he give the teraphim to Lot, the descendant of his firstborn Haran? Or should he give them to his oldest *living* son Nahor? Lot, being the only son of Haran, would fully inherit Haran's portion. As third in line either way, the decision would not affect me.

"First I expressed my discomfort with the use of teraphim. Father could announce his decision to the family in front of ten witnesses, I said, then put the decision in writing. There was no need of teraphim to seal the deal.

"I suggested that Father give Nahor the double portion, as he was presently taking the most active role in watching out for his father in his old age. Father countered with the argument that it was Lot who had traveled with him from Ur. Nahor had stayed behind. Furthermore, if Father had died *before* Haran, this discussion would not even be taking place. Lot would already have the firstborn's portion—the double portion.

"As I left Father to make the final decision, I told him that Yahweh had commanded me to leave my country and my people *and my father's household*. I also told him about Yahweh's promises to me. Father didn't say anything, but I could tell that he was not pleased.

"The next day Father was determined to persuade me to stay in Haran. He had hoped that I would stay near him for the rest of his life, he said. He dismissed Yahweh's accompanying promises to me as wishful thinking. I had concocted the promise of becoming a great nation because I had no children, he said. As for blessings and prosperity, he could help me with that, he said. Then he pulled out his most convincing argument. He presented me with his teraphim.

"I understood the gesture. Not only was he asking me to stay. He was also bribing me with the double portion of his estate. He was reminding me that I would get half the estate, and Lot and Nahor would each get one quarter of it."

"What did you do?" Isaac asked.

"I got very angry. I was disappointed, angry, hurt, sad—all at the same time. I was deeply disappointed that Father had turned from Yahweh and returned to the familiar gods of his past. The people of Haran, like the people in Ur, also worshipped a moon god. They called him by a different name, Sin, but there was little difference in their worship practices.

"I was angry that Father could so easily dismiss all that he had learned of Yahweh. I was angry that he didn't share with me my love of Yahweh. I was puzzled and angry that he could imagine that I would turn my back on the God of glory after such an awesome encounter with him.

"I was sad for Father's sake that he could not see for himself how wonderful and real Yahweh is. Some time before I heard Yahweh's voice for the second time, Father began dropping not-so-subtle hints that I should take a second wife—or at least a concubine—since Sarai was barren. But I had told him that Yahweh was in control, and if he chose not to give me children, that was alright with me. I would still worship Yahweh.

"But most of all, I was hurt that Father could think my world was centered around my possessions, that he could bribe me with more. I was so upset that I smashed the teraphim on the floor and stomped on them."

"You defied your father?!" Isaac could not fathom such disrespect for an elder.

"Yes, Son," Abraham said. "Under normal circumstances I showed my father the utmost respect. But when I had to choose between Father and Yahweh, Father lost. Father looked at me in disbelief.

"That day a firm resolve was born in my heart. I resolved to believe Yahweh for his blessing. And I resolved never to give anyone the opportunity to claim he had made me rich. Only Yahweh would get the glory if and when I became rich. Since coming to Haran, I had accumulated many possessions, and my household had increased dramatically. Besides hiring new servants, I had gained more by having children born to those who worked for me. In many people's eyes, I was already rich. I chose to give Yahweh the credit for it all. So I told my father, 'I don't want a sheep or a shekel of your estate. Give it all to Lot and Nahor.'"

"What did Grandfather say?"

"He said, 'Be careful what you wish for. Get out!' and opened his tent door for me to leave. I left without another word."

"What happened next?"

"Sarai and I made preparations to leave. Soon Lot showed up. He had heard from Father that we were leaving, and he wanted to get my version of the story. While traveling from Ur to Haran with Terah, Lot had really caught his grandfather's excitement about going to Canaan. Almost every year he brought up the topic of moving on. And every year, when Terah found some reason for postponing the trip, I could see the disappointment on Lot's face. As soon as he heard that Sarai and I were planning to leave for Canaan, he wanted to know more.

"As I talked about hearing Yahweh's voice and hearing His promises, Lot became excited again and wanted to come with me. He wanted to share the adventure of following Yahweh and living by faith."

"Wasn't Lot part of your father's household?" Isaac asked. "Weren't you supposed to leave him behind?"

"I wondered about that myself," Abraham replied. "Nahor, as the oldest living son, had become part of our father's household. Leaving him was not much of a problem because he didn't want to go to Canaan. He was very comfortable with life in Haran.

"But Lot was another story. When I told him what Yahweh had said to me, he argued that he was not part of Father's household. He was married and had lived independently for quite some time. Besides, he was an ardent follower of Yahweh. If I was leaving to follow Yahweh, he wanted to come along. He did not want to stay behind with half-hearted followers of Yahweh either. Right or wrong, I let him convince me."

"What did Grandfather do then?" Isaac asked.

"He got very angry. He hurried to the marketplace and bought another pair of teraphim and presented them to Lot. But Lot was not tempted by them to stay in Haran. So Father called for Nahor and presented the teraphim to him. When I went to visit my brother Nahor to say goodbye, he showed me the teraphim as legal proof that he would inherit the double portion. Nahor told me I could claim my portion any time after Father's death. 'You can have my portion,' I told him. 'My blessings come from Yahweh.'"

"How did Uncle Nahor respond to that?" Isaac asked.

"He didn't think I was serious about the estate. And the teraphim were not a problem to him. 'Why rock the boat?' he said. 'I can accept the teraphim without worshiping the moon god of Haran or whatever gods they represent.' He couldn't understand that my faith in Yahweh had to be exclusive of other gods. He had been rather half-hearted in following Yahweh all along, and now he didn't want to displease Father.

"Sarai and I continued our preparations to leave Haran with mixed feelings. Part of us was excited about embarking on a new adventure. But we were grieved by the strained relationship with our father. We also felt sad about Nahor—that he didn't understand that Yahweh has to be worshipped exclusively or not at all.

"The next day I was surprised to receive a message from Nahor. Father had died unexpectedly in his sleep. His intense anger must have resulted in a heart attack. We buried him later that day. Then I told Nahor that I was leaving in the morning. He wanted me to stay long enough for him to divide up Father's estate.

"'I meant what I said to Father,' I told him. 'The entire estate is yours and Lot's. I don't want you or anyone to be able to say, 'I made Abram rich.' Nahor looked surprised, but he didn't argue with me. He respected my stand, but he didn't understand it."

"Be careful what you wish for," Isaac said under his breath.

"What did you say?" Abraham asked.

"Be careful what you wish for," Isaac repeated. "Grandfather said that to you. But he also had a wish—that you would stay until he died. Yahweh granted his wish."

Abraham nodded solemnly in agreement. "Scary, isn't it? Yahweh never forces us to go against our will, but sometimes he makes us more willing to go. Father's death made it easy to leave Haran."

"How did you know where to go?" Isaac asked. "Did Yahweh tell you to go to Canaan?"

"No, he just said, 'I will show you.' When Father and I had left Ur, Canaan was our intended destination, so I decided to head in that direction. Besides, as Sarai reminded me when we discussed where to go, Yahweh through Noah had prophesied that Canaan would be a slave to Shem. Yahweh may intend to fulfill the prophecy through us."

Abraham paused thoughtfully. "You know, Son, Yahweh doesn't always give us specific directions. More often he expects us to use our heads. If we desire to please him, we will carefully weigh our options. God can direct us even in the silence. Then we have to step forward in faith, believing that the logical thing is God's will for us. We must act upon what we already know before he will give us further direction."

"I wish I could hear Yahweh's voice," Isaac said wistfully.

"Some day you will, Son, some day you will," Abraham assured him. "But first you must learn to walk by faith in obedience to what you already know. If your heart is right, but your steps are wrong, Yahweh will redirect you."

Abraham resumed his story.

"So we moved slowly toward Canaan. Every morning, six days a week, we packed up our tents, loaded them on our camels and drove our livestock forward. Every evening we unloaded the camels and pitched our tents. We traveled only as fast as the slowest animal. On the Sabbath we rested.

"Eventually we reached Canaan. It was a good land. Fertile. Well watered—especially in the north. Many of the Canaanites lived in well-fortified, walled cities. We were careful not to provoke them. We also made sure that our servants were well trained to defend ourselves against marauders. If we showed any sign of weakness, we would become targets, and our flocks and herds would quickly dwindle.

"My best defenders were the servants who had been born in my household. They took ownership of their duties—as if they were defending their own property and not someone else's.

"One day I spotted a giant tree in the distance, and decided that would be my target—the place to reach before nightfall. The place turned out to be Shechem. Talking to some people from that city, I learned that we were right in the heart of Canaanite territory. Whatever direction we traveled from there, we would be on our way *out* of Canaan.

"That evening was the beginning of the Sabbath. I was relieved not to be packing up in the morning because I needed time to think. How much farther did Yahweh want me to go? When would he show me?

"I sat outside my tent watching the stars and wondering. Sarai withdrew to her personal quarters. She sensed my contemplative mood and knew better than to disturb me by talking about the trivia of the day.

"Then *he* appeared again."

"Who?" Isaac asked.

"The God of glory! Just when I needed to hear from him. I watched that glorious light and waited to hear what he would say. Then I heard his voice—that rich, powerful, compelling voice. Oh, how I love that voice!"

"What did he say?" Isaac asked.

Abraham did not reply right away. He was lost in wonder at the thought of Yahweh's voice.

"What did he say?" Isaac asked again.

"He said, 'To your offspring I will give this land.'[20] Actually he said, 'To your *seed* I will give this land', meaning my offspring."

"Did he say anything more? Any commands? Any more promises?"

"No. I wanted to ask questions, but the light disappeared as quickly as it had appeared. Now I had to use my head again and think through what he meant.

"*This land.* How much was 'this land'? Was it this city and the surrounding fields and vineyards? Was it the entire land of the Canaanites? Or was it more? I chuckled at the audacity of the thought. I had no offspring. What possible need would I have for the entire land of the Canaanites? Of course, Yahweh didn't mean *more* than the land of the Canaanites—if he even meant that much!

"But he said *my offspring*. Earlier he said he would make me into a great nation. That could be loosely interpreted to mean I would *lead* a great nation. My nephew Lot was following me. His servants and mine had grown to many hundreds. Our people probably numbered half the population of some of the smaller cities we had passed, but we were hardly a nation.

"*To your offspring I will give this land.* But Sarai was barren. God knows we had both done our part to produce children. That was no chore—with Sarai as beautiful as she is! We would continue to try. Maybe Yahweh would do a miracle.

"I went to bed still pondering Yahweh's promise. Sarai was still awake. So I told her what had happened, and we talked long into the night. The more we talked of Yahweh, the more we wanted to worship

---

[20] Genesis 12:7, NIV. Compare with KJV.

him. In the morning I looked for large stones and started gathering them into a pile.

"'What are you doing?' Sarai demanded. She was horrified that I was working on the Sabbath.

"'I'm not working for myself. I'm preparing to worship Yahweh,' I said. 'If *this land*, however much that entails, is to belong to our children, we have to change it. Have you noticed that every city we have passed has a shrine to pagan gods outside its gates? I'm going to prepare this land for our children. I'm going to make it a place where Yahweh is worshiped.'

"'In that case I will help you,' Sarai said, and together we built an altar to Yahweh. We tried to remember the altar Shem had used in the land of Elam and to make ours the same way. We brought the largeststones we could carry, arranged them in place and filled the spaces with dirt and smaller stones. For some reason that day the stones didn't seem as heavy as usual.

"When we were finished, we built a fire on the altar. We selected a young lamb without blemish, laid our hands on the head of the lamb and confessed ours sins to Yahweh. Then we killed the lamb, burnt the fat, the liver and the kidneys on the altar, and roasted the meat."

"Why did you put your hands on the head of the lamb?' Isaac asked.

"We did it in recognition that because of our sins, we deserve to die. God told Adam and Eve in the Garden of Eden that if they disobeyed him by eating of one specific tree, they would die."

"I know what tree that was," Isaac said. "It was the tree of the knowledge of good and evil."[21]

"That's right, Son. And when they ate of it, they died spiritually. Eating of the tree of the knowledge of good and evil made Adam and Eve aware that they were naked. Whereas before they had looked forward to walking with God everyday in the cool of the evening, now they hid from him in fear and shame—emotions that were new to them. They made crude garments for themselves out of fig leaves because they

---

[21] See Genesis 2:7

felt ashamed to be naked. They also knew they deserved to die, even though they didn't fully understand what death was.

"God showed them what death was. He killed a couple of lambs right before their eyes. They had never seen blood before. They had never seen anything die. They were horrified to see beautiful frolicking animals turned into something so ugly and still. Their horror continued as God skinned the animals and cut them into pieces. So much blood and gore! God told them that because they had sinned, they too would die some day. Fear almost choked them.

"As Adam and Eve continued to watch, their horror turned into wonder. God turned the bloody hides into beautiful leather garments for them. They were relieved to have their nakedness covered, and happy to discard their inadequate fig leaves.

"Then God built a fire. Adam and Eve watched from behind the bushes because they still were not comfortable in his presence. They saw God put pieces of meat on the fire. They had never smelled anything like it. When the meat was cooked, God called them over to join him. Hesitantly they sat down with him and together they ate the meat. Adam and Eve had never eaten meat before. With each bite, they were reminded that a living creature had died so they could be fed and clothed.

"But as they ate, God talked with them and explained the significance of all he had done. The animals had died as a substitute for Adam and Eve. The death of the animals had satisfied Adam and Eve's felt need for clothing and food. But more importantly, God had been satisfied with the death penalty. Fellowship with God was restored. God went on to explain that the sacrifice was temporary. When Adam and Eve sinned again, they would need another sacrifice. But some day God would provide a permanent solution."

"What was the permanent solution?" Isaac asked.

"I don't know yet," his father replied. "But in the mean time we use God's temporary solution. That's why we put our hands on the head of the animal that is being sacrificed."

Abraham resumed his story.

"As Sarai and I waited for our lamb to cook, we savored its smell and sang songs of praise to Yahweh. All the while, we sensed Yahweh's approval. I think he enjoyed the smell of the roasting lamb as much as we did."

"So did you settle down there in Shechem?" Isaac asked.

"No," Abraham said. "The morning after the Sabbath we were slower than usual in breaking camp and moving on. Sarai and I felt a special attachment to that place. For the first time *she* had felt Yahweh's presence. Prior to that, she had experienced him only indirectly through my experiences with him. But we both agreed that Yahweh had more to show us before we settled down. He had told us to go, but we hadn't heard him say, 'Stop!' We kept going southward.

"A few days later we were camped on the hills just east of Luz. The town of Luz was on a low rocky ridge situated above a point where two wadis join. It was just high enough to be safe from the flooding caused by seasonal rains. On our west was Ai.

"With the Sabbath approaching, Sarai and I were still thinking of Shechem and our experience there. We wanted to recapture that sense of fellowship with Yahweh. So we decided to stay at Luz until the Sabbath. But this time we wanted to share our experience with everybody.

"So we told our servants that we would not be moving again until after the Sabbath and that we wanted them to join us for the Sabbath celebration. Some of my most trusted servants helped me build another altar and organized preparations for the Sabbath.

"In the afternoon before Sabbath, I shared with all my people what Yahweh had said to me the week before, and I related to them how Sarai and I had spent the Sabbath. Then we slaughtered enough animals to feed the entire crowd, and we encouraged as many as wished to do so to place their hands on the head of an animal before it was slaughtered in confession of their sin and in recognition of the substitute Yahweh had provided by the death of that animal."

"Did everybody do it?" Isaac asked.

"Not everybody, but I was pleased that many did. I called on the name of Yahweh, and they reverently joined in. While the food cooked, we sang songs of praise to Yahweh."

"You couldn't cook all that meat on one altar!" Isaac exclaimed.

"No, of course not," Abraham replied. "The altar was never used for cooking food. The blood of each animal was sprinkled on all four sides of the altar. Then each animal was skinned, and the fat, the liver and the kidneys only were placed on the burning wood. We waved the meat briefly over the flames on the altar while thanking Yahweh for forgiving our sins and thanking him for our food. Then our servants cooked the meat in roasting pits they had prepared for the occasion. As the sun went down and the food was served, we felt a sense of fellowship with our families and servants and their families that we had not sensed before.

"The next morning there was a different atmosphere in the camp. The people seemed quieter and happier. Many of them hummed or sang softly to themselves the tunes of the previous day. People gathered in clusters, quietly talking. Several people gathered around me to ask more about Yahweh. Before I knew it, I was preaching to a crowd!

"As the Sabbath drew to a close, someone commented, 'This place feels like the house of God.' Everybody agreed. So that's what we call the place now. Bethel. House of God. The Canaanites still call it Luz, but my people call it Bethel."[22]

---

[22] See Genesis 12:8-9; 28:13

3

Detour to Egypt

"From Bethel we continued southward," Abraham said to his son Isaac. "As we got closer to the Negev, the land got drier. I remember being camped on a ridge with a spring and greenery on one side and the desert on the other. It seemed strange to have such contrasting views from the same spot. Camels and desert on one side; sheep and cattle and green pastures on the other. If I wanted a change of view, all I had to do was turn around!

"Even the desert has its beauty—especially when the sun is low in the sky. And the stars! How the stars shine over the desert! The dry air seems to make them shine so much brighter. I felt that if my arms were just a little longer, or if I stood on tiptoe, I could touch them.

"And Yahweh felt close, too. During the day the warmth of the sun on my skin felt like an embrace from God. At night the moon smiled at me and the stars twinkled at me. I distinctly felt Yahweh's approval—even when He didn't say anything to me.

"But then things changed. For a long time there was no rain. I was told that in most of Canaan six months without rain is normal. But the rainy season came and went with hardly enough rain to settle the dust. The land dried up. The streams dried up. Where springs used to flow, there were only mud puddles. Lot, Sarai and I wondered what direction to go. Should we backtrack? As we made inquiries, we learned that famine was widespread. Places we had already been were dry, so there was no sense in retracing our steps.

"South of us was even more desert. But to the west was Egypt. The Nile never dries up. The soil is fertile, with good grazing land for livestock. So we went westward. The first part of our journey was worse than anything I had ever experienced. We struggled to survive from one oasis to the next. We always took as much water as we could carry, but even then some of the young animals died along the way. When we reached the River of Egypt, it was dry."

"You mean even the Nile ran dry?" asked Isaac in shock.

"No," Abraham said. "Not the Nile. The River of Egypt. That's what the Canaanites call it. It's the only river between the southern border of Canaan and the Nile delta. The Egyptians would never call it a river because it dries up between rainy seasons. 'A real river never dries up,' they say with a sniff. 'That's only a wadi.' Wadi el Arish they call it. The Egyptians think you haven't seen a river until you've seen the Nile.

"Being dry, the river—or wadi if you prefer—was easy to cross, but we would rather have had water. Finally we came within sight of the Nile delta. Everybody was excited at the thought of an easier life. Even the animals smelled the moisture in the air and seemed eager to move forward.

"But that last day before reaching the Nile, I couldn't sleep. I began to think of everything I had heard about Egypt. They had grand cities and palaces. I wasn't interested in their cities. I just wanted water and good pasture for my flocks and herds.

"Pharaoh's power extended into Canaan and beyond. Whenever Pharaoh needed money to build another palace, or whatever his latest project was, he sent tax collectors into the cities of Canaan. The Canaanites hated to pay, but if they didn't, able-bodied family members would be taken as slaves. Paying taxes was easier than slavery. And paying taxes was easier than going to war against the Egyptians. Whatever Pharaoh wanted, Pharaoh got.

"Thankfully I didn't have the things that Pharaoh wanted, I mused. I had sheep and cattle, donkeys and camels, but the Egyptians had those too. What they were really interested in were Arabian horses. And I didn't have one horse. They liked exotic spices and fancy jewelry. I didn't have spices, and I could warn Sarai to keep her jewelry out of sight of strangers.

"I was about to drift peacefully off to sleep when another thought startled me wide awake. Sarai! That's what interested Pharaoh. Beautiful women! Pharaoh would kill to add someone as beautiful as Sarai to his court.

"For the first time since I left Ur, I was afraid. My servants were very protective of Sarai, and had often fought off lecherous Hittites and Canaanites. I had never feared for Sarai's safety during all of our travels. Even the local Egyptians would be no problem for me. But Pharaoh! My few hundred servant guards, though well-trained and well-armed, were no match for Pharaoh's armies. If I resisted his wishes, I would be dead.

"What could I do?

"Then I had an idea. I could pose as Sarai's brother and guardian. They would have to negotiate with me for her bride price. In that role I would not be killed. Pharaoh would expect to pay for a beautiful woman. And I wouldn't even have to tell a lie! Our father was dead. I would just say our father was dead and I was her brother. Pharaoh would expect me to look after any unmarried sisters."

"But she was married. She was married to *you*," Isaac objected.

"I wouldn't tell Pharaoh that," Abraham said. "I would just let him draw his own conclusions."

Isaac looked critically at his father. "Wouldn't that get you into worse trouble when Mother told them the truth?"

"She was part of the problem, alright. I had to explain to her the gravity of the situation. It was a matter of life and death to me. Someone of her exceptional beauty would inevitably come to Pharaoh's attention. His officials were always on the lookout for beautiful women to add to Pharaoh's harem. So whenever anyone asked questions about her, she was to say she was my sister. Under no circumstances was she to say 'wife'. Did she want me to get killed? Better not to even say 'half-sister'. That would just invite more questions."

"Besides, thinking of my deceased father Terah reminded me of something he had said. He had dropped hints that, since Sarai was barren, I should take a second wife. How could I become a great nation without children? he had asked. I had replied that I was already a small nation, if you considered my entire household of a couple thousand servants. Many hundreds of them were second generation servants, born in my household.

"But since Yahweh had told me 'To your offspring I will give this land,' I could no longer use that argument. I wondered if Yahweh would take away my wife's barrenness, but soon dismissed that thought as ridiculous. Not only was she barren, but she had also ceased having her monthly cycle.

"So what was Yahweh trying to tell me? That I should take a second wife? How did that fit with God's instruction that a man and wife become one? All of my God-fearing forefathers had adhered to the one-man-one-woman concept of marriage. Those who didn't take God seriously weren't inhibited by his idea of marriage. Kings in surroundings nations seemed to think the more wives the merrier. Many had huge harems. Was God trying to tell me that I should have faith that it was alright to bend his rules?"

Abraham noticed that Isaac was beginning to squirm.

"I'm sorry, Son, but it's the truth. That's what I was thinking. I know you love your mother dearly, and it hurts to hear that I didn't always treat her well. I tell you this only so that you will not make the same mistake as I did. Yahweh does want one man to have only one wife. More than that leads to trouble. There can be no unity in a household with multiple marriage partners."

"Did Mother agree to being called your sister?"

"Not at first," Abraham said. "She said she would cover up in public."

"That would have worked, wouldn't it?" asked Isaac.

"Not really. She could wear a head scarf, but that wouldn't hide her beauty. In Egyptian society, trying to cover up would draw more attention than not doing so. Egyptian women didn't cover up like the wives of desert nomads. It took some convincing, but she eventually came around to my way of thinking."

"What happened then?" Isaac asked.

"For a day or two, life was great. We had plenty of pasture for the animals, and for the first time in many months, we didn't have to worry about water. But it wasn't long before Sarai had to go shopping. And that worried me."

"Couldn't *you* do the shopping?" Isaac asked.

Abraham gave his son a withering look.

"Have you ever seen me shopping for vegetables? That's women's work! I would have been laughed out of the marketplace."

"Oh," Isaac said sheepishly. "I didn't think. So what happened?"

"Just what I feared," his father replied. "Sarai went shopping. Sarai didn't know the local language, but she did her best by pointing and gesticulating to make her needs known. At one stall she met a young woman named Hagar who could speak a little Eber. Sarai was very surprised to find someone who understood her. It turns out that merchants from the land of Eber had been through there many times, and Hagar had learned some of their language. Hagar made a practice of learning other languages. She found it increased her sales. Foreigners preferred shopping at the booth where she was working because she could converse with them. As a result, her master treated her better than his other slaves.

"Sarai purchased Hagar on the spot by offering her master a price he couldn't refuse. Hagar's master wasn't pleased to lose his best worker, but he couldn't afford to turn down Sarai's offer. With Hagar's help Sarai finished her shopping in no time.

"I had worried about Sarai the whole time she was away. I was relieved to see her come back from the marketplace, and was about to welcome her with a big hug and a kiss, when she brushed me aside and introduced me to Hagar as her 'brother'. I was glad for the reminder and determined to watch my actions more carefully in the future.

"As Sarai continued her shopping trips, the merchants took more than a casual interest in her. Sarai was oblivious to any reaction she got from the men, mainly because she couldn't speak their language or answer their questions. But Hagar noticed how people stared appreciatively at Sarai. Hagar was often asked questions about her mistress. Then one day some of Pharaoh's officials passing through the marketplace noticed Sarai. Hagar saw them look each other and then start talking amongst themselves while casting frequent glances in Sarai's direction.

"It wasn't long before a contingent from Pharaoh's palace came to the place where we were camped. One was driving a chariot. The others were on horseback. They were armed to the teeth. I was so afraid, but I tried to hide my fear and stay calm. I received them royally. Pharaoh had heard of Sarai's extraordinary beauty and wanted her in his palace."

"Did they take Mother by force?"

"No, they were polite but businesslike. I tried with my limited knowledge of the Egyptians' language to dissuade them by saying that at her age Sarai was barren. They were surprised to learn that Sarai was 67 years old, because she didn't look anywhere near her age. But Pharaoh's officials assured me that didn't matter. Pharaoh could have children by his other wives, they said. What he wanted was a beautiful woman at his side. He wanted everyone to know that the mighty Pharaoh could have the most beautiful women in the world. Not only would Pharaoh show off his wives to visitors to the palace, but he would also put them on public display from time to time as he drifted down the Nile in his royal barge.

"When I saw that reasoning would get me nowhere, I reluctantly let Sarai go. I feared the officials would draw their swords in an instant if I didn't cooperate. They let Sarai take Hagar with her as her personal handmaid and translator. And they paid me generously in sheep and cattle, donkeys and camels, and extra servants to help care for them. I didn't want payment. I just wanted Sarai. But I was too afraid to do otherwise.

"And so began one of the darkest periods of my life. I couldn't say goodbye to Sarai the way I wanted or the officials would know that she was my wife. Sarai went to live in Pharaoh's palace."

There was silence between father and son as they pondered the story. Isaac couldn't imagine his mother living anywhere but with him and his father.

"I'm not proud of what I did, Son," Abraham said finally. "I had not lied in word, but I had deceived by my actions—and by my silence. Maybe it was my imagination, but I didn't feel the respect I usually felt from my servants. When they called me 'Abram', I felt like asking them to call me something else. I didn't deserve to be their 'exalted father'.

"Worst of all, I knew I had failed to trust Yahweh. I felt his displeasure. The sun burned me by day, and the moon mocked me by night. The moon seemed to say, 'I'm smiling on Sarai and Pharaoh, but laughing at you.' The stars no longer twinkled in the sky. The days were long, and the nights without Sarai seemed endless. I tried not to think what Sarai might be doing.

"I was very conscious that I was no longer walking by faith, but I didn't know how to get back onto the path of faith. All I could think was, 'Without faith it is impossible to please Yahweh.'[23]

"I had been thinking of Yahweh as my friend. But then *this* happened. Sometimes I longed to hear his voice again. At the same time I was afraid to hear his voice again for fear of what he would say to me."

"How did Mother get back to you?" Isaac asked. "Did she run away from the palace?"

"No. She knew there was no place to get away from Pharaoh. Even Canaan was not far enough away.

"A few days after Sarai left, some of Pharaoh's officials came by again. This time they brought even more livestock and servants—and more camels. The camels told me that Pharaoh was really pleased.

"'Pharaoh wants to express his pleasure with your sister,' the officials said.

"I bowed and smiled on the outside, but I was crying inside.

"I cried out to Yahweh. 'O God, what have I done? How can I live without Sarai? How can I live without you smiling upon me? Will I ever hear your voice again?'

---

[23] See Hebrews 11:6

"The heavens were like brass. My words echoed back at me. Yahweh was silent. The days and weeks dragged by. I wasn't much good for anything. But my servants handled everything efficiently, and my business prospered in spite of me. The livestock fattened up and multiplied quickly with the abundance of food and water. My sheep and cattle commanded good prices in the marketplace.

"Then one day a chariot from Pharaoh pulled up in a cloud of dust. Two officials jumped out. What now?

"'Pharaoh wants to see you. Now!' was all they said. With rough hands they pulled me into the chariot and raced toward the palace.

"I was frightened to see Pharaoh, but I also feared I wouldn't live long enough to get there. I had never traveled so fast in my life as in that chariot. I had often ridden camels and enjoyed their rhythmic rocking pace. But the chariot driver kept the horses at a gallop. The two officials stood and held to the railing. They could brace themselves against the bumps. But I was forced to sit. I could easily have jumped out if I had stood, so they made me sit.

"Not only did I feel every bump in the road, but I also got the full force of the dust. The men standing were above the dust as it rose from the hooves of the horses. I covered my head with my mantle as I would in a dust storm. Finally the driver took pity on me and slowed the horses to a trot. The three hours' ride to the palace seemed like forever.

"I was so glad when the chariot stopped. My legs were so stiff and cramped that I could hardly get up. When the officials pushed me for walking so slowly, my fears about facing Pharaoh returned. I had survived the chariot ride, but would I survive the next hour? Would Pharaoh execute me swiftly, or would he torture me first?

"When I was ushered into Pharaoh's presence, I was too full of fear to absorb the grandeur of his palace. All I noticed was a series of wide steps with his throne above it.

"'What have you done to me?' Pharaoh's voice thundered from above me.

"I didn't say anything. I was trying to think what he meant. I hadn't done anything to Pharaoh.

"'What have you done to me?' he repeated. 'Why didn't you tell me she was your wife?'

"I still didn't answer. I had no excuse for being deceitful about Sarai. I couldn't explain to him my fears and apprehensions. But I also couldn't understand Pharaoh's intense anger. What did it matter to him whether the beautiful woman he wanted was someone's sister or someone's wife? If he wanted her, he got her.

"While I was trying to sort things out in my head, Pharaoh kept shouting at me.

"'Why did you say, "She is my sister," so that I took her to be my wife? Now then, here is your wife. Take her and go!'[24]

"It was only then that I noticed that Sarai was standing nearby. She looked pale and drawn. Pharaoh shouted some more orders to his men, and before I knew it, Sarai and I were hustled outside. Then Hagar appeared, and the three of us were on our way back home. This time we traveled in a wagon, not a chariot, which was much more comfortable.

"I had to pinch myself to see if I was awake or dreaming. Was I alive or dead? What had happened back there? And why? Were we really free?

"I turned to ask Sarai, and noticed an amused smile on her face. When I asked her what had happened, she burst into hysterical laughter. I looked questioningly at Hagar, but she just shook her head. I waited impatiently for Sarai to get control of herself.

"When Sarai finally stopped laughing, she started to cry. A soft wailing cry. That was when I realized she was in shock. I drew Sarai close to me, held her tight, and gently kissed her face and her hair. I felt her body slowly relax. We traveled the rest of the way home in silence.

"Later, between Sarai and Hagar, I was able to piece together their story.

"When Sarai arrived at Pharaoh's palace, she was immediately taken into the women's quarters where she was bathed in steam, soaked in mineral waters, then rubbed down head to foot with scented oils. Then hairdressers washed her long, thick hair and set it in an elaborate style. After that, makeup specialists came in to do her face. Then Sarai was

---

[24] Genesis 12:19

taken to the wardrobe, and consultants helped her choose the most becoming clothes.

"Sarai had seen many beautiful clothes, but nothing compared to these! Some fabrics were so delicate and silky, others were incredibly soft. 'Silks from the Orient,' they said. 'And Egyptian cotton—the best, softest cotton in the whole world.'

"And the colors! The colors were as brilliant as flowers. Where did they get such dyes? Sarai wondered.

"At last the consultant settled on what Sarai would wear when she was presented to Pharaoh."

Abraham looked over at his thirteen-year-old son, who was following every word. He decided not to go into any more detail.

"Women were presented to Pharaoh in a group for inspection. If any of them caught Pharaoh's attention, they would be introduced. After presenting the women, the servants quietly withdrew.

"Pharaoh was used to seeing beautiful women, but when Sarai was ushered into his court along with several other women, the mighty Pharaoh was visibly impressed. Pharaoh caught Sarai's eye and started to move toward her. He was interrupted on the way by a messenger.

"'Didn't I give orders not to be disturbed?' Pharaoh said angrily.

"'Yes,' the messenger replied, 'but you wanted to be kept informed about your favorite wife. She is in labor, and is in great difficulty.'

"'See that she has the best midwives attending her,' Pharaoh said.

"'She already has the best in the land.'

"Pharaoh's anger subsided. 'Keep me informed.'

"As the messenger departed, Pharaoh called after him, 'I hope it's a boy.'

"With that news, Pharaoh was distracted. So he called for a servant to take Sarai and the other women to their quarters to return at a more opportune time.

"By morning the whole palace was whispering the news. After a long, hard labor, Pharaoh's favorite wife had delivered a baby. It was a boy. It was stillborn. The wife was weak, but she was expected to recover.

"Pharaoh asked to have Sarai brought into his court several times, but it seemed that every time he tried to approach her, he was interrupted by a messenger. After receiving the message, Pharaoh appeared disturbed.

"Hagar heard more from the palace grapevine than did Sarai, because she understood the language and could converse with the other servants. There seemed to be a contagious disease spreading throughout the palace, but it wasn't spreading in a normal fashion. It was a disease usually found only amongst prostitutes and their patrons, but now people in monogamous relationships were getting it.

"Though Pharaoh himself didn't get the disease, one by one his other wives came down with it. The first time one of his wives contracted the disease, Pharaoh was considering executing her for being unfaithful to him. But she swore loudly that she *had* been faithful, and all of her servants swore to her innocence. Pharaoh's wives could not be unfaithful without the knowledge and cooperation of their personal attendants.

"Then Pharaoh's officials started showing symptoms of the disease. As rumors spread, those who worked outside the palace were afraid to come inside for fear they too would catch this strange disease. They believed a curse of the gods was upon the palace.

"Hagar told Sarai what was happening in the palace and told her about the rumor that a curse of the gods had fallen upon the place. That was when the truth dawned on Sarai. It was not a curse of the gods but the curse of the true God, Yahweh. Yahweh was fighting for her!

"Hagar had never heard about Yahweh until she met Sarai, but if Yahweh was stronger than the Egyptian gods, that would surely explain this unexplainable disease.

"'But why is your god so angry?' Hagar asked. 'You have done nothing wrong. And Pharaoh has done nothing wrong. All he did was bring you into his harem. And he has been very generous to your brother Abram.'

"That was when Sarai confessed to Hagar that she was my wife," Abraham said to Isaac, "and she poured out the whole story about my fears—and my solution. Sarai begged Hagar to understand. In light of what was happening in the palace, our little deception about her being my sister seemed pretty silly.

"'You must tell Pharaoh.' Hagar said to Sarai.

"But Sarai was too afraid to tell him.

"The next day there was more bad news. Another of Pharaoh's wives had a miscarriage.

"'You must tell Pharaoh.' Hagar insisted again. But Sarai was still afraid.

"'If your god Yahweh is more powerful than the Egyptian gods, as you claim he is, why are you afraid?' Hagar asked. 'If he has brought these diseases and disasters upon Pharaoh when Pharaoh thought you were Abram's sister, won't he protect you even when Pharaoh knows the truth?'

"That made sense to Sarai, so she arranged to have a private conversation with Pharaoh. In fear and trembling, she told Pharaoh that she was already married. She also told him she thought that the disasters that were falling on the palace were because of her.

"We will never know what Pharaoh would have done if he had known from the beginning that Sarai was my wife. But in light of what was happening in the palace, Pharaoh wanted nothing more to do with Sarai no matter how beautiful she was. He was afraid of Yahweh and angry with me. Pharaoh wanted us as far away as possible—out of the country. We planned to leave the next day. Back to Canaan. There was no other alternative.

"As we were packing up our tents the next morning, officials from Pharaoh's palace came by again. Seeing the looks on our faces, they quickly said, 'Don't be afraid. We are not here to harm you. We are here to escort you out of town to make sure you leave.'

"Just then herdsmen driving sheep and cattle came into view, so I stepped back to let them pass.

"'These are for you,' the official said. "A final gift from Pharaoh. Everybody in the palace is healthy again, and Pharaoh sends his thanks.'

"On our way out of town, we met a caravan coming into Egypt from Canaan. We enquired about the famine there. They said there had recently been heavy rains in Canaan, and things were rapidly turning green again. Yahweh was good to us in spite of ourselves."

Isaac was trying to absorb the whole story. Finally he spoke up.

"Father?"

"Yes, Son."

"When you left Haran and Uncle Nahor, you renounced your inheritance. You said you didn't want anyone to be able to say they made you rich."

"That's right."

"Well, when you left Egypt, you were wealthy, weren't you?"

"Yes, very wealthy. When Lot and I took stock after leaving Egypt, we couldn't believe how much livestock and silver and gold we had accumulated."

"So didn't Pharaoh make you rich?"

"I didn't see it that way. Pharaoh treated me well for Sarai's sake, but his gifts were within the bounds of a shrewd business transaction. We accumulated far more from good animal husbandry and from marketing our livestock than from Pharaoh.

"Besides," Abraham smiled as the thought struck him, "I don't think Pharaoh will boast that he made me rich. He never wants to hear my name again!"

Abraham paused again, pondering the question his son had raised.

"No, Pharaoh didn't make me rich. Yahweh did. He kept his promise to bless me even when I didn't deserve it."

4

Abram Separates from Lot

"What happened after you left Egypt, Father?" Isaac asked.

He was in the mood for a story, and Abraham was always happy to oblige.

"Well," Abraham began, "the first place Lot and I came to in Canaan was the Negev. But we didn't stay there long. If fact we didn't stay anywhere long. Our flocks and herds were so large that we had to move them frequently. They would quickly graze any pasture right to the ground.

"People in my line of work are always wandering, but I felt an unusual restlessness. Something I couldn't put my finger on. I just kept going.

"Then one day the terrain around me started to look familiar. It wasn't until I saw the altar that I realized where we were. My most trusted servant, Eliezer, spotted it at the same time.

"'It's Bethel!' he exclaimed. 'We're back at Bethel.'

"From the tone of his voice, I knew that he was as pleased to be back there as I was.

"'Let's do it again,' I said to him. 'Let's stay until the Sabbath and worship Yahweh here together.'

"Eliezer was more than pleased to agree.

"'In Egypt we acquired many new servants,' he said. 'They know little or nothing about Yahweh. They need to learn more about him.'

"And so the preparations began.

"I, more than anyone, needed to get right with God. If I was to teach my people to walk with God, I would have to lead by example. I could not tell them one thing then do another. I needed to make things right before Yahweh, Sarai, Lot and all of my people.

"I instructed my people to quit work mid morning so we could be ready to eat at sundown, when the Sabbath began. We gathered on a hillside so everyone could see and hear me.

"Because so many servants were new, I started from the beginning—back in Ur. I told of my early, limited knowledge of Yahweh and how that grew as I learned from my forefathers. I told of hearing Yahweh's voice promising to bless me and make me a blessing. I told of Yahweh's command to leave my country and my people in Ur. I told of hearing Yahweh's voice again in Haran, telling me to leave my father's house. I told of coming to Canaan, hearing Yahweh's voice again in Shechem, then worshiping Yahweh there and in Luz. I explained that we called Luz Bethel, because it felt to us like the house of God. I told of going to Egypt to escape famine.

"Then the story got harder to tell. Haltingly I confessed what I had done. My worry. My fears. My deception. Worst of all, my lack of faith in Yahweh. I had trusted him all the way from Ur to Egypt. I couldn't explain why I didn't trust him when I got there. In hindsight I looked so foolish. So self-absorbed. In Yahweh's sight I had sinned. Because Yahweh is perfectly holy, my fellowship with him was broken. Worse, in Yahweh's sight I deserved to die for what I did.

"But—this was the good news—fellowship with Yahweh could be restored. Yahweh had taught the first pair, Adam and Eve, that fellowship with him could be restored by having a substitute die in one's place. If a perfect innocent animal dies, that satisfies Yahweh's sense of justice. It's a mystery that I don't fully understand, but somehow it makes sense to God. Some day he will explain it to me. All I know is that it is a picture of something God plans to do in the future. Yahweh makes the rules. I just follow them. With justice done, fellowship is restored.

"Then I showed my people how it was done. I called Sarai to my side, and in front of everybody I apologized to her and asked her forgiveness. With tears she accepted my apology. Then she confessed her own sin. With her powers of persuasion and her influence over me, she could have made me see reason. She could have believed Yahweh would protect her from Pharaoh, but she chose to obey me, her husband, rather than Yahweh.

"I motioned to Eliezer, and he brought a lamb to us. Sarai and I both put our hands on its head, explaining that we were placing our sins on this animal. As I slit the lamb's throat and sprinkled its blood on all four sides of the altar, I was fully aware that I deserved the same fate. I placed the lamb in pieces on the burning wood. As the fire totally consumed the animal, I called on the name of Yahweh in confession, thanksgiving and worship.

"Seeing that some of my people were moved, I had an idea. I called Eliezer to bring a heifer. Then I asked anyone who wanted to begin serving Yahweh to step forward. Hagar was the first to respond. She wanted to follow Yahweh rather than the gods of Egypt. Several dozen others also came forward. One by one, they confessed their sins and laid their hands on the animal's head. Its blood was sprinkled on the altar and the animal was consumed by fire.

"When I asked if anyone wanted to have broken fellowship with Yahweh restored, Eliezer was the first to respond. Many others joined him. This time we didn't consume the animals by fire. We butchered the animal into pieces. We burned the fat, the liver and the kidneys on the fire, then we waved the pieces of meat briefly over the altar, symbolically giving them to Yahweh. We killed enough animals to feed those who came.

"It was some time after noon when the people stopped coming forward. We then killed enough animals to feed the rest, but didn't sprinkle the blood of those animals on the altar, nor did we burn the fat or the inner parts of those animals on the altar. Those animals were only for food. The rest of the afternoon was spent in preparation for the evening meal.

"When everything was ready, I thanked Yahweh for the food and we began to eat as we watched the sun set. After the meal we sang songs of worship and praise to Yahweh.

"As had happened the last time we were at Bethel, the next morning there was a different atmosphere in the camp. Again my people gathered around me to ask more about Yahweh. And again, conversations that began with a few turned into conversations with a crowd.

"There is something special about that place. My people will always call it Bethel, the house of God.

"After the Sabbath we moved again. This time we went southward. I didn't hear Yahweh's voice right away, but I was able to think more clearly than I had for a while, certainly more clearly than when I was in Egypt! And that strange restlessness was gone.

"I came to the conclusion that Lot and I should separate. The land couldn't support us while we stayed together. His herdsmen and mine were always quarrelling as they fought for the best pastures for their animals. Even pitching all the tents was a problem. Sometimes we had trouble finding enough level ground for all the tents.

"Lot and I were not the only ones to consider. The Canaanites and Perizzites were in the land before us. If we didn't leave them enough space, they would fight against us. Though Lot and I had well-trained guards, we were not interested in war.

"Eventually the crowding began to affect the relationship between Lot and me. When we began to be short with each other, I knew something had to change, so I spoke to Lot about it. 'Let's not have any quarrelling between you and me, or between your herdsmen and mine. We're brothers. Let's part company. The whole land is before you. You choose. If you go to the left, I'll go to the right; if you go to the right, I'll go to the left.'[25]

"Lot's face brightened. He liked the idea. Why should he always live in my shadow? He needed his independence.

---

[25] See Genesis 13:8-9

"We were camped on a ridge that gave us a sweeping view of the land in all directions. It was a very clear day, and we could see all the way from the Great Sea in the west to the Jordan River in the east. The river widened into a deep lake, then ended up in a plain, well watered by the river. It reminded me of the description of the Garden of Eden passed down by my forefathers. It reminded Lot of another place.

"'It looks like Egypt,' Lot said. 'Like the Nile delta where we escaped famine and our flocks and herds multiplied so quickly. This place is so well watered, it will never experience drought.'

"'That's true,' I agreed. 'If I had seen this place, I wouldn't have gone to Egypt.'"

"And you wouldn't have run into Pharaoh," Isaac added.

"If only . . .," Abraham sighed. "But we can't change the past."

Abraham continued his story.

"It didn't take Lot long to make up his mind. He would go east. He would have the whole plain of Jordan in which to roam. We parted on friendly terms and promised to keep in touch."

"He took the best land," Isaac said. "Why did you give him first choice?"

"He was older than I, even though he was my nephew. I loved Lot as a brother, and I wanted the best for him. I was happy to see him get the best land. But I had Yahweh's promise to bless me. That promise was not conditional upon my location.

"Besides, from time to time since leaving Haran, I had wondered if 'leaving my father's household' should have included Lot. And there was another reason."

"What was that?" Isaac asked.

"Yahweh's prophecy to Noah. *Canaan will be the slave of Shem*. I still had the feeling that somehow Yahweh wanted me to be part of the fulfillment of that prophecy. So I was content to stay in Canaan while Lot moved away. The little town of Bela looked like a good place for him to begin."

"Wasn't Bela near Sodom and Gomorrah, the cities that God destroyed?" asked Isaac.

"Yes, Son. I wasn't aware at the time how wicked the men of Sodom were. But the more I learned about the cities in that plain, the more I was concerned for Lot. When I heard that he had pitched his tents near Sodom, I was even more concerned. I often prayed that he would remain true to Yahweh and be a spiritual light in that darkness.

"Immediately after parting with Lot, I knew it was the right decision."

"How did you know?" asked Isaac.

"Yahweh spoke to me again," said Abraham. "I heard his voice."

"What did he say?"

"He said basically what he had said the last time—when I was in Shechem. But he added a lot more detail. He didn't leave so much for me to figure out on my own. This time he spoke in the light of day. I was looking east toward the plain of Jordan where Lot was and wondering how he was faring in that wicked part of the country.

"'Lift up your eyes from where you are,' Yahweh said, 'and look north and south, east and west. All the land that you see I will give to you and your seed forever. I will make your seed like the dust of the earth, so that if anyone could count the dust, then your seed could be counted.'[26]

"The first thing that struck me about Yahweh's message was talk about my offspring. I had almost forgotten about having children. Sarai was barren. She had been ever since we were married. Now she was beyond the age when people use the term 'barren.' She no longer had a monthly flow. Yet Yahweh was saying my offspring would be uncountable—'like the dust of the earth', he said.

"I must have stood there with my mouth open in surprise, because Yahweh spoke again, this time urgently.

"'*Go*,' he said, 'walk through the length and breadth of the land, for I am giving it to you.'[27]

"With Yahweh's words ringing in my ears, I ran toward my tent to tell Sarai. On the way there, I saw Eliezer, my chief servant. I shouted to him to start packing up the camp. We were moving.

---

[26] Genesis 13:14-16, NIV. Compare KJV.
[27] Genesis 13:17

"'Where to?' he asked.

"I hadn't thought that far.

"'I'll let you know when I figure it out,' I said.

"Eliezer shook his head and started passing the word. We were moving on.

"I repeated to Sarai word for word what Yahweh had said. Just talking about it helped to clarify my thinking.

"'I was looking down at the plain of Jordan when Yahweh spoke,' I said, thinking out loud. 'But he said to lift up my eyes from where I am. I looked up and saw that the ridge on which I was camped continued to rise to the north.'

"Sarai's eyes followed mine, and she said what I was thinking.

"'If we follow that ridge to the summit, we will have an even better view of the land,' she said. 'Let's begin there.'

"So that's what we did.

"As we walked along, Yahweh's words kept echoing through my mind. *Walk the length and breadth of the land. I am giving it to you.* I started to feel the excitement of his promise. I chose to believe it.

"My eyes kept going toward the summit. It was dotted with huge oak trees. They would be ideal for shade on a hot day. Those trees have been a landmark to me ever since."

"Hebron," Isaac said.

"Yes," Abraham replied, "but it wasn't called Hebron at the time. I will explain later how it got to be called Hebron.

"At the summit I stood with my arm around Sarai, and we drank in the view. *Look north and south, east and west,* Yahweh had said. So we turned slowly and looked in all directions. *All the land that you see I will give to you and your offspring forever.* Other than quoting Yahweh, we said nothing. We were trying to absorb the promise. It was so hard to visualize when we didn't have any children.

"The view was awe-inspiring. My heart rose in praise to Yahweh. The One who made all this beautiful land could surely give us a child. I chose to believe it.

"I was jarred back to the present when Eliezer asked me where we should pitch our tents. I looked around at the huge oak trees. Right where we were was an ideal spot. As we were unloading our animals, a man approached us. He had been sitting under one of the trees and watching us, but we had not noticed him until he approached.

"He introduced himself as Mamre, and I introduced myself, my wife, and Eliezer. We were on Mamre's land, so we would not be able to pitch our tents here, but Mamre was very helpful in pointing out a place nearby where we could camp without trespassing on someone's land. There were some large shade trees there, too, for which we were grateful.

"Mamre left us alone to set up camp but invited several of us to join him for a visit when we were settled. That was the beginning of a wonderful lifelong friendship.

"Almost every evening we got together to drink coffee and talk. Sometimes we met in his tent, sometimes in mine. When one of us smelled the coffee beans roasting, we knew the other was finished work for the day. The smell of coffee served as an invitation to the other to come and relax. We talked about anything and everything.

"When I asked what they called this place, Mamre said, 'It depends on whom you ask.' The walled city nearby was called Kiriath Arba, the city of Arba. It was named after a giant of a man who had founded the city. But Mamre was an independent sort of man who lived outside the city. He called his place Mamre.

"Before our first Sabbath in that place, I built an altar. I just had to worship Yahweh for all his goodness to me. My new friend came by and watched with interest. He wondered what gods I worshiped. He seemed surprised when I said I worshiped only one god, the true God—Yahweh. Mamre had never heard of Yahweh. Over time I would have many opportunities to share about Yahweh.

"Another favorite topic of conversation was politics. Since leaving Haran, I had not kept up with the developments in the Babylonian empire, but Mamre told me that the empire was expanding. Four kings from the east and north had joined forces and were moving west and south, subjugating territory as they went.

"I was interested to learn who the four kings were. One king was the king of Shinar, which I knew as the heart of the Babylonian empire— southern Babylonia. Another king was from northern Babylonia, which I was familiar with, having lived in Haran for so long. I pricked up my ears when I heard that the ringleader of the four kings was Kedorlaomer, king of Elam. I had heard the name Elam before. The territory was named after one of the sons of Shem and was inhabited by his descendants. After the Flood and before the Dispersion my ancestors had lived in Elam. After the Dispersion Eber, whose language we speak, moved away and settled north of Haran. The fourth king, king of Ellasar, was practically an old neighbor. He ruled the cities just across the Euphrates River from Ur.

"A year or two before Lot and I separated, these four kings from the east had subjugated the territory south of the Salt Sea. The cities in that area—Sodom, Gomorrah, Bela, and several other cities—were already paying taxes to Egypt, but when Kedorlaomer's soldiers moved in, the inhabitants were forced to pay taxes to them as well! The people in that area were not happy with the situation.

"From time to time I heard news from Lot, and it was always the same story—he loved the country, but he hated the heavy tax burden. His flocks and herds were prospering, and he was gaining respect and prestige among the people.

"Mamre soon introduced me to his brothers, Eshcol and Aner. Eshcol was a vintner who lived in the nearby valley. When he visited Mamre, he usually brought fresh grapes or raisins, depending upon the season, and a skin of wine with him. His raisins were larger and sweeter than any I had ever seen. When I exclaimed about the wonderful quality of his wine, he said it was due to the grapes from which it was made. The slope of the land gave just the right exposure to the sun. And the nearby lake provided the perfect moisture conditions. He offered to bring me a cluster of grapes from the next harvest.

"I could hardly believe my eyes when, a few months later, two of Eshcol's servants came to my tent. They were carrying a single cluster of grapes between them, slung on a pole which they carried on their shoulders. The grapes hung almost to the ground!

"Mamre and his brothers were powerful enough that they were able to resist the attempts of Egypt to tax them, but they were keeping a close eye on the actions of Kedorlaomer and his confederates. If enough people banded together, they might be able to resist a takeover.

"Mamre and his brothers were aware that due to my nomadic lifestyle I had not paid taxes since coming to Canaan. It was mainly those who lived within walled cities who paid taxes for protection from outsiders.

"'Yahweh is my protection,' I told Mamre.

"'I have yet to see what he can do,' Mamre replied skeptically. 'But I am impressed with your numerous well-trained servants.'

"'When it comes to fighting,' I said, 'I rely on the men born in my household—born to my servants. They are like my sons, and would fight to the death for me.'

"'How many do you have?' Mamre asked.

"'I'm not sure, but I'll find out and let you know,' I told him.

"I took a count. Three hundred and eighteen. I had well over a thousand servants, male and female, but 318 fighting men had been born, raised and trained in my household![28] I hadn't realized I had so many.

"Not long after learning that, Mamre and his brothers came by with a proposal for me. They invited me to form an alliance with them in case Kedorlaomer and his confederates became a threat. After some consideration, I accepted his invitation.

"And that gave me the idea to name my location. Hebron. 'Alliance.' I had toyed with calling the place Ebron, meaning 'company', because I enjoyed the company of Mamre and his brothers, and also because it was suggestive of 'Eber', my language. But 'Hebron' incorporated all three ideas—company, language (Eber), and now alliance. Hebron it would be.

"When I told Mamre I had named my place Hebron, he nodded his approval. Then he commented, 'Now we know what to call your *place*, but what do we call *you*?'

"Puzzled, I replied, 'My name is Abram. But you already know that. What do you mean?'

"'Who are you collectively? What tribe are you from? When a man has a large family and becomes prominent, his relatives and descendants

---

[28] See Genesis 14:14

are named after him and the area in which they live is also named after him. Canaan's descendants are Canaanites. Their territory is called Canaan. Heth's descendants are Hittites. None of my ancestors was particularly prominent, but we live in the hill country. So I'm called an Amorite, literally a "high one", because I'm a highlander. What kind of "ite" are you?'

"I didn't know what to say.

"'I have never called myself an "ite",' I confessed. 'None of my forefathers was particularly influential or famous. The best known was Noah. But everyone is descended from Noah. Next best known is Shem—probably because he lived so long. But calling ourselves Shemites is not very descriptive. That would include a third of the world's population.'

"I thought down through the list of my forefathers.

"'My forefathers were all followers of Yahweh,' I told Mamre. 'They were more interested in living for him than in conquering territories or making a name for themselves. The only one who possibly stands out is Eber. After the incident at the Tower of Babel, he and his family spoke a different language. But that didn't make him famous.'

"Mamre kept pressing the issue.

"'Maybe none of your ancestors were powerful, but you certainly are. Look at all the tents around you. These people act at your bidding. They are your tribe. Shouldn't we call you Abramites?'

"'We can't call them Abramites,' I objected. 'That would imply that they are my descendants.'

"'*None* of them are your descendants?' Mamre reacted in surprise.

"'Not one,' I replied. 'Not even Eliezer, my most trusted servant and my right arm. I recruited him in Damascus on my way to Canaan. I have no children. Sarai is barren.'

"'So, take another wife,' Mamre suggested. 'A young one. That's what I would do.'

"Mamre paused.

"'I was going to say take a pretty one,' he continued sheepishly, 'but you already have that. Sarai certainly is beautiful.'

"'Yahweh intended a man to be the husband of only one wife,' I told Mamre. 'He intended the two to become one. That oneness is not possible for a man with multiple wives to relate to, or for a woman who has to compete with other wives for her husband's attention. Besides, I have never had eyes for anyone but Sarai.'

"'I can see why,' Mamre replied.

"Returning to our former conversation, he persisted, 'So, what is the language you speak? Eber? I understand that all your people speak Eber. Why not call you Eberites?'

"Again I objected, 'Sarai and I are descendants of Eber, but most of our servants are not.'

"'What about a place name?' Mamre suggested. 'If I am an Amorite because I live in the highlands, you could be Hebronites.'

"'I have no intention of settling permanently in Hebron,' I replied. 'My flocks and herds force me to keep moving. Besides, any kind of "ite" suggests blood relationship. I could argue that you are the son of a highlander and your father was the son of a highlander, but I have no sons.'

"'So let's find a compromise,' Mamre said. 'Language seems to be the major tie with your people. If not Eber-*ites*, how about just plain Ebers?'

"'Combine Hebron and Eber and get Hebber,' I suggested, falling into the spirit of the search for a name. 'Abram the Hebber.'

"'Hebber.' Mamre rolled the name on his tongue a few times. 'Hebbers. Heebers. Hebrews! That's easier to say.'

"We both liked that, so that's what Mamre called me from then on. Abram the Hebrew.[29] The name stuck, and in time we referred to our language as Hebrew as well."

"I always wondered how we got to be called Hebrews," Isaac said.

"So now you know, Son. Now you know."

One of the oil lamps flickered and went out, reminding Abraham of the passing of time.

"It's getting late, Son. Time to go to bed."

---

[29] Genesis 14:13 is the first mention in the Bible of the name "Hebrew."

5

Abram Rescues Lot

The next evening Isaac again wanted to hear a story, so Abraham continued.

"My flocks and herds kept us on the move, but every year we spent some time in Hebron. Mamre always greeted us warmly upon our return, and I was always eager to get caught up on the latest news. How was Lot doing? Were Kedorlaomer and his confederates still a threat?

"For twelve years there hadn't been much change politically. But Lot's situation had changed. He had given up his nomadic lifestyle and moved into the city of Sodom. There he was steadily growing in influence."

"I hope he was able to influence people to follow Yahweh," Isaac said.

"I hoped so too," Abraham replied. "But his influence in Sodom was mainly political. He became a city elder and often sat at the city gate. Lot didn't mind paying taxes locally for protection, roads, water and other tangible benefits. But paying taxes to Egypt and providing labor for Egypt benefited only Pharaoh and his need to build grand cities and temples in Egypt. Paying taxes also to the Babylonian Empire, which was headquartered even further away, was an insult!

"Lot convinced the elders and the king of Sodom to form a confederation with other cities in the area and throw off the yoke of Babylon. So in the thirteenth year, they refused to pay Kedorlaomer's tax collectors.

"They got away with it for a year, then Kedorlaomer went on the warpath. If the cities in the Valley of Siddim, where Lot lived, rebelled successfully, other cities nearby would soon join the rebellion.

"We followed the news with interest as Kedorlaomer and his confederates moved steadily southward conquering the territories east of the Jordan River. By conquering the strongest cities in each territory, they were assured of facing no resistance from the smaller cities. We became aware of their conquests when they arrived across the river from Canaan's northern border.

"First they defeated the Rephaites in Ashteroth Karnaim, across the river Jordan and directly east of the Sea of Galilee. The Rephaites were a giant race, who brought fear into the hearts of most of their enemies, but Kedorlaomer had little trouble defeating them. Then he continued south and conquered the Zuzites."

"Zuzites!" Isaac laughed. "What a strange name!"

"If you think that's funny," Abraham replied, "their original name was even stranger. Zamzummites."

Isaac laughed harder.

"Each language has a distinctive sound," his father explained. "To outsiders the Zuzites sound like a swarm of bees. Their talk sounds like murmuring or humming or buzzing. Zam-zum-zam-zum. So they became known as Zamzummites. Eventually it was shortened to Zuzites.

"The kings in the Valley of Siddim thought they would be targeted next. But Kedorlaomer went right past them. He continued marching south. He defeated the Emites in Shaveh Kiriathaim, and the Horites in the hill country of Seir. Then he went still further south—right to El Paran on the shore of the Gulf of Aqaba! By the time he conquered El Paran, he had control of the entire length of the King's Highway from the northwestern edge of Babylonia to the Gulf of Aqaba. This made Babylon the strongest empire in the world—even stronger than Egypt.

It also meant that no country east of Sodom would join in the rebellion against Kedorlaomer.

"He was targeting Lot and Sodom and the other cities in the Valley of Siddim because he knew that was the centre of the rebellion. But he didn't go straight for Lot. Instead he conquered all the territories in a circle around the Valley of Siddim, so they would not be able to add other armies to their alliance and so they would have no place to run.

"Only after conquering El Paran did Kedorlaomer swing west and north, continuing in a circle around the desert of Paran."

"I hear that Paran is very mountainous," Isaac said.

Abraham gave his son a nod of approval for his knowledge of geography.

"Yes," he replied. "It would have been pointless to go right into Paran itself. The territory is very mountainous and is protected by rugged passes which are easy to defend and almost impossible to conquer. But Kedorlaomer made his point. Nobody would be able to escape into the desert of Paran. He followed the highway around it, going as far west as En Mishpat, the stronghold of the Amalekites.

"En Mishpat has an abundance of water, making it the most livable part of the Sinai Peninsula. But that advantage has a dark side. Their water brings life, but it also brings strife as other empires seek to control it. Because they have water, the international trade route runs through En Mishpat, but that same highway makes it easier for invaders to approach them.

"So the Amalekites often found themselves under attack. They began to feel persecuted by the gods. That is why the place became known as En Mishpat—'fountain of judgment'. 'Fountain' because of their rich water supply, and 'judgment' because they had to fight to maintain control of it."

"I understand that the Amalekites are a wicked people," Isaac said. "Do you think Yahweh was bringing judgment upon them through Kedorlaomer?"

"It could be," replied Abraham. "God is in control of the whole universe. He sets up kings and deposes them according to his purpose. He can use one king to bring judgment upon another. Then a third king to bring judgment upon the second one if he does not acknowledge Yahweh.

"Once En Mishpat fell to the Babylonians, the whole territory of the Amalekites capitulated. El Paran and Amalekite territory were right on the border of Egypt, so Kedorlaomer was sending a message to Egypt: This is our battle. We are stronger than you. Don't interfere with us or we will invade Egypt as well!

"Kedorlaomer wanted to make sure that the kings in the Valley of Siddim would not be able to join forces with any other nation—not even the Egyptians, whom they resented for taxing them without receiving any benefit in return.

"The last people Kedorlaomer targeted before tackling the Valley of Siddim were the Amorites in Hazezon Tamar."

"That's straight east of us on the shore of the Salt Sea!" Isaac exclaimed.

"Yes," Abraham replied. "I visited that area with Mamre once. I was going to Sodom to visit Lot. Mamre offered to accompany me as far as Hazezon Tamar, where he stopped to visit his relatives. He introduced me to his family and friends there.

"The area is beautiful but very rugged—an oasis with plenty of palm trees, and the best water you ever tasted! I guess that is why the Amorites chose to live there.

"You have to be part mountain goat to live there. I scrambled around the rocks and caves and springs and waterfalls with Mamre for a day, and ruined a perfectly good pair of sandals. We saw lots of wild goats and a few coneys."

"What's a coney?" Isaac asked.

"It's a hyrax or rock badger about the size of a rabbit," his father replied. "They are easy to spot in the morning when they sun themselves on the rocks. They retire to the shade when the day gets hot.

"Hazezon Tamar means 'row of palms', which is descriptive of the place as you see it from the Salt Sea shore, but it could just as easily have been called En-Gedi, 'spring of a young goat'."

"I think En-Gedi is a more romantic name," Isaac interjected.

"I agree," said his father. "Anyway, Kedorlaomer knew he had to conquer the place. He had excellent military intelligence. The closer he got to the Valley of Siddim, the more information he gathered concerning conditions there. He knew that Lot had been instrumental in convincing the kings in the Valley of Siddim to rebel. He knew that the Amorites in the highlands were an independent people, therefore they would be sympathetic to the cause of the kings in the valley and would likely join forces with them. He knew that if he conquered Hazezon Tamar, the centre of Amorite territory, the nearby Amorites would likely stay out of the battle.

"He may even have heard rumors that the independent Amorite, Mamre, who avoided taxes by living outside Kiriath Arba, had founded his own town, and had made an alliance with his brothers and a powerful nomad alien."

Abraham paused to see if his son would catch the reference to himself.

"That was you!" Isaac exclaimed. "Do you really think Kedorlaomer knew about you?"

Abraham laughed.

"Maybe, maybe not. He knew a lot. If his intelligence was good enough, he would even have known that I was related to Lot. We kept in touch with each other at regular intervals.

"The Amorites put up a good fight. They had the advantage of knowing their mountains. Many observers would have bet on the Amorites. But Kedorlaomer's forces scrambled up into the mountains, adapted to the Amorites' guerrilla tactics, routed them from their caves, and defeated them as soundly as they had defeated all the other nations in their path.

"Mamre and his brothers feared that we would be the next target for Kedorlaomer's armies, so they and I made sure that our men were as prepared for battle as possible. My 318 trained men practiced war games against Mamre's men. Mamre commented that he was glad his men weren't fighting mine for real, or he would lose!

"To our relief, Kedorlaomer didn't come as far north as Hebron. He had proved that he could fight in any terrain using any tactics. Finally he was able to focus on the ones who had dared to stand up against the Babylonian empire. So the kings marched out and drew up their battle lines in the Valley of Siddim—four powerful kings from the east against five rebellious but not so powerful kings in the valley.

"It wasn't much of a fight. In fact from an observer's point of view, it was rather comical. I heard the story from a man who escaped from Sodom. He could hardly keep from laughing as he told it. Lot had asked him to be sure to report to me. As soon as the escapee arrived, I sent a message to Mamre to come quickly so he could hear the full report.

"Kedorlaomer, coming from the western shore of the Salt Sea, had gathered enough intelligence about the terrain to know how to defeat the rebel kings without much of a fight. His forces had noticed the tar pits and sink holes along the southern shore of the sea, and scouts were sent out to survey the territory ahead. They learned that those tar pits became more frequent between their location and the Valley of Siddim.

"Kedorlaomer came just close enough to let the valley kings know he was ready to engage them in battle. The rebel kings had known for months that Kedorlaomer was coming for them. Putting on a brave front, the local armies marched out in battle to fight the Babylonian forces. The land between them was flat and looked like a good place to engage the enemy. But they had forgotten why there was no road through this plain.

"As the local armies advanced, several of their men fell into tar pits. They changed course, only to have more men fall into more tar pits. The Babylonian soldiers began to roar with laughter. Demoralized and not knowing how to advance, the remaining rebel forces headed for higher ground. While they were fleeing into the nearby hills, the Babylonian forces advanced unchallenged along the highway around the salt flats to the Valley of Siddim. The conquest of the valley couldn't have been easier.

"With no fighting men to resist them, Kedorlaomer and his confederates entered the two largest cities, Sodom and Gomorrah. They arrived so quickly and quietly that the elders sitting at the city gate didn't notice their approach until it was too late. They kidnapped the elders, ransacked the cities, seized all the goods and carried everything away—including all the food. Loaded down with goods, the armies didn't even bother with the smaller cities in the valley, but headed back home along the King's Highway.

"Mission accomplished. No one would dare to stand up against the Babylonian empire again."

Abraham paused.

"No one," he continued, "but an alien who did not fear the Babylonian gods."

Isaac's eyes widened in surprise.

"You don't mean that you went to war against Kedorlaomer, do you, Father?"

"Now you're sounding like Mamre, Son. Kedorlaomer was only a man. His gods were nothing. I had Yahweh on my side. The living God. God Most High, Creator of heaven and earth.

"As the escapee from Sodom finished his report, it dawned on me that kidnapping the elders involved my nephew Lot. I had laughed at the account of the battle which wasn't much of a battle, then sobered up when I remembered that Lot had been chosen to be an elder in Sodom and spent much of his days sitting at the city gate.

"I questioned the man from Sodom, and he confirmed that Lot had been taken captive. So had his wife and daughters. And his household servants. They had been conscripted to help carry away all Lot's possessions.

"Everybody with wealth had been captured, along with their families and servants, and all their possessions and stores of food had been seized. Babylon wouldn't need to bother sending around tax collectors for a long while, as there was nothing more worth taxing.

"I questioned the messenger to get as much detail from him as he knew, paid him well for the information, then called to my fighting men to get ready for action.

"Mamre reacted just like you did, Son. He couldn't believe I was planning to tackle Kedorlaomer.

"'The Rephaites were giants. The Amalekites were fierce warriors. The Amorites were cunning in battle. Yet Kedorlaomer defeated them all, and more!' Mamre reminded me. 'Kedorlaomer controls everything east of the Jordan River from the Euphrates River to the Gulf of Aqaba. You can't be serious!'

"'But I *am* serious,' I said. 'Yahweh commanded me to leave my country—the country of Kedorlaomer and his confederates. I obeyed. I left my country at Yahweh's command. Lot left with me. Now Kedorlaomer is taking him back to Babylon. I can't let that happen.'

"'But the gods are with Kedorlaomer,' Mamre objected. 'How else could he have defeated the giants and the highlanders and all those other nations? How else could he have taken Sodom and Gomorrah without a fight?'

"'What gods?' I argued. 'The Babylonian gods are nothing but wood and stone. I know. Some of my family worshiped them. I smashed a couple of them at my father's feet. But Yahweh is above all gods. He is God Most High, Creator of heaven and earth,' I told Mamre. 'He is real. He is alive. I have heard His voice. Yahweh fought for us in Egypt and rescued Sarai from Pharaoh even when we didn't trust Him to protect us. Now I look forward to seeing what Yahweh will do for Lot.'

"'But Kedorlaomer defeated *five* kings and their armies in the Valley of Siddim,' Mamre objected again. 'Your men and mine and my brothers' men all put together barely make *one* army.'

"'Kedorlaomer didn't defeat those five kings,' I replied. 'Yahweh did. Who do you think created the tar pits and sink holes?'

"Mamre looked at me with an expression that told me he wasn't convinced.

"'Okay,' I said. 'Don't come with me. I will go alone. I and my 318 trained men. Yahweh will deliver my enemies into my hand.'

"'My brothers and I made an alliance with you,' Mamre said, 'so if you go, we will go with you. I think you are crazy, but our word is our word.'

"With that settled, we sprang into action. We knew Kedorlaomer was traveling up the King's Highway on the east side of the Jordan River. He would not be expecting any opposition because all the nations around him had been conquered. With his captives and all the goods they were carrying, they could not move very fast.

"We hurried along the west side of the Jordan, past the Salt Sea and the Sea of Galilee, all the way to Dan, where the river begins. Some men were on camels, some were on foot. All along the way I was praying to Yahweh to help us. As we went, a plan started to develop in my mind—a plan from Yahweh.

"We stopped at Dan. There at the base of Mount Hermon it was easy to cut across to the King's Highway. There I explained our next move. By now we were directly west of Kedorlaomer's forces.

"We would attack in the dark, so Kedorlaomer would not have any idea how many of us there were. We would spread out and attack from the east, south and west all at once to increase the perception that we were a mighty army. Those on camels would attack first and run back and forth through the camp to give the impression that they were many. The enemy soldiers would be asleep. They would not be ready for action. In the dark and rudely awakened, their first reaction would be to escape the hooves of the camels. Hopefully, they would not even be able to find their swords in the confusion. During the pandemonium our foot soldiers would move in, making lots of noise with ram's horns—again, to give the impression of numbers.

"We would not worry about trying to find Lot and his family in the dark. The captives would not run. Nor would the enemy soldiers be concerned about the goods they had carried off from Sodom and Gomorrah. We would concentrate on routing the enemy forces. Once the enemy was on the run, most of our men would continue to chase them, but some would remain behind. At the first hint of daylight, they would collect the people and their possessions and start escorting them home.

"Mamre and his brothers were impressed with the plan.

"'Brilliant!' they exclaimed in unison.

"'It was Yahweh's idea,' I told them. 'He is the Lord of Hosts—the greatest general in the universe.'

"So that's what we did. We divided our men, attacked in the middle of the night from every direction but north, and the result was utter chaos. Absolute pandemonium! Our men fought as they had never fought before. The Babylonian forces panicked. They must have thought that all the nations they had recently conquered had united against them. Some of them fled without their shoes. Some fled with only one shoe! Most fled without their weapons and armor. It was a complete rout!

"Our men chased the Babylonians all the way to Damascus. The people of Damascus were just waking and starting the activities of their day. You should have seen the looks on their faces as the Babylonian soldiers went running past with our men in hot pursuit! We chased them as far as Hobah, north of Damascus. The last we saw of them, they were still running!"

"I wish I had been there to see it," Isaac said laughing.

"You will see Yahweh at work, Son. It's amazing to watch! Just keep your eyes open."

"Did the Babylonians ever return?" Isaac asked.

"No. They never bothered us again. They lost face in our part of the country. Once people figure out that an enemy can be beaten, that enemy loses some of his power. Often the difference between winning and losing is more mental than physical.

"Anyway," Abraham continued, "we found Lot and his family amongst the people who had been captured. We recovered all his possessions, and we recovered all the goods that had been taken from Sodom and Gomorrah. The only thing missing was the food the armies had eaten along the way and a few small items, such as jewelry. But Lot's wife and daughters didn't lose any of their jewelry.

"The return trip was a celebration. The fighting men were happy with the weapons and armor the enemy had abandoned in their confusion. The people laughed and talked and sang as they walked. But Mamre was unusually quiet. He seemed to be in deep thought. Finally he spoke.

"'This Yahweh you talk about,' he said to me, 'he really is real, isn't he?'

"'Absolutely,' I replied.

"'*He* generated the panic,' Mamre continued. '*He* set them on the run. Our few men couldn't have done it alone.'

"I nodded in agreement. Mamre fell silent. A few minutes later he spoke again.

"'I wonder how many men they thought were chasing them?'

"I grinned at him.

"'I'd like to know that, too!'"

"Me, too!" Isaac chimed in.

"It would be interesting to know, Son, but with Yahweh numbers don't matter. When you are on Yahweh's side, you are always in the majority."

"Is that the end of the story?" Isaac asked.

"No. As we were returning home, Mamre's brothers, Aner and Eshcol, began talking about the belongings they would claim as spoils of war. They were checking out the goods people were carrying and deciding what they would like to claim for themselves. Mamre reminded them that Abram had first claim on those spoils. They would never have tackled Kedorlaomer's forces if Abram hadn't shamed them by saying he would go alone.

"Then Mamre noticed that I wasn't paying any attention to the people's belongings.

"'Wake up, Abram,' he said to me. 'Quit daydreaming. If you don't make any claims soon, all the best goods will be claimed by me and my brothers for ourselves and our men. You and your men will get only leftovers. Just kidding! I know you have first claim. By the way, I saw you with your hand up in the air. Your lips were moving. At first I thought you were waving and talking to somebody, but then I noticed you were looking up, not forward. Be careful. Watch where you are going, or you will trip and fall.'

"'I wasn't daydreaming,' I told Mamre, 'I was talking to Yahweh. I was remembering what I told my father when I left Haran. I renounced my inheritance so that he could not use it as a bribe to keep me from following Yahweh. I just realized that this victory could tempt me to live for power and possessions instead of living for Yahweh. I felt a real rush when the Babylonian armies were running from us in panic.'"

"'Me, too,' Mamre agreed. 'What a feeling!'

"'I realize that I could easily forget that Yahweh won the victory for us,' I told Mamre. 'I know that when we return to Sodom with Lot and the rest of the captives, the king will reward us for their return. But I fear that accepting that reward will lessen my dependence on Yahweh. I will be tempted to say that I earned it, rather than to give Yahweh glory for the victory.

"'I want always to walk by faith, to receive everything I have from Yahweh's hand. So I made a vow to him just now,' I told Mamre. 'I raised my hand in a solemn oath to Yahweh, God Most High, Creator of heaven and earth. I vowed that I will accept nothing when we return the captives to Sodom—not even a thread or the thong of a sandal. I don't want anyone to be able to say, "I made Abram rich"[30]—least of all, the king of Sodom! He has done nothing to curb the evil in his city.'

"When we reached the Valley of Shaveh, in the plain just east of Salem, we stopped to determine the best route home. For Mamre and me the shortest way home was to continue straight south to Hebron and Mamre's town nearby. But the people of Sodom and Gomorrah didn't want to travel to Hebron. If they went that route, they would have a steep climb all the way to Hebron, only to have an even steeper descent to their homes in the Valley of Siddim, which is well below sea level.

"'Don't you want to see the best view in the land?' I joked. 'On a good day you can see all the way to the Western Sea and all the way to your homes in the Valley of Siddim!' But they weren't persuaded.

"We could part ways in the Valley of Shaveh. That would mean a short downhill trip for them to the shore of the Salt Sea. Their journey from there would be level all the way home. But I was reluctant for them to travel without military escort. There were women and children and servants of all ages among the captives. None of them were fighters.

"I had just volunteered some of my fighting men to escort them, when we noticed a small army approaching from the south. At the front was Bera, king of Sodom. I was happy to see him. It meant that I wouldn't have to escort the captives home.

---

[30] See Genesis 14:22-23

"As Bera king of Sodom was approaching from the south, Melchizedek king of Salem was approaching from the west. He brought out bread and wine to me and raised his voice in blessing. That is when I realized that he was not only a king, but also a priest of God Most High."

"What did he say?" asked Isaac.

"He greeted me in my own language. 'Shalom.' Then he pronounced a blessing over me."

> *"Blessed be Abram by God Most High,*
> *Creator of heaven and earth.*
> *And blessed be God Most High,*
> *who delivered your enemies into your hand."*[31]

"He spoke in poetry!" Isaac exclaimed.

"In his blessing, yes, Son. His voice reminded me of the voice of Yahweh. It had that same ring of authority. It produced the same sense of awe in my spirit. God Most High was blessing me! When Melchizedek said it, I knew it was true.

"And the word he used for Creator—it was a word that also carried the meaning of Possessor. I was reminded that Yahweh not only made everything, he owns everything. All that I have is on loan from him.

"My immediate response was to give to Yahweh what belonged to him. All that had been retrieved from the Babylonian armies was legally mine, because I had retrieved it. I asked the people to pass in front of Melchizedek with their possessions, and I carefully counted out one in ten of everything and gave it to him."

"That's like paying taxes to him!" Isaac exclaimed. "Doesn't paying tax signify subjection to a government's authority? Wasn't this whole war about taxes? Lot started it by rebelling against paying taxes to Babylon on top of paying taxes to Egypt. You never paid taxes to Egypt or Babylon, yet you paid taxes to Melchizedek without him even asking! Why?"

"Earthly kingdoms aren't the only governments needing taxes, Son," Abraham replied. "Earthly kingdoms have to pay for roads and defense

---

[31] Genesis 14:19-20

and salaries of civil servants. But God also needs taxes to run his Kingdom here on earth. Egypt and Babylon tried to tax outside their legitimate jurisdiction. But Yahweh's jurisdiction extends to the ends of the earth—and farther.

"I felt that Melchizedek would spend wisely for God's Kingdom, so I gave him my tenth. You can think of it as a tax if you want to. I also resolved to send him a tenth of everything I had back home."

"Wasn't that overdoing it?" Isaac asked.

"God has chosen to put his creation into our hands, Son. He asked Adam and Eve to rule over it—to use it wisely. We can never give too much to God. He wants us to freely give back to him what is already his. We limit what God can do here on earth when we are stingy toward him.

"Melchizedek received my gifts graciously, then proceeded to distribute bread and wine to the troops and the former captives."

"He fed everybody?"

"He didn't exactly feed them," Abraham replied. "It was a toast. Melchizedek and his servants gave each person a piece of bread and a sip of wine, saying to each one, 'Shalom. To Salem. To peace.'

"Apparently this was a tradition with Melchizedek whenever people came to his city. Having just come back from battle, we felt it was especially appropriate. I had the strangest sensation of being in another time and another place. A future time and a place far away. A heavenly place. In my imagination Yahweh, King of kings, was welcoming me to the heavenly City of Peace.

"Bera king of Sodom shattered my reverie by approaching. He had been standing in the background impatiently waiting while Melchizedek welcomed everybody. He didn't dare to interrupt Melchizedek. Though Melchizedek was not surrounded by soldiers and his servants carried no weapons, he projected a sense of power. I could not imagine anyone waging war with him. I sensed that Bera was not on good terms with the king of Salem but didn't dare to oppose him.

"'Give me the people,' Bera said to me, 'and keep the goods for yourself.'[32]

"Something about Bera bothered me. I had just freely given my tithe to Melchizedek, and now the king of Sodom was offering me wealth—all the goods that had been retrieved from Kedorlaomer. The timing was wrong. The contrast was unmistakable. For some strange reason my thoughts flashed to the story of the serpent tempting Eve in the Garden of Eden. In my imagination Bera seemed to slither and hiss.

"Something inside me snapped. I drew myself up to my full height and spoke to the king of Sodom in an officious voice.

"'I have raised my hand to Yahweh, God Most High, Creator of heaven and earth, and have taken an oath that I will accept nothing belonging to you, not even a thread or the thong of a sandal, so that you will never be able to say, "I made Abram rich." I will accept nothing but what my men have eaten and the share that belongs to the men who went with me—to Aner, Eshcol and Mamre. Let them have their share.'[33]

"Bera looked as if he had been slapped in the face. He turned without a word and distributed to Mamre and his brothers their fair share of the spoils. Then he ushered his people away without a backward glance.

"'What was that all about?' Mamre asked me.

"'I'm not sure that I can explain,' I replied. 'I didn't mean to be rude. I just couldn't help myself.'

"I never saw the king of Sodom again. But Melchizedek and I remained friends. He always welcomed me whenever I passed through Salem."

---

[32] Genesis 14:21
[33] See Genesis 14:22-24

6

The Covenant Promise

"Who is God?" Isaac asked his father.

It was the Sabbath again. Isaac loved the Sabbath. His father Abraham insisted that his family and his people do no work except that which was absolutely necessary. Where possible, such as in food preparation, they did things in advance so they would have less to do on the Sabbath. That gave them time to focus on God.

That focus gave them rest of body, mind and soul, which energized them for the next week. Isaac could see the difference between his father's people and the nations around them. The Canaanites, Hittites, and whatever-ites worked seven days a week, but they worked at a slower pace. Abraham got more work out of his servants in six days than the pagan taskmasters got from their servants or slaves in seven. Beating their slaves might result in a short-term burst of activity, but as soon as the taskmaster turned his back, the slaves slowed down again. Their pain made them even slower than before the beating.

Was it Isaac's imagination, or did even his father's working animals—the donkeys, oxen and camels—work harder than the Canaanites animals? The animals benefited from the rest as much as did the people.

Abraham was contemplating Isaac's question.

"Who is God?" Abraham echoed. "I don't know."

When Isaac looked at him in surprise, Abraham added, "And I *do* know."

Abraham had a twinkle in his eye, and Isaac knew his father would explain himself.

"What answer do you want first? There are things I know about God—from what my forefathers taught me and from experience. But there are many things about God that are unknown and unknowable."

"You use different names for God," Isaac said. "El. Elohim. Yahweh."

"Yes, Son. Different names convey different aspects of God's nature and character. 'El' is a generic word for God. Even the Canaanites call their gods El. I use El sometimes for simplicity's sake. But more often I use the plural of El—the name 'Elohim'—not in the Canaanite sense of 'gods' plural, but in recognition of the majesty and supremacy of the one true God. He is the God of gods, the highest of all.

"But my favorite name for God is Yahweh. When Yahweh says it, it sounds as if he is saying, 'I Am.' He is. The Canaanite gods came into being when people dreamed them up, then carved them out of wood or stone. But Yahweh had no beginning. He was there before the creation of the earth. He created the earth and everything in it.

"When he first spoke to me in Ur, he was just a voice out of the blue. But he was real. Not visible, but real. More real than the wood and stone carvings of the Canaanite gods. He was just there. He *was*. He is. Period. That was and still is a comfort to me.

"As I journeyed from Ur to Canaan, he was there. Sometimes he talked to me, sometimes he didn't. But he was there. Always.

"As I journeyed into Canaan, then out of Canaan and into Egypt, I got to know Yahweh better. I saw how powerful Yahweh was. He was powerful enough to protect Sarai and me from Pharaoh. He was there even when I didn't trust Him.

"He was with me from Egypt back to Canaan, and He was faithful to his promise to bless me. He blessed me so much that Lot and I had to part company. The land could not support us when we were together.

"After I rescued Lot from the Babylonian kings, I learned another name for God. Melchizedek, king of Salem, taught it to me. When he greeted me after the victory, he referred to Yahweh as 'El Elyon',

God Most High. I had heard the Canaanites use that name for their highest gods, but not even their highest gods could save them from Kedorlaomer and his confederates.

"My personal little army consisted of only 318 men. Sure, Mamre and his brothers supplemented my army with their men, but we still weren't much compared to the most powerful army in the world! I knew the victory was not my doing. But I had the most powerful ally in the *universe*—'El Elyon'. He won the victory.

"Before we went to rescue Lot, while our fighting men were in training exercises with Mamre's men, Sarai and I had a discussion. What if I was killed in battle? Who would inherit my estate after she and I were dead? The most logical choice was my chief servant Eliezer. He was not a fighting man, therefore not as likely to die at the hands of the Babylonians, and he had proved himself both capable and worthy. So we told him our plans to make him our heir.

"Eliezer was overwhelmed at our generosity, but he had reservations.

"'I thought Yahweh promised to make you into a great nation,' he objected.

"'That's what he said,' I replied, 'but maybe he changed his mind. And at a time like this, it would be irresponsible of me not to make arrangements in case of my death.'

"'Alright,' Eliezer said, 'but at the birth of your first child this agreement is null and void. How will all peoples on earth be blessed through you if you have no child and I inherit your estate?'

"'Agreed,' I said. 'At this point you have more faith in Yahweh than I do!'"

"I thought you always believed Yahweh for a son!" Isaac exclaimed.

"All logic said otherwise," Abraham replied. "At that point in my life, all I had were promises."

"Yahweh promised to bless you," Isaac argued. "He had fulfilled *that* promise."

"Yes, but that was a promise I could explain away," Abraham said. "I can't explain away your existence. A child born to a barren woman. At the age of 90, no less! But you hadn't been born yet. Sometimes my faith was strong. Sometimes it waned. I still had much to learn about God.

"Every once in a while I would learn a new name for God," Abraham continued. "That new name would give me a new perspective of God. A new window to his personality. A new understanding of his character.

"In the evening after returning from rescuing Lot, I watched the sun set and darkness fall, then I went inside my tent to wind down after the excitement of the day. As I reviewed the events of the last few days, I began to shake. I had chased after Lot almost instinctively. What if things had turned out differently? What if the Babylonians had not run but had put up a fight? Would I be alive to tell the story? Have you ever done something dangerous and not realized until later how dangerous it was?"

Isaac nodded. "But not as dangerous as tackling the Babylonian army!"

Abraham smiled in agreement.

"I also began to question my decision not to take any reward for rescuing the people of Sodom," Abraham continued. "Should I have taken the reward as insurance against some future reversal of fortune?"

"You didn't even have faith that Yahweh would provide for you?" Isaac asked in surprise.

Abraham shook his head sadly. "How could I doubt Yahweh after such a victory? But I did. As I was saying, I had just watched the sun set outside my tent. Then while I was sitting inside, the sun rose again and moved toward me. I realized I was having a vision. The sun became a shield. A bright, softly glowing shield. Not made of layered cowhide, but of purest gold. The shield came toward me, then it slowly turned around so I could hold it. I realized that I was holding incredible wealth in my hand.

"Then the shield began to grow bigger and heavier. Just when I could no longer hold it, an arm reached around from behind me and held the shield for me. The shield continued to grow and change shape until it was wrapped completely around me. I remember feeling completely safe. The shield continued to grow until it encompassed my wife, my tent, and all my flocks and herds. Then it faded and disappeared.

"While I was pondering what I had seen, a voice spoke. Yahweh's voice.

"'Don't be afraid, Abram,' he said. 'I am your shield, your very great reward.'[34]

"The word he used for 'shield' also carried the meaning of 'sovereign'. I was struck by the bitter incongruity of what I had just heard. Yahweh was sovereign. He was in total control. Yes, he had protected me. Yes, he had made me rich. But there was a kind of wealth that I still lacked—the wealth of children. Sarai was barren. I felt poor. If Yahweh was sovereign, why hadn't he given us children? Now it was too late. Sarai was too old.

"I had already come to the conclusion that God's promise to make me a great nation was figurative. It did not mean my own flesh and blood. What good was material wealth if I had no one to bequeath it to? In my bitterness and frustration I lashed out at God.

"'O Sovereign Yahweh, what good are all your blessings when I don't even have a son? Eliezer of Damascus will inherit my wealth.'[35]

"I used the word 'sovereign' because Yahweh's choice of word for 'shield' had suggested it. I didn't really believe Yahweh was sovereign. I was throwing his claim of sovereignty back into his face. I half expected Yahweh to strike me dead for being so disrespectful. His silence emboldened me to continue. I explained the situation to him as if he didn't already know who Eliezer was.

"'Because you have given me no children, the steward of my household will be my heir.'

"There. I had said it. It was all Yahweh's fault that I had no child.

"Then the word of Yahweh came to me. He spoke as if making an announcement—not just to me, but to the whole world. *'This man won't be your heir. A son from your own body will be your heir.'*[36]

---

[34] Genesis 15:1
[35] See Genesis 15:2-3
[36] See Genesis 15:4

"I felt an arm lifting me up from my sitting position and gently propelling me outside my tent. It was a beautiful cloudless night. The stars were so bright!

"'Look!' Yahweh said gently to me. 'Look up into the sky! Count the stars—if you can.'[37]

"I looked and marveled at their beauty. I forgot my problems. I forgot my disappointment at having no child. I was aware only of God's greatness. God Most High, Creator of heaven and earth. Yahweh, my Yahweh, had created all those stars! I tried to count the stars in a tiny corner of the sky and estimate how many stars were out there. Hundreds, thousands, hundreds of thousands, millions! Just as I thought I had succeeded in counting the stars in that one tiny patch, a few more would twinkle faintly at me. I didn't have words for that many. Only Yahweh could know how many stars there are!

"'*So shall your seed be*,'[38] he said gently to me. "That's how many descendants you will have!"

"I caught my breath at his words. At that moment I believed him. My God, Yahweh, was sovereign—sovereign over all creation. My *seed*, from my *own body*, he said. If he could create the stars, he could create a child. Even for an old man and a barren old woman. If I ever doubted Yahweh again, all I had to do was look at the stars. I would remember this moment. His voice. His promise! *So shall your offspring be!*

"I sensed Yahweh's approval as he continued speaking to me.

"'I am Yahweh, who brought you out of Ur of the Chaldeans to give you this land so you can take possession of it.'

"Ur! That seemed so far away. So long ago. I thought back to my life in Ur, then traced my steps from there to here. I could see Yahweh's sovereign hand all along the way.

"'O Sovereign Yahweh!' I exclaimed. This time I was sincere. 'O Sovereign Yahweh, I believe! Help me when my faith wavers. How can I know I will gain possession of this land?'[39]

---

[37] See Genesis 15:5
[38] See Genesis 15:5, KJV
[39] See Genesis 15:8

"As soon as the words were out of my mouth, I could have kicked myself. How could I believe and then ask him for a sign? My faith was so small. Yet I still felt Yahweh's approval, little as my faith was. What did it matter that my faith was small? What really mattered was that Yahweh was so great. If he made a promise, he would keep it. Any amount of faith is enough, provided it is placed in Yahweh—the One who can deliver on his promise."

Abraham looked at his son as he said it, hoping Isaac would absorb the lesson. Then he continued his story.

"'Bring me a heifer,' Yahweh said, 'and a goat and a ram, each three years old, along with a dove and a young pigeon.'[40]

"My heart rejoiced at his words. I knew what he was about to do. Yahweh had already given me a promise—three promises actually—a son from my own body, countless offspring, and land, this land I had been walking on. Now he was going to strengthen that promise with a covenant, using our local covenant rituals. I couldn't get the animals in the dark, but I would do it first thing in the morning. I didn't sleep much that night in anticipation of Yahweh's covenant.

"Over breakfast I told Sarai about what I had seen and heard, then I rushed out to locate the best heifer in my herd. From there I went to my flocks of sheep and selected a ram. While looking for a goat, I began to think, 'This must be some covenant Yahweh is making!' Usually a heifer is sufficient. Or a goat. Or a ram. A little promise or a covenant between poor people can be sealed with a dove and a young pigeon. But Yahweh wanted me to bring one of each!

"Yahweh had said, 'Bring them to me.' But where? I wondered. I decided to take them to a little knoll near my altar. There I killed the animals and carefully cut them in two right down the spine. I arranged the halves opposite each other, mirror images, bloody side up, with a pathway between them. I didn't cut the birds in half, but laid them opposite each other. Then I sat down on a large rock and waited for Yahweh to come.

"The one making the covenant was supposed to walk through the pieces as a visual statement that this is what will happen to the one who

---

[40] Genesis 15:9

breaks his covenant. *In what form will Yahweh appear?* I wondered. *He is not a man. Will he appear as a bright light? As a golden shield?*

"My thoughts were interrupted as a vulture started circling over head. Soon there were more vultures. As one settled on a carcass, I shouted at it, and it flew a little distance away before returning. Then several vultures descended at once, emboldened by their numbers. I ran at them, shouting and waving my arms.

"As the day wore on, more and more birds of prey came—vultures, kites and gier eagles. The big black kites were especially bold. When my shouts and arm-waving no longer scared them, I grabbed a couple of sticks to whack at them. I didn't want my arms and hands ripped by their razor-sharp talons and beaks. Of course they were quick enough to elude my swinging sticks.

"All day I drove them off. Finally, as the sun was setting, the birds flew off to wherever they sleep for the night. I was so exhausted that I lay down and soon fell into a deep sleep. That was when Yahweh finally came to make his covenant. I thought I heard someone calling my name and tried to shake off my sleep. I opened my eyes, but couldn't see a thing. Usually there is a little light on the horizon where the sun has set. The sky before sunset had had very little cloud, so I should have been able to see some stars. But I could see nothing. The darkness was scary. It was so thick I could almost feel it.

"Then Yahweh started to speak, and I no longer felt afraid.

"'*Know for certain that your descendants will be strangers in a land that is not theirs, where they will be enslaved and mistreated four hundred years. But I will punish the nation that enslaves them, and in the end they will come out with great wealth. (As for you, you will die in peace and be buried at a ripe old age.) After four generations your descendants will return here to this land, for the sins of the Amorites do not yet warrant their destruction.*'[41]

"I didn't fully grasp what he was talking about, but I would remember the words and ponder them. Yahweh was giving me a glimpse of the future. My future. Your future, Son, the future of your descendants and mine."

---

[41] Genesis 15:13-16. Compare NIV and NLT.

Isaac didn't comment. He was comforted to learn that his father would live to a good old age, but this talk about slavery was disturbing. Fortunately the fulfillment sounded a long way off. Not in his father's lifetime, maybe not even in his own lifetime.

Isaac had heard about the Covenant and wanted to hear more.

"While I was wondering about the future," Abraham continued, "a movement in the distance brought me back to the present. The thick darkness had lifted somewhat so that I could see in the distance a small light moving towards me. Then it separated into two lights, one brighter than the other. As it got still closer, I could identify the lights as a blazing torch and a smoking fire pot. They were moving in a swinging motion as if held by an invisible man walking."

"Yahweh!" Isaac exclaimed.

"Yes, it was Yahweh. He came right towards me, then turned as he came opposite the carcasses on the ground and walked between the pieces. Not just once, the way we customarily do, but back and forth several times. He was making it abundantly clear that he would fulfill his covenant with me. Then Yahweh brought the torch and the fire pot, set them on the ground, and sat down beside me to talk."

"You could actually see Yahweh!" Isaac exclaimed in astonishment.

"No, Son, but I could see the torch and the fire pot, and I knew Yahweh was there. His voice was right close to my ear. He identified himself as my shield and my very great reward. He repeated the promise that I would have a son from my own body. He pointed out the stars, which at last were visible, and said, 'So shall your offspring be.' He said he would give this land to me and my descendants. When I asked what he meant by 'this land', he told me.

"*From the river of Egypt*—you know that's not the Nile—'"

Isaac nodded. "I remember. The Egyptians call it Wadi el Arish." Abraham continued, "'*From the river of Egypt to the great river, the Euphrates—the land of the Kenites, Kenizzites, Kadmonites, Hittites, Perizzites, Rephaites, Amorites, Canaanites, Girgashites and Jebusites.*'"[42]

"Wow!" Isaac exclaimed. "How do you remember them all?"

---

[42] Genesis 15:18-19

"If you heard Yahweh's voice list them all, you would remember them, too, Son. Then the torch and the fire pot faded from sight."

"The land of the Amorites," Isaac mused. "Your friend Mamre is an Amorite. Will you seize *his* land?"

"No, Son. Yahweh said that the sins of the Amorites don't yet warrant their destruction. He also said he would give it to me. I will wait to see how he does that. I am slowly learning not to 'help' Yahweh fulfill his promises."

Abraham gave Isaac a rueful smile. Just then Sarah walked in.

"I heard that last comment," she said. "You had better revise that to: *We* are slowly learning not to help Yahweh fulfill his promises!"

7

"Helping Yahweh"

"What did you and Mother mean by 'learning not to help Yahweh fulfill His promises'?" Isaac asked Abraham.

"After Yahweh confirmed his promises by walking between the pieces, your mother and I watched with renewed hope for signs of fulfillment. But months went by and nothing happened. Sarai didn't get pregnant.

"She began quizzing me.

"'What did Yahweh say?' Sarai asked. 'When you were 75 years old, he promised to make you into a great nation. That was ten years ago. Now he says a son coming from your own body will be your heir. But he didn't say anything about *me*, did he?'

"That took me by surprise.

"'Yahweh didn't need to mention you,' I replied. 'You are my wife. What are you suggesting? That I divorce you and find another wife?'

"'Of course, not!' she replied.

"'What then? Find a mistress?'

"'No. Not exactly.'

"'What does "not exactly" mean?'

"'When the Amorite or Canaanite men have no children, they sleep with their wife's maidservant,' Sarai explained. 'It is strictly a business arrangement. They don't continue the relationship once a child is conceived.'

"'Or so they would have you believe,' I replied. 'That sounds so pagan to me.' I didn't admit to my wife that I found Hagar attractive. 'Yahweh knows I have always had eyes only for you,' I said, hoping Sarai would believe me.

"'Yahweh!' Sarai exclaimed. 'He's the one who has kept me from having children. Go! Sleep with my maidservant. Close your eyes and pretend it's me. Perhaps I can build a family through her.'[43]

"I still had reservations.

"'Don't think of it as being unfaithful to me,' Sarai continued. 'Hagar is *my* maidservant. My slave. *My* property. I am using her to do what I cannot. Her child will be *my* child—*our* child—yours and mine.'

"The more I thought about it, the more reasonable it seemed. So I agreed to what Sarai said. I guess ten years of living in Canaan had colored my thinking.

"It wasn't long until Hagar knew she was pregnant. Normally the maidservant would inform her mistress first. But Hagar waited until I was present with Sarai before she made the announcement. I still remember the pride and satisfaction in her voice.

"Sarai jumped up and hugged Hagar, then me, then both of us together. Sarai and I laughed and cried at the same time. But the laughter didn't last long.

"Sarai and Hagar had gotten along very well for many years. She had been content as the handmaid of Sarai, beautiful wife of the esteemed Abram. Though she was in reality a slave, she had always been treated with respect. Sarai often referred to Hagar as her 'maidservant', making it sound as if she worked for Sarai by choice. But when Hagar got pregnant, everything changed. Suddenly Hagar was no longer just a slave. She was about to become a mother—mother of the child of the highly respected Abram. That made her much more than a slave. Hagar also began to look down on Sarai for being barren. Without a child, in Hagar's eyes Sarai was a nobody.

---

[43] See Genesis 16:2

"Things also changed between Sarai and me, both from her perspective and from mine. Even though I had gone to Hagar at her suggestion, Sarai now became jealous and suspected that it was more than a one-time event. For my part, I couldn't forget that night in Hagar's arms and it affected my relationship with my wife. Our lovemaking became increasingly strained.

"Hagar became very uppity around Sarai. She started to treat Sarai as if she were her handmaid, and Sarai couldn't stand it. Sarai had never been treated with anything but respect all her life. She didn't know how to handle it, so she blamed me.

"'*You* are responsible for the wrong I am suffering,' Sarai accused me. 'I put my servant in *your* arms, and now that she knows she is pregnant, she despises *me*! May Yahweh judge between you and me.'

"'What are you accusing me of?' I asked. 'Sleeping with Hagar? Guilty. But we share the guilt. We did it because we didn't believe Yahweh's promise to give us a child.'

"'No, I'm not faulting you for sleeping with Hagar,' Sarai replied, 'but you must have said something to make her treat me the way she does.'

"Sarai thought I had encouraged Hagar to despise her! My wife was suggesting that in a court of law with Yahweh as judge, she could accuse me of inciting Hagar to hatred and win her case!

"'I was right to use Hagar to give us a child,' Sarai insisted. 'How else could Yahweh fulfill his promise? But I know you have poisoned her against me.'

"I was flabbergasted! First she had blamed Yahweh for not giving her a child. Now she blamed me for Hagar's bad behavior! It reminded me of the story of Adam and Eve in the Garden of Eden. Adam blamed Eve for giving him the fruit and blamed God for giving him Eve. Eve, in turn, blamed the serpent for deceiving her.

"I wanted to say, 'You told me to sleep with Hagar,' but then I would be like Adam and Eve—passing blame. What could I do about Hagar? She wasn't my servant. Neither Sarai nor I could dismiss her, because she was bearing my child.

"I was in a no-win situation. If I spent time with Hagar trying to talk reason to her, Sarai would see me as continuing my relationship with Hagar. I had never given Hagar orders in the past, and I wasn't about to start now! She was Sarai's handmaid—Sarai's property. If Yahweh was truly on Sarai's side, he would show her how to handle Hagar. I could see the possibility of more trouble brewing, but I didn't dare say so.

"'Your servant is in your hands,' I told Sarai. 'Do with her whatever you think best.'

"I washed my hands of the affair. I was sorry to see Sarai and Hagar quarrel. Ever since their return from Egypt years ago, they had been the best of friends, not just mistress and servant. Now from time to time I heard angry voices coming from Sarai's tent, but I said nothing. Occasionally I even heard blows and cries, but I still said nothing.

"Sarai was no longer her carefree self. She walked around with a grim face. She was determined not to let Hagar have the upper hand. Hagar seemed equally determined to assert her position as mother of the master's child.

"It was a clash of cultures. In Egypt or anywhere else in Canaan, Hagar would have been elevated in position. But not in this household! Sarai was determined that once the child was born, *she* would be looked upon as the mother.

"'*I* want to be the one to teach *my* child—our child—about Yahweh,' Sarai insisted.

"'Hagar also loves Yahweh,' I countered. 'She won't teach the child about the Egyptian gods. We will both teach our child about Yahweh.' I felt like saying that the way Sarai was behaving toward Hagar would teach the child the wrong things, but I bit my tongue.

"The next day Sarai and Hagar had a particularly bad quarrel. I heard loud angry voices, blows and cries. The following few days were unusually quiet, and Sarai seemed serene. I was pleased that she and Hagar were finally getting along better, and I said so.

"Sarai said nothing. Her silence puzzled me.

"'What's wrong?' I asked.

"'Hagar,' she replied softly. 'She's gone.'

"'What do you mean, gone?'

"'Just gone. She ran away.'

"'How do you know she is really gone?'

"'Her belongings are gone. I asked around the camp,' Sarai replied. 'Several people saw her walking south carrying a large bundle. Someone said she was going back home to Egypt.'

"'When did she leave?' I asked.

"'Several days ago. Right after we had a really bad fight. At first I was glad to see her go. Then I thought about our baby and was afraid to tell you.' Sarai had treated Hagar so badly that she ran away!"

Isaac had a distressed look on his face.

"I'm sorry to have to tell you this, Son," Abraham said. "But I know you will always have questions about your half brother Ishmael, and I would rather that you hear the story from me. Neither your mother nor I handled the situation right. Your mother behaved badly, and I turned a blind eye to what was happening. Hagar's running away was a wake-up call for both Sarai and myself.

"I began to panic. What if we never saw Hagar again? What if she had my child and I never knew it? I might never know whether I had a son or a daughter. What if Sarai had treated Hagar so badly that she miscarried?

"We organized several search parties, but they all returned empty-handed. If Hagar did not want to be found, we had little chance of finding her. About a week after we had given up the search, Hagar returned.

"Sarai took her back with mixed feelings. Both Sarai and Hagar were changed. Hagar was submissive toward Sarai, and Sarai treated her better; but they were never close friends like they had been.

"Sarai tried to find out where Hagar had been and what had happened while she was away, but Hagar was reluctant to say much. Sarai did notice one thing—Hagar was sure the child she was carrying was a boy. She never said, 'My baby.' It was always, 'My son.' When Sarai asked how she could be so sure, Hagar always said, 'I just know.'

"One day as Hagar's due date was approaching, Sarai was wondering out loud to me whether the baby would be a boy or a girl and began suggesting possible names for the baby. Hagar overheard our conversation and came in without being summoned.

"'His name is Ishmael,' she announced firmly.

"Both Sarai and I were startled. It was not the handmaid's place to name the baby. This would be our baby, and Sarai and I had the right to name it.

"'How can you be so sure it will be a boy?' I asked.

"'Yahweh told me,' Hagar replied, 'and he told me to name him Ishmael.'

"Then Hagar poured out the whole story. She had run away with no thought except to get as far away as she could from her tormenter, Sarai. Since she was carrying all her belongings, she had to stop frequently to rest.

"The first Sabbath that she spent on the road, Hagar found it strange to be traveling. It had been ten years—before she began working for Sarai—since she had worked or walked any distance on the Sabbath. Part of her wanted to stop and rest for the day. Another part of her wanted to put as much distance as possible between her and Sarai. Besides, if Sarai could treat her so badly, and Sarai claimed to follow Yahweh, Hagar wanted nothing to do with Yahweh and his Sabbath rules. So she walked all that day.

"A week later she was nearing the border between Canaan and Egypt. As the day wore on, she could see palm trees in the distance, and she knew she was approaching an oasis. She quickened her steps at the thought of water. Her skin of water was empty.

"When she reached the oasis, she wasn't disappointed. There was a well with cool, clean, refreshing water. She drank deeply and filled her lambskin flask with water. Then she purchased some food from a vendor near the spring and found a quiet place to eat and rest. As she was finishing her meal, a man approached. Hagar didn't recognize him, but he obviously knew her, because he addressed her by name.

"'Hagar, servant of Sarai,' he said, 'where have you come from, and where are you going?'[44]

---

[44] *Genesis 16:8*

"Hagar wanted to say, 'None of your business,' she told us, but since the man knew her name, she admitted that she was running away from her mistress Sarai. When he told Hagar to go back to her mistress and submit to her, Hagar thought he had been sent by Abram to fetch her back. She was about to object when the man continued.

"'I will so increase your descendants that they will be too numerous to count,'[45] he said.

"Sarai and I looked at each other. This is what Yahweh had said to me when he asked me to count the stars in the sky. This must be confirmation that Yahweh was about to fulfill his promise to us through Hagar's child, we said.

"Hagar agreed. Sarai had told her about the promise. Hagar knew instantly that this man was no ordinary man but an angel from Yahweh—maybe even Yahweh himself in visible form.

"Sarai and I wanted to know more. Had Yahweh said anything else?

"'Yes,' Hagar said, her eyes shining.

"Then she closed her eyes and started to recite a poem, one she had obviously recited to herself every day since she first heard it. She rocked slowly back and forth as she quoted Yahweh in a quiet voice.

> "'*You are now with child*
>   *and you will have a son.*
> *You shall name him Ishmael,*
>   *for Yahweh has heard of your misery.*
> *He will be a wild donkey of a man;*
>   *his hand will be against everyone*
>   *and everyone's hand against him,*
> *and he will live in hostility*
>   *toward all his brothers.*'[46]

"'*El Roi*,' Hagar continued. 'That's what I called him—the God who sees me.[47] I fell at his feet, but when I looked up, he was gone.

---

[45] Genesis 16:10
[46] Genesis 16:11-12
[47] See Genesis 16:13

Disappeared into thin air. I kept repeating his name. *El Roi. El Roi.* I actually saw the One who sees me!'

"Hagar turned to us, a look of wonder on her face.

"'You may call him Yahweh,' she said. 'But to me he will always be *El Roi.* I even named the well after him. *Beer Lahai Roi.* The well of the Living One who sees me.'

"The three of us sat in silence for a while, thinking about Yahweh's words. They were partly comforting, partly disturbing.

"'Ishmael,' I mused. 'Ishmael means God hears.'

"'Were you praying when Yahweh appeared and spoke to you?' Sarai asked Hagar. 'Is that why he called the baby Ishmael? Because he heard your prayer?'

"'No,' Hagar replied. 'Frankly I had been toying with the idea of forgetting Yahweh altogether. Life seemed unbearable. But as I pondered Yahweh's—*El Roi*'s—words and thought about the name Ishmael, I realized that *El Roi* had seen and heard everything. He had seen and heard when Sarai and I fought. He heard the angry and cruel words. He saw the blows and the bruises. But he saw and heard even more. He saw the pain in my heart. He heard the longings that I could not—dared not, didn't have the words to—express. He heard the prayer I didn't pray.'

"Hagar paused and let out a deep sigh. Unconsciously, Sarai and I sighed too. When we realized what we had done, the three of us looked at each other and laughed.

"'I guess we all have desires, spoken and unspoken,' Sarai concluded. 'Sometimes all we can do is sigh. It is comforting to think that Yahweh hears and understands them all.'

"So Hagar taught you another name for God," Isaac remarked to his father. "El Roi. The God who sees me."

"Yes, Son. God sees me. And he also hears me—as I am reminded often when I think of Ishmael. Hagar's baby was a boy, and there was no argument over his name. I named him Ishmael."

"But you haven't answered my question yet. What did you and Mother mean by learning not to help Yahweh fulfill His promises?"

"The day that Hagar told us what happened when she ran away, I asked her to repeat what Yahweh had said to her. She did so, quoted the poem once more, then left.

"After Hagar left, Sarai and I looked at each other for a long time without saying anything. Finally Sarai broke the silence.

"'Are you thinking what I'm thinking?' she asked.

"I nodded. 'Hagar's baby is not the child of Yahweh's promise to us,' I said.

"Sarai agreed. Ishmael would have descendants too numerous to count, but from there on, the promise to Hagar was very different from the promise to me. Sarai and I discussed the differences.

"Yahweh's first promise said, 'I will make you into a great nation.' Nations have geographical boundaries. In subsequent promises Yahweh specifically promised land and even defined its boundaries. But Ishmael will be a wild donkey of a man. Wild donkeys don't belong to any specific piece of land.

"Secondly, Yahweh promised me, 'You will be a blessing . . . and all peoples on earth will be blessed through you.' That is the opposite of 'his hand will be against everyone and everyone's hand against him.' Hostility is the opposite of blessing.

"So, we concluded, if Ishmael was not to be our child of promise, what then? And what about Ishmael's brothers?"

"Another child was coming," Isaac answered the question that his parents had asked each other.

"Yes," Abraham agreed. "That much was clear. But how many more sons were coming? And who would the mother be?

"The questions were too big for us to answer. Sarai and I had tried to figure out how Yahweh planned to fulfill his promise and had tried to help him fulfill it. But our reasoning turned out to be wrong. It had caused a lot of grief to Hagar, Sarai and me. And it sounded from Yahweh's promise to Hagar as if a lot more grief was coming.

"If Ishmael was not the child of promise, then a second child from Hagar was not likely to be. Who then would the mother be? Another handmaid? The disaster with Hagar scared us away from contemplating that thought. Sarai? She was my wife, and the most logical one, but she was still barren—and getting older every day.

"We finally concluded that Yahweh's ways were not our ways. We could not fathom how he would fulfill his promise. But he had promised that a son coming from my own body would be my heir. And he had showed me the stars.

"That evening Sarai and I sat outside our tent and looked at the stars again.

"'*So shall your offspring be,*' she quoted.

"That's the promise," I agreed. "I don't know how Yahweh is going to do it. But he is going to have to do it all by himself. I'm not going to help him with that one. And your mother heartily agreed."

Father and son were silent for a while, each lost in his own thoughts.

"So we waited for Yahweh to fulfill his promise without any help from us," Abraham finally said.

But Isaac's imagination had been captured by another thought.

"El Roi. The God who sees me," he said quietly. "One day I would like to see where God appeared and spoke to Hagar, where he announced the name of my half-brother. I would like to see Beer Lahai Roi—the well of the Living One who sees me."

8

The Covenant Sign

Abraham and Isaac had been working in the rain, driving a flock of sheep to a new pasture, when the sun came out and a beautiful rainbow filled the sky.

"Look!" Isaac exclaimed, pointing to the rainbow.

Father and son paused from their work to admire the sight.

"Do you remember what the rainbow means?" Abraham asked. He had told his son the story many times.

"It's a reminder of God's promise to Noah that he would never again destroy the earth by flood. It's the sign of the everlasting covenant between God and all living creatures on the earth."

"Very good, Son." Abraham smiled.

The rainbow reminded Isaac of another covenant—one in which he had a very personal interest.

"Father, you were telling me the other day about when Yahweh made his Covenant with you. He walked between the pieces. But you said nothing about the sign of the Covenant. Why did you omit that part? I thought that was the most important part."

Abraham never tired of talking about the things of Yahweh with his son. He was pleased that Isaac was so interested in spiritual things.

"Do you remember what I told you about covenants, Son? What are its components?"

"I remember by thinking of a marriage covenant," Isaac replied. He had attended a wedding not long ago. "The covenanters identifies themselves by name.

"They also symbolically walks between the pieces when they walk down the aisle between the families and friends of the bride and of the groom. They don't walk between bloody animal carcasses, for which I'm glad! It's scary enough to walk down the aisle. Whoever breaks the wedding vow will have to face the wrath of their spouse's family and friends!"

Isaac continued, counting the components of a covenant on his fingers.

"The covenanter gives a command—like, love and obey me for the rest of your life. He gives a promise—like, I will love you and look after you forever. He gives a new name.

"At the wedding we recently attended, the groom changed the bride's name from Rahel to Rachel. I don't know what Rahel means, but Rachel means ewe or lamb. The groom saw his bride as a sweet lovable lamb.

"And to top it all off, the covenanter gives a sign of the covenant. God gave a rainbow to Noah. At a wedding the groom traditionally gives jewelry to his bride. The richer the groom, the more jewelry he gives."

"Very good, Son! You remembered them all. Yahweh included all those components in his covenant with me—but not all at once. He walked between the pieces when he promised me a son from my own body before Ishmael was born. He also identified himself and made promises. But it was years later—fourteen years later—before he added the other components—the name change and the sign.

"Ishmael was just your age, Son—thirteen—when Yahweh appeared to me again. The years since Ishmael's birth had been happy ones for me. During his infancy I didn't see a lot of Ishmael. He was with his mother most of the time, and by the time I finished my work for the day, he was usually asleep. Hagar often carried Ishmael on her back while working for Sarai. Sarai and Hagar treated each other respectfully, and Sarai enjoyed having the little fellow around. Who doesn't love a baby or a little child?

"But I saw more of Ishmael as he grew older and began to spend more of his time with me. I enjoyed making toys for Ishmael to play with. I tried my hand at carving animals out of wood. They were no great works of art, but he liked them because I had made them for him. When I made him a sling, he used the wooden animals as target practice. If they were barely recognizable before, they were totally unrecognizable afterwards!"

Both Abraham and Isaac laughed at the thought.

"But Ishmael's favorite toy was the bow I made for him. He liked it so much and got so good at archery that I introduced him to a craftsman that was very skilled at making bows. Ishmael learned how to make bows for himself, and today he makes his living from archery."

Isaac noticed the pride in his father's voice. But he looked up, saw that the rainbow was still visible, and was again reminded of covenants.

"You said Yahweh appeared to you again when Ishmael was thirteen." Isaac didn't want to get side-tracked by talk of Ishmael. "What happened?"

"He introduced himself as *El Shaddai*, God Almighty. 'I am *El Shaddai*,' he said, 'walk before me and be blameless. I will confirm my covenant between me and you and will greatly increase your numbers.'"[48]

"There are three components of the covenant right there," Isaac interrupted. "The covenanter's name, a command, and a promise." Abraham acknowledged Isaac's comment, then continued.

"*El Shaddai*. That really hit me. For the past fourteen years, every time I looked at the stars, I was reminded of God's power on a grand scale and also of his promise, *'so shall your offspring be.'* I believed that God created the universe. I believed that he sustained it—that he reigned supreme from eternity past to eternity future. But somehow when it came down to applying his mighty power to my personal situation, when it came to believing that God would give Sarai and

---

[48] Genesis 17:1,2

me a son, my faith faltered. Your mother and I believed enough not to attempt to help Yahweh fulfill his promises, but some days our faith wore pretty thin.

"Sometimes it's like that, Son. Sometimes it's easier to believe in God's power on a grand scale—creating the universe, sustaining it through time, reigning over the centuries—than it is to believe in his power to keep one simple promise."[49]

Isaac nodded. From his perspective—as the fulfillment of the promise—it was easy to see Yahweh as *El Shaddai*. But he had never had to believe God for the impossible. He was trying to put himself in his father's sandals.

"With the declaration that Yahweh was God Almighty," Abraham continued, "I fell facedown in worship. While I was face down, God Almighty confirmed his covenant with me. '*You will be the father of many nations,*' he said, and he changed my name from Abram, 'exalted father', to Abraham, 'father of many'. He said the Covenant would be everlasting. Not just between him and me, but between him and my descendants. He again promised me land. '*The whole land of Canaan, where you are now an alien,*' God said, '*I will give as an everlasting possession to you and your descendants after you; and I will be their God.*'[50]

"'I will be their God.' I looked forward to sharing my God—my Yahweh, the One Who Is, my God Most High, my Shield and Sovereign, my God Almighty—sharing him with my descendants, starting with Ishmael."

"Don't forget *El Roi*, the God who sees me," Isaac said.

"Right," Abraham replied. "Then God gave me the sign of the Covenant—circumcision. It was a strange sign. The rainbow, the sign of God's covenant with Noah, is highly visible. The sign of the marriage covenant is jewelry, the more the better—again, very visible. But circumcision! That is very private. Virtually invisible. The only ones who see are the person circumcised and, if he marries, his wife."

"*El Roi* sees," Isaac reminded his father. "He sees everything."

---

[49] Ann Spangler, *Praying the Names of God*, Zondervan, p. 43.
[50] Genesis 17:4,8

"You're right, Son. Maybe that was the point God was making. He sees what others do not see. He sees our hearts. And that is what is important. So much of what is important to God is invisible to others. Faith is invisible, yet without faith it is impossible to please God. Some people make a show of practicing their religion, but that is all it is—show. God looks at their hearts and sees nothing—only coldness and indifference toward him.

"While *El Shaddai* was talking to me about circumcision, I had risen from being flat on my face. But then he said something that flattened me again. First he changed my wife's name from Sarai to Sarah, 'princess'. Then he said, '*I will bless her and will surely give you a son **by her**.*'[51]

"Yahweh had never specifically mentioned Sarai before, though I had assumed she was to be the mother when he originally promised me children. He had promised to bless me, but now he specifically promised to bless her. '*I will bless her*,' Yahweh continued, '*so that **she** will be the mother of nations.*'[52]

"When God said that, I fell facedown again, partly in worship, but mostly to hide my unbelief. I laughed at the thought of us having a child at this late stage of life. Even if Sarah got pregnant tomorrow, I would be a hundred before the child was born. That was rare, but not unheard of. But Sarah! She would be ninety! Surely God was joking!

"I changed the subject rather than tell God I didn't believe him. 'If only Ishmael might live under your blessing!'[53] I babbled, hoping to hide my unbelief. I would be perfectly happy if God would transfer this impossible promise into something that was possible. I already had a son—Ishmael—but God had called him a wild donkey of a man. He had said his hand would be against everyone and everyone's hand would be against him. Why not just change that part? Why not bless him and make him a blessing?

---

[51] Genesis 17:16
[52] Genesis 17:16
[53] Genesis 17:18

"But God would not change his promise, nor would he let me change the subject. 'Yes, but,' he said. That sounded so much like me. Yes, but.... It sounds as if you are agreeing, but really you are not. *'Yes, but your wife Sarah will bear you a son,'* God said, *'and you will call him Isaac. I will establish my Covenant with him as an everlasting covenant for his descendants after him.'*[54]

"I caught my breath so quickly that my giggle turned into a hiccup. *El Roi* had seen me laugh. I was to name my son Isaac, meaning 'he laughs', as a reminder that *El Roi* had seen my unbelief. Yet *El Shaddai*, Almighty God, had not struck me dead. Or had he? I pinched myself to make sure I was still alive. Yahweh, the eternal I AM, was still my God. When I was 75, he promised to make me into a great nation, and now, 24 years later, he had not changed his mind. *El Shaddai*, Almighty God, had spoken and he would do it.

"I chuckled as I thought about it. If there was any doubt that Yahweh's promises were true, this was it. A son born to an old man and a barren old woman would be proof. A ninety-year-old woman giving birth! Nobody could explain this away as coincidence or nature. *El Shaddai* was about to do the impossible.

"My chuckle turned into outright laughter. I laughed long and hard, but this time it was a laugh of faith. I looked forward to my son's birth. I looked forward to announcing to the whole world that his name was Isaac—'he laughs'!

"I sensed Yahweh's approval of my laughter this time. He waited until I could laugh no more before continuing.

"*'And as for Ishmael,'* Yahweh said, *'I have heard you: I will surely bless him; I will make him fruitful and will greatly increase his numbers. He will be the father of twelve rulers, and I will make him into a great nation.'*

"Yahweh is so gracious. In the midst of my unbelief he heard and granted my request for Ishmael. But he made sure I knew that was just an incidental thing. His parting words to me told me that the long-awaited promise was soon to be fulfilled.

---

[54] Genesis 17:19

"'*But my Covenant,*' he emphasized, '*I will establish with Isaac, whom Sarah will bear to you by this time next year.*' Then he was gone."

"How did Mother react to that news?" Isaac asked. "I bet she was ecstatic."

"Frankly, Son, I didn't tell her right away. Not about the Isaac part. Not that she would be a mother at the age of ninety. She would probably laugh at me the way I had laughed at God, and my tender faith could not stand up to ridicule. I thought I would just let God Almighty fulfill his promise, then when she got pregnant, we could both laugh with joy. Then I would tell her Yahweh said your name would be Isaac.

"I did tell her about Yahweh introducing himself as *El Shaddai*, God Almighty, and about his confirming his Covenant as an everlasting covenant between him and me and my descendants. I even told her that Yahweh promised to bless Ishmael and make him into a great nation. I told her about the name changes for her and me. She seemed very pleased with the new names. I would be 'father of many', and if she couldn't be mother of many, she could at least be 'princess'. The fact that she was not Ishmael's birth mother did not diminish her rank.

"Then I told her about the sign of the Covenant. We pondered its meaning. Usually the covenanter gives the sign. God puts the rainbow in the sky. The groom gives his bride jewelry. But God didn't give me circumcision. I even checked to see!

"Then I remembered God's command to me: '*Walk before me and be blameless.*' God Almighty wanted two things from me—faith and obedience. I can't always control my thoughts. I can't manufacture great faith. But I can offer up my tiny little scrap of faith to God and ask him to grow it. And I can control my actions. I can choose to obey.

"So that's where circumcision came into the picture. I could choose to be circumcised, and I could have all males in my household circumcised—whether born in my household or bought from a foreigner. That very day I explained to 13-year-old Ishmael that God had confirmed his Covenant with me. If he wished to be part of that Covenant and remain in my family, he would have to be circumcised. Ishmael consented, and I circumcised him.

"Then I called all the men in my camp together and told them what God had said to me. God had confirmed his Covenant with me, and as a sign they would all have to be circumcised. Any who refused would be cut off from me. They would no longer be my people.

"I organized a team of men to circumcise all the males. There were hundreds of them, so it was a long process. Those who had young sons went back to their tents to get them. The youngest one was eight days old. When we were sure no one had been missed, I circumcised the team, then it was my turn. I, at age 99, was the oldest one to be circumcised.

"And a strange thing happened. As I obeyed in the matter of circumcision, my faith was strengthened. During the healing process, in my moments of greatest pain, I found myself laughing, and that eased the pain. I laughed at the strange sign of the Covenant. I was awed that God would choose such an intimate sign. At first blush it seemed ridiculous. In some crazy ways it made sense, but in other ways it baffled me.

"Why he had chosen a sign so specific to males? Wasn't Sarah an integral part of the Covenant promise? Without a mother there could be no son. Weren't the women in my camp just as much a part of my people as the men? Some of them loved Yahweh more than their husbands did.

"I still don't have answers to some of those questions, but even as I struggle for answers, my faith grows. I believe that Yahweh is. That he is sovereign and he is almighty. I believe he is able to fulfill every promise he makes. I believe he can be trusted to fulfill his promises. But most of all I believe that Almighty God, Creator of heaven and earth, cares about me and wants to have an intimate relationship with me."

Abraham looked up at the sky again when he spoke of the Creator of heaven and earth. Isaac followed his gaze to the fading rainbow.

"The rainbow is almost gone," Isaac said, "but Yahweh's promise is as sure as ever."

9

Sarah Laughs in Unbelief

"So, when did you finally tell Mother that I would be born? Or did you wait until she knew she was carrying a baby?"

Isaac and his father were still watching the fading rainbow.

"My plan was to wait a while. If you, the son of promise, were to be born within a year, it would not be long until Sarah knew she was pregnant.

"But Yahweh had other plans. Shortly after everybody had healed and life had returned to normal, my tent was again pitched in Hebron.

"I love staying there. I can see so far in all directions. I love to dream of the day when all this land will belong to my offspring—to you, Isaac—or to your offspring. But I know it won't happen in my lifetime. I am a nomad. I am content to live in tents in this life while looking forward to the next life. There I will live in a heavenly city—a city with solid foundations, whose architect and builder is God. What a city that will be! Only such a city could lure me away from this nomadic lifestyle."

Abraham turned around slowly, staring far into the distance in all directions with a dreamy look in his eye. Isaac brought him back to the present.

"Yahweh had other plans, you said. What were they, and how did you find out?"

"I was in Hebron," Abraham continued, "sitting at the entrance to my tent in the heat of the day. I looked toward the great trees of Mamre—the trees that got my attention when I first set eyes on this part of the land—and saw three men standing nearby. At first I thought it was Mamre with friends. But Mamre didn't usually drop by until late afternoon or evening, when the day's work was done. These men were total strangers.

"I hurried out to meet them and extend to them the common courtesies of shade, water and food. I gave them water to drink, then brought more water so they could wash their feet. That's the quickest way to get comfortable on a hot day. I asked them to rest under the tree nearest to my tent. I invited them to stay and eat, and they politely accepted.

"Something about the three made me think that they were no ordinary men. Their eyes captivated me. I got the feeling that they could see right through me. The voice of one especially caught my attention. It reminded me somewhat of Yahweh's voice. If these were messengers from God, I could not offer them merely dates and yesterday's bread. I must put on a feast!

"While they were washing their feet, I hurried back into my tent and asked Sarah to bake a big batch of bread. While she was doing that, I ran to the herd and selected a choice, tender calf and gave it to a servant with instructions for him to hurry and prepare it. When the meat and bread were ready, I brought them, together with some curds and milk, and set these before them. While they ate under one tree, I stood near them under another, ready to fetch them anything they needed.

"When they had finished eating, the one with the voice reminiscent of Yahweh asked, 'Where is your wife, Sarah?'

"With that question I instantly knew he was Yahweh himself in human form. How would anyone outside our camp know my wife's name? More importantly, how would he know her *new* name? It had been changed only a few days ago.

"I answered his question, 'There, in the tent,' and pointed in Sarah's direction while wondering what would happen next. Yahweh had never spoken directly to my wife. Would he ask to speak to her now? Instead he spoke to me, but he raised his voice a little to make sure Sarah could hear even though his back was toward the tent.

"'I will surely return to you about this time next year,' Yahweh said, 'and Sarah your wife will have a son.'[55]

"I heard a stifled snicker coming from the tent and knew that Sarah had reacted the same way I had. I also knew I had been wrong not to tell Sarah the whole story about Yahweh confirming his covenant with me. Better to have her laugh at me than to laugh at Yahweh. I hoped Yahweh had not heard. But of course he had. If *El Roi* sees all, he must also hear all.

"'Why did Sarah laugh?' he asked. 'Why did she say, "Will I really have a child, now that I am old?" Is anything too hard for Yahweh?'[56]

"Yahweh had not only heard Sarah's laughter, he had also heard her thoughts! She now knew it was Yahweh speaking to her, and she was terrified. Sarah, who had been hiding just behind the entrance to the tent, did the first thing that popped into her head. She stepped into full view and said, 'I didn't laugh.'

"She was lying, and everyone knew it.

"'Oh yes, you did,' Yahweh said, and looked Sarah straight in the eye. Sarah lowered her gaze and stepped back out of sight.

"Yahweh looked at me and I knew I was no better than Sarah. I, too, had laughed when Yahweh first told me Sarah would have a son in her old age. But Yahweh is so gracious. He didn't rub it in. Instead he and the two men with him quietly got up to leave.

"'I'll be back this time next year,' he said quietly, 'and Sarah will have a son.'

"Later that evening I asked Sarah what had gone through her mind when Yahweh announced that she would have a son. Her reaction had been almost identical to mine. We were both old and Sarah was long past the age of child-bearing.

---

[55] Genesis 18:10
[56] Genesis 18:13-14

"'How could a worn-out woman like me enjoy such pleasure, especially when my master—my husband—is also so old?' Sarah wondered when she heard the announcement.

"She used a word for pleasure that suggested the Garden of Eden with all its luxurious delights. I asked her about it.

"'To have my own child to suckle and nurture would be heaven on earth. Paradise!' she explained. 'But impossible at my stage in life. I already have every luxury money can buy. I have all the pleasures this life offers. Since you were circumcised, even our personal relationship has improved. We have experienced a greater intimacy than I can remember. Now Yahweh is going to add to my delight by giving me a child? No. The gate to paradise was shut when Adam and Eve were driven out of Eden.'

"Yet the promise of a child had been given, first to me, now to Sarah."

10

Bold Enough to Bargain

"The heavenly visitors had a second reason for their visit," Abraham told Isaac, "but they were slow to disclose it. As they departed, I walked along with them for a short way. They were looking toward Sodom, which was visible from the ridge near my tent. I had often stood there and prayed for my nephew Lot, who lived in Sodom and did his best to witness to his neighbors. He had often spoken at the city gate and tried to convince the elders and the common people to change their wicked ways and follow Yahweh. But the city elders were among the worst offenders.

"When Kedorlaomer pillaged Sodom, some people's consciences were stirred, and some people believed that Yahweh was judging them for their sin. But when all the people and their belongings were retrieved, the incident was soon forgotten, and the people continued in their wicked ways.

"Lot had often told me how difficult it was living among the people of Sodom day after day. He was tormented in his soul by the lawless deeds he saw and heard. Some things were so disgraceful, he wouldn't even talk about them."

"Why didn't he move away from Sodom?" Isaac asked.

"I asked him the same thing," Abraham replied. "But his wife liked the city life—living in a real house. She had accumulated really nice furniture and a lot of things that are not easily carried around when you have to move regularly. There was no way she would consider living in a tent again. Besides, their two youngest daughters had been raised in Sodom. They were so young when Lot moved there that they had no memory of nomadic life. Increasingly Lot let his hired help take care of his flocks and herds, and Lot spent most of his time at the city gate performing his duties as an elder of the city.

"As I walked with my three visitors in the direction of Sodom, Yahweh turned and spoke to the other two.

"'Shall I hide from Abraham what I am about to do?'[57] Yahweh asked. 'One day Abraham will become a great and powerful nation, and all nations on earth will be blessed through him. I have chosen him to be a model of righteousness to the nations. If he is to teach his children and his household what is just and right, he must know how I look upon sin.'[58]

"One of the men brought up the subject of Noah and the Flood, arguing that evil must be punished or it will spread unchecked. The other countered that God had promised never again to destroy the whole earth with a flood. Yahweh reminded the men that there were other ways to stop evil. He had slowed the spread of evil at Babel by changing people's language so they wouldn't understand each other. He could destroy Sodom and Gomorrah selectively without destroying the whole country.

"Yahweh reminded the two men that the sin of Sodom and Gomorrah was so grievous that the outcry against them had reached him in Heaven. Lot's and Abraham's prayers had been heard! Even the angels in Heaven were coming to God's throne asking that something be done to stop the wickedness.

"When it dawned on me that Yahweh was considering destroying both cities entirely, I was immediately concerned for Lot and his family

---

[57] Genesis 18:17
[58] See Genesis 18:18-19

and any other righteous people who might be living in that spiritual cesspool. I stood before Yahweh and blocked his way as the other two continued toward Sodom.

"'Are you serious?' I exclaimed. 'Are you really going to sweep away both the righteous and the wicked! What if there are fifty righteous people in the city? Won't you spare the place for the sake of the fifty righteous people in it? Surely you wouldn't do that, kill off the good and the bad alike as if there were no difference between them! You can't treat the righteous and the wicked the same! That would be unthinkable!'[59]

"I was surprised at my own audacity—talking to Yahweh like that. But I had to fight for Lot and his family. Had I rescued them from the Babylonian armies only to lose them to Yahweh's anger over their wicked neighbors?

"I pleaded with Yahweh, 'Will not the Judge of all the earth do what is right?'[60]

"To my relief Yahweh agreed with me. 'If I find fifty righteous people in the city of Sodom,' he said, 'I'll spare the whole place for their sake.'

"My relief was short-lived. I could see that Yahweh was making no move to stop the two men who were heading toward Sodom. There weren't fifty righteous people in Sodom! Lot would be destroyed.

"The thought that Yahweh as Judge of the whole earth would do what was right emboldened me to keep negotiating. 'What if the number of the righteous is five less than fifty?' I asked. 'Will you destroy the whole city because of five people?'

"'If I find 45 there,' Yahweh said, 'I won't destroy it.'

"Again Yahweh made no move to stop the two men heading for Sodom.

"I asked Yahweh to spare Sodom for the sake of forty righteous people, and he agreed. I asked for the sake of thirty, then twenty righteous people, and each time he agreed. Each time, I realized from Yahweh's actions that there weren't enough righteous people to stop him from judging Sodom.

---

[59] See Genesis 18:23-25
[60] See Genesis 18:25

"I asked Yahweh not to get angry with me, but I had to make one final request. 'What if only ten can be found there?' I said, almost in a whisper.

"'For the sake of ten, I will not destroy it,'[61] he declared.

"I knew from the look in his eyes that there weren't even ten. Neither of us said another word. Yahweh left, and I returned home with a heavy heart. All that evening I thought about Lot and wondered what would happen to him when Yahweh judged Sodom and Gomorrah, but I clung to the thought that the Judge of all the earth would do right.

"Early the next morning I got up and returned to the place where I had stood before Yahweh. Sodom and Gomorrah were gone! The once-lush green plain was black. Dense smoke was rising from the land.

"Fear gripped my heart. What had happened to Lot and his family? Had they, too, been destroyed? But then again I was comforted by my own words of the day before, 'Will not the Judge of all the earth do what is right?'

"A few days later a message came from Lot. He and his two daughters were safe. They were living in a cave in the mountains somewhere east of the plain where Sodom had been. His wife had not survived."

"I heard that Lot's wife was turned into a pillar of salt," Isaac said.

"Unfortunately, yes," Abraham replied. "She escaped the initial destruction; but she looked back, against the angels' instructions. Her heart was still in Sodom."

Abraham looked around for the rainbow, but it had completely disappeared.

"So balance the rainbow with the picture of fire and brimstone, Son. The rainbow is a reminder of God's promise that he will never again destroy the whole world with a flood. But that is no excuse for godless living. Sodom and Gomorrah are reminders that God will still judge evil. But you don't have to live in fear and hide in a cave as Lot and his daughters are doing. If you keep the way of Yahweh by doing what is right and just, you have nothing to fear. Live for him and he will bless you."

---

[61] Genesis 18:31

11

Another Faith Detour

"Father, you said that your faith in Yahweh was sometimes strong and sometimes weak. But I was wondering, after Yahweh told you that within a year Mother would have a son, did you have faith from then on?"

Isaac's question took Abraham by surprise, but he was pleased that his son wanted to talk about faith.

Abraham took his time answering. He did not want to leave a false impression. If he made himself out to be a giant of faith, his son would likely put him on a pedestal. That would result in one of two outcomes. One, Isaac could conclude that he could never live up to his father's example, and not even try to emulate his father's faith. Or if—God forbid—Abraham should ever fail and fall from that pedestal, Isaac would be devastated, and might reject Yahweh entirely. Isaac would think, "If my own father, the great Abraham, can't have faith in Yahweh, how can I possibly have faith?"

Abraham did not want to put himself on a pedestal—especially not a faith pedestal. He just wanted to be real. If his son could see him as human, with all his successes and failures, he could learn to emulate the successes and use the failures as warning signs of what not to do. Isaac could then learn to walk by faith as Abraham was trying to do.

"Faith is a strange, elusive thing, Son. It is like the sun trying to shine through clouds. It glows through faintly at times, and more brightly at other times. Sometimes the clouds disappear altogether, and sometimes the clouds completely obscure the sun. The sun is always there, just as Yahweh's promises are always there. It is we who put clouds in the way—clouds of unbelief.

"In my case, my faith or lack thereof depended partly on what I was asked to believe. I never once doubted that Yahweh would bless me. His blessings were evident right from the start. I accumulated wealth almost effortlessly. Everything I did succeeded. I also never doubted that Yahweh would give me land, a permanent homeland for my descendants."

"That seems strange," Isaac remarked, "since you are an alien in Canaan and a nomad."

"It does seem strange, doesn't it?" Abraham agreed. "But it is true. I love the life of a nomad. I love the freedom that comes with living in a tent. Being able to move to wherever the pastures are best. Having a change of scenery regularly. Meeting new people. Making new friends.

"But something deep inside me longs for permanence. Not now, but eventually. My descendants will experience that permanence. I have no trouble believing that. And I, too, will live in a city. Not in this foreign land, but in Heaven. I look forward to the City With Foundations, whose architect and builder is God.[62] Every city I have ever seen has some good features and some things that, in hindsight, could have been better planned. Every house I have ever seen has some good features and some things that, in hindsight, could have been better planned. But God's city will be perfect! The home he builds for me will be perfect.

"Maybe I believe Yahweh for land and permanence precisely because I know that promise is future. It is the immediate promises that I struggle with. That's what happened with believing Yahweh for a son. When he first promised me descendants, I believed. When he asked me to count the stars and said, 'So shall your offspring be,' I believed. But when your mother and I stopped trying to count the stars and started

---

[62] See Hebrews 11:10

to count our wrinkles and gray hairs instead, our faith wavered and we tried to help Yahweh fulfill his promises."

Isaac chuckled at the thought of his father counting wrinkles instead of stars.

"There's a lesson there, Son. Whenever you start to doubt Yahweh, it is because your focus is too short-sighted. Don't look at your wrinkles."

Isaac gave his father a blank look. Wrinkles were too far into his future to comprehend. Abraham quickly realized his mistake and revised his advice.

"In your case, Son, don't look at your minor human flaws! Take a step back and look at the big picture. Look at the stars, and your faith in Yahweh and his promises will be restored. Then don't just *look* at the stars. Try to count them!"

"Is that what you did when your faith wavered, Father? Counted the stars?"

"I wish I could say yes, Son. Often I did, but not often enough. Do you know what I struggled most with believing Yahweh for?"

Isaac tried to think of what Yahweh had promised that his father had not already mentioned.

"That you will be a blessing?" Isaac guessed.

"No. I don't concern myself about how others see me. I just live my life and leave the impact on others to Yahweh."

"It can't be that your name will be great. It already is. You are the best known, best respected alien in Canaan. People still remark about your rescuing Lot and the people of Sodom from Kedorlaomer. They still laugh that a few hundred nomads could put the Babylonian forces on the run."

Abraham shook his head. Isaac had no more guesses.

"My greatest faith struggle has been believing Yahweh for something so basic that he didn't even bother promising it to me. I should have taken it for granted."

Isaac still couldn't guess.

"My personal protection!"

Isaac couldn't have been more surprised. "But you chased the Babylonians! Nothing could have been more dangerous!"

"I wasn't thinking about myself at the time, Son. I was thinking only of Lot. He was family. Besides, I was indignant that Kedorlaomer was dragging him back to the country Yahweh had commanded me to leave."

"I have never feared for my safety," Isaac exclaimed. "When did you need protection? From whom? Or from what? Besides, you have hundreds of trained fighting men to protect you."

"I know, Son," Abraham sighed. "It doesn't make sense, but it is my weakness. Remember I told you about being in Egypt and fearing that Pharaoh would kill me to get my wife?"

Isaac nodded. "Yahweh fought for you by inflicting serious diseases on Pharaoh and his household, so Pharaoh let Mother go. But you learned from that."

Abraham dropped his head in shame.

"I wish that were true, Son."

"What are you telling me?"

"I failed Yahweh the same way twice. I failed to believe him for protection."

This was news to Isaac.

"What happened? Did you go back to Egypt? Did Pharaoh . . . ?"

Isaac couldn't force himself to ask the unthinkable question.

"No, Son."

Abraham hated to admit his failures, but he knew Isaac would find out some day, and he would rather have his son hear it directly from him.

"I never again went far enough into Egypt to attract Pharaoh's attention. But Pharaoh isn't the only powerful man in the world."

"The most powerful man I know is Abimelech in Gerar," Isaac said, "but you made a treaty with him a few years ago."

Isaac noticed a pained look come across his father's face. "What?" Isaac asked. "Does this have something to do with Abimelech?"

Abraham sighed and nodded. Slowly he began the story.

"After Yahweh destroyed Sodom and Gomorrah, I needed to move my flocks and herds, so I moved southward from Hebron into the Negev. In my wanderings I ended up in Kadesh.

"Kadesh means holy. Consecrated. Sanctuary. And what a sanctuary it was! The water supply was so abundant and refreshing! Having so recently talked with Yahweh, I pondered his promise. Within a year Sarah and I would see the fulfillment of the promise. A son! From Sarah, the barren one! Sarah and I were so excited.

"Hagar, too, was excited. We were on the same path that she had taken when she had run away from Sarah's mistreatment of her. If we went a little further northwest, we would come to Beer Lahai Roi—the well of the Living One who sees me. Hagar wanted to show Ishmael the place where Yahweh had named him and prophesied about him. Ishmael begged me to go there. Sarah and I were also interested in seeing the place, so we went.

"We all had a good time there. We worshipped El Roi, the God who sees me. We celebrated Ishmael and recounted to him the prophecies that had been made about him. He had been named Ishmael, 'God hears', because God had heard Hagar's unspoken cries of misery and desperation.

"We talked about the things God had prophesied about Ishmael.

"Some were good. 'I will surely bless him; I will make him fruitful and will greatly increase his numbers. He will be the father of twelve rulers, and I will make him into a great nation.' Hagar's descendants would be 'too numerous to count.'

"Some prophecies were not so good. 'He will be a wild donkey of a man; his hand will be against everyone and everyone's hand against him, and he will live in hostility toward all his brothers.'

"And we told Ishmael again what I had told him the day he was circumcised. He was not the Son of Promise. Yahweh's covenant would be established with Isaac, the son not yet born."

"How did Ishmael respond to that?" Isaac asked.

"All his life Ishmael had enjoyed his status as son of the exalted father Abram, now known as Abraham. And he obviously was enjoying being the centre of attention at Beer Lahai Roi. But he seemed thoughtful that day, as if he was pondering what changes he would experience with the birth of a brother—or rather, a half-brother. A younger brother who would take his place as the centre of attention. A younger brother who would be recognized as the firstborn. A younger brother who would replace him entirely!

"Ishmael, his fellow-servants had reminded him recently, was only the son of a slave woman. That they used the term 'slave woman' took Ishmael by surprise. He was used to hearing his mother referred to politely as a 'maid servant' or sometimes as the slightly less politically correct term 'handmaid', but never 'slave woman'! As long as he was Abraham's only son or as long as Abraham had no children by his wife, Ishmael was told, he would be considered a son. But if Sarah had a child, Ishmael would have no right to an inheritance from Abraham and would be considered illegitimate. 'You will have no more status than we do,' he was told by his peers.

"Ishmael was shocked!

"I told him the day he was circumcised that he was not the Son of Promise, but Ishmael had not absorbed the full implication of that statement. My people don't feel like slaves because they have never been treated like slaves."

"How about when Mother mistreated Hagar?" Isaac asked.

"You're right," Abraham agreed sadly, "but that was a brief exception. Hagar had stepped out of line when she found out she was pregnant. She treated your mother as if *she* were the slave woman. Your mother didn't stand for that, though she may have overdone it. Hagar was treated respectfully when she returned and behaved herself.

"To get back to my story, Ishmael enjoyed thoroughly our time at Beer Lahai Roi, but he was more subdued after that. Maybe even morose. For the first time I could believe the prophecy that he would live in hostility to any future brothers.

"Beer Lahai Roi is right on the border between Canaan and Egypt. From there it is not far to the wilderness of Shur, Hagar's original home. Being that close to her home, she wanted to visit her relatives and introduce them to her son Ishmael. So we went, but we didn't stay for long because my large flocks and herds needed more water and pasture than was readily available there.

"I had no desire to continue further into Egypt, so we headed back to Canaan and ended up in Gerar, halfway between Beersheba and the Great Sea, on the southern edge of the land of the Philistines.

"The Philistines were a powerful sea people who had come from far way, across the Great Sea. They were taller than the Egyptians and the Canaanites, and had distinctly different features. I was told that they resembled their Greek ancestors, who had migrated via Caphtor, which the Greeks call Crete, to the western coast of Canaan. They settled along the coast, claiming the best land in the area—the fruitful, well-watered maritime plain from Joppa to Gerar. The Canaanites had long given up trying to evict them from the land. The Egyptians kept a watchful eye out lest the Philistines try to expand further south into Egypt. As long as the Philistines did not try to conquer more territory, there was peace.

"The Egyptians regarded the Philistines as highly civilized, but my first impression of the Philistines was how godless they were."

"Godless!" Isaac exclaimed. "I heard that they were intensely religious."

"Oh, they have gods alright," Abraham replied, "many gods—but no concept of the true God. Their worship is not only misdirected, it also involves highly immoral practices, especially with respect to their worship of the fertility goddess Ashtoreth. Being a seafaring people, they worship Dagon, meaning "little fish", a god with the hands and face of a man and the tail of a fish. They pray to Dagon for rain and give him credit for their good crops. They carry images of Dagon with them into their battles both at sea and on land. Their prince of demons is Baalzebul, meaning 'Baal the exalted'."

Isaac started to laugh.

"I overheard one of our servants teasing a Philistine by calling the god Baalzebub instead of Baalzebul—calling him 'lord of the fly' instead of 'Baal the exalted'. Luckily the Philistine didn't catch the joke or there would have been a big fight! The Philistine thought our servant was just mispronouncing the name. If the servant had said Baalzebub*im*, lord of the flies plural, the Philistine would have known it was not just a slip of the tongue."

Abraham laughed too.

"Actually the name Baalzebub is very appropriate," Abraham added. "Dagon is a dead god—a dead fish, so to speak—and dead fish certainly attract flies!

"But, back to my story about Abimelech . . . ."

"I knew that the Philistines were not only powerful and prosperous and well organized politically, but also warlike in nature. With their zealous worship of gods like Ashtoreth, Dagon and Baalzebul, that makes them dangerous. They are eager to conquer any people and territories that show any sign of weakness. They have no concept of living peaceably with their neighbors unless it is politically expedient to do so.

"I went to Gerar because my sheep and cattle needed the water from the river and the pasture from the well-watered plain. But I went with some trepidation because of the Philistines' reputation. Being aware that Sarah's beauty would attract attention, I went back to the old ploy of introducing Sarah as my sister."

Isaac's face registered disbelief and disapproval.

"You didn't!"

"Don't be too quick to condemn me, Son. You haven't walked in my sandals. Besides, married Philistine women wear veils, and Sarah didn't, which added to the misunderstanding.

"In Gerar, I discovered later, my reputation—and my God's reputation—had preceded me. The Philistines knew I had stood up to the Babylonian confederation of kings, sent them running for home, and rescued the hostages taken from Sodom and Gomorrah. In the fourteen years since that event, my name had become almost legendary. When Sodom and Gomorrah were destroyed by fire from heaven, word soon spread that Abraham's God had done it and had spared Abraham's nephew Lot. Some of the Philistines had seen the pillar of salt that used to be Lot's wife and had heard the rumor that she had been destroyed for disobeying Abraham's God.

"I didn't know when I went to Gerar that the Philistines feared me as much as I feared them. Their king was Abimelech. 'Abimelech' among the Philistines, like 'Pharaoh' among the Egyptians, is a title of royalty. It literally means 'father of the king', but is more loosely translated 'royal father.'

"When Abimelech came to meet me shortly after my arrival, he was very friendly. He came with a contingent of his officials but not with Phicol, his ever-present military commander-in-chief. I learned later that this was a sign that he came in peace. Sarah helped me extend hospitality to Abimelech and his officials, and Abimelech asked to be introduced to her. Of course I said she was my sister.

"It was not very many days later that he sent for Sarah and took her into his harem. I should have understood his gesture, but I didn't at the time. He was trying to make a pact with me so that I would not declare war against him and he would not make war against me. Such treaties were common in the nations around me. But I had my head in the sand, and all I could understand were my selfish fears. I didn't even think to ask Yahweh what was happening and what should I do. I didn't dare object to Abimelech's taking my wife.

"With Sarah gone, I relived the time when we were in Egypt and Pharaoh took her. I relived the fear and anxiety. I relived the feeling that Yahweh was not pleased with me. Why could I not trust him to protect me? Only two months ago Yahweh had sent his angels to rescue Lot from Sodom before destroying the city. Could he not do the same for me? If Yahweh could destroy two whole cities where no one feared God, could he not destroy one man who would harm me and mine? Besides, Yahweh had promised that Sarah would have a son within a year, and two months had already passed since the announcement. Where was my faith now? When I believed Yahweh, I sensed his pleasure. When I disbelieved, his displeasure pressed heavily upon me.

"After a few days of turmoil and anguish, I could stand it no longer. I had scorned the Philistines for having no *fear* of God, but Yahweh scorned me for having no *faith* in him. I cried out to Yahweh in repentance. I confessed my unbelief and asked him to forgive me. With my repentance and confession of sin, my burden of guilt lifted. I asked Yahweh to strengthen my faith. I promised Yahweh that if he would just bring Sarah back to me, I would never doubt him again.

"'Yahweh,' I prayed, 'I never want to doubt you again. Make me a man of faith. I want to believe you for everything—for everything you have promised me and for everything you have promised my descendants, even though I haven't seen any legitimate descendants yet. I want to believe you for everything you will fulfill because you are Almighty God.'"

Abraham looked at his son.

"I pray that for you, too, Isaac. That you will be a man of faith. That you will believe Yahweh for everything he has promised to me, because those promises are yours, too. Those promises will be your inheritance. I pray that you will surpass me as a man of faith."

Isaac looked at his father with tears in his eyes.

"I want that too," he said softly. "But I doubt that I will ever have more faith than you, Father."

Abraham resumed his story.

"My repentance made a difference. Early the next morning I heard a clap of hands outside my tent and I heard someone calling my name. It was a contingent of Abimelech's officials. My instant reaction was fear, but I quickly refused it. Instead I chose to believe that this was the beginning of answered prayer.

"When I was brought before Abimelech, he dispensed with the usual polite greetings and got right to the point.

"'What have you done to us?' he shouted. I knew what he was talking about even without his mentioning Sarah. His anger reminded me of Pharaoh. 'How have I wronged you? What crime have I committed that deserves treatment like this, making me and my kingdom guilty of this great sin? No one should ever do what you have done!'

"'I'm sorry,' I said, dropping my head in shame.

"Abimelech waited for me to say more, but all I could do was to repeat lamely, 'I'm sorry.'

"His anger turned to puzzlement. 'Whatever possessed you to do such a thing?' he asked.

"'I just assumed that there was no fear of God in this place,' I told him, "and that they will want my wife and kill me to get her.'"

"I looked up and saw that Abimelech couldn't believe his ears. I tried to explain my actions, but all I did was babble and talk faster.

"'Besides, she really is my sister—my father's daughter but not my mother's. She is also my wife. And when God sent me out as a wanderer from my father's home, I said to her, "Do me a favor. Wherever we go, tell people that I'm your brother."'[63]

"I ran out of words and fell silent. Abimelech, too, was silent for a moment. Finally he spoke.

"'So, you think there is no fear of God in this place. You think I don't fear your God?' His voice rose with the question and continued rising as he talked. 'Well, you're wrong! I've heard stories about your God—how he sent the Babylonians running for home. I know you couldn't have done that all by yourself—you and your puny little army. And just recently your God bombed Sodom and Gomorrah with fire from heaven because their morality didn't match his concept of right and wrong. For your information, I didn't approve of the things that went on in those cities either. And he turned Lot's wife into a pillar of salt! For what? For turning around and looking back? Of course, I fear your God!' he thundered.

"Then Abimelech lowered his voice and told me his side of the story.

"'I was shaking in my sandals when I heard that you were coming to Gerar. So my solution was to marry someone you really cared about. That's why I took Sarah into my harem. To make peace. I had no idea she was your wife. She doesn't wear a veil. I wouldn't have dared to touch your *wife*!

"'Last night your God came to me in a dream. "You're a dead man!" he said. 'Why?' I asked him. 'What have I done?' 'Because of that woman you took,' he told me. 'She's a married woman.' Thankfully I hadn't slept with her yet, so I proclaimed my innocence.

"'Didn't Abraham say to me, "She's my sister," and didn't she herself say, "He's my brother?" I acted in complete innocence! My hands are clean.'

---

[63] See Genesis 20:11-13

"'Then God said to me in my dream, "Yes, I know your intentions were pure, that's why I kept you from sinning against me; I was the one who kept you from going to bed with her. So now give the man's wife back to him. He's a prophet. He will pray for you, and you will live. But if you don't return her to him, you may be sure that you and all your people will die."'[64]

"I looked around at Abimelech and all his officials," Abraham told Isaac. "It was obvious that they were all terrified. Looking at their faces, I realized for the first time that they were more afraid of me and my God than I was of them. As long as I walked closely with El Shaddai, God Almighty, I had nothing to fear.

"The next thing I knew, Abimelech was showering me with gifts. In a long parade he brought sheep and cattle, with male slaves to care for the livestock and female slaves to handle domestic duties. And at the end of the line was Sarah. How happy I was to see her again! Magnanimously Abimelech announced, 'My land is before you; live wherever you like.'

"Just when I thought it was all over, a servant came forward carrying a heavy bag. It was filled with silver coins.

"'I'm giving your 'brother' a thousand pieces of silver,' Abimelech explained to Sarah. 'A covering for your eyes,' he said with a wink.[65]

"We squirmed at his rubbing in our deception. We also understood his comment as being both literal and figurative. There was enough money to buy a thousand veils for Sarah to wear when she was in Philistine territory. With all but her eyes covered, no one would mistake her for being unmarried. His payment would also cover the offence of having taken Sarah into his harem, even though it had been done with the best of intentions. Abimelech was hoping we would cover our eyes, so to speak, look the other way, and forget the incident ever happened. Sarah and I were happy to cover our eyes.

"While Abimelech had been bringing gifts to us, I had the distinct impression that Yahweh had closed up every womb in Abimelech's

---

[64] See Genesis 20:6-7
[65] See Genesis 20:16

household because of Sarah, but I had no proof. I hadn't heard Yahweh's voice. I was about to dismiss the thought when Abimelech reminded me that God had said I was a prophet. I was to pray for him so that God would not kill him.

"Before I prayed for Abimelech, I chose to step out in faith and tell him what I believed God's Spirit was telling me. It was the first time I had acted on God's silent voice.

"I asked Abimelech to bring out his wife and all the women, slave or free, in his household. When I told them that God had shut all their wombs, I saw some of them look at each other knowingly and nod. They believed me. They must have had some indication that it was true.

"I asked Abimelech for permission to touch each of the women—to lay my hands on them as I prayed. Abimelech considered this a highly unusual request, but he wasn't about to argue with me if that was what my God was asking me to do. Starting at the end of the line, I prayed for each woman. That Yahweh would spare her from death. That Yahweh would heal her. That Yahweh would bless her and the fruit of her womb.

"I looked around to make sure I hadn't missed any of the women. I was about to turn to Abimelech when it struck me that the only woman I hadn't prayed for was my own wife. 'Why not?' I thought to myself. I moved toward Sarah and saw the surprise in her eyes. Then I laid my hands on her and prayed for her.

"As I prayed, I felt the Spirit of Yahweh upon me, speaking through me. I prayed that Yahweh would heal Sarah of her barrenness. I prayed that he would give her faith to conceive. That she would have faith to believe that Yahweh would be faithful to his promise. That he would bless her and the fruit of her womb.

"Sarah bowed her head fervently while I prayed, and when I finished praying for her, she looked up with tears in her eyes and an appreciative smile on her face.

"Last of all I prayed for Abimelech. That Yahweh would spare him from death. That Yahweh would bless him. That he and his people would learn to know Yahweh as the only true and living God. That they would follow him and his ways.

"Sarah and I departed in peace—a peace that did not need to be sealed with marriage to a foreign king. And I learned a little more that day about trusting Yahweh.

"So did Sarah.

"'So you're a prophet, eh?' Sarah mused later that night. 'I believe it. I could feel Yahweh speaking through you, rebuking me for my unbelief. I had given up believing that Yahweh had the power to blow away my barrenness. While you were praying, I confessed my unbelief and repented. For the first time in years I can truly say that I believe Yahweh will give me a child. A son. We'll call him Isaac.'

"Then Sarah laughed. Not the laughter of derision, but the relaxed happy laughter of faith."

12

Living Water

The sun was rising over a lush river valley on a quiet Sabbath morning. Abraham, Sarah, and Isaac were in Beersheba enjoying the prospect of a leisurely day. After breakfast they emerged from their tent and settled under a tamarisk tree. Abraham let out a long sigh of pleasure.

"I love this place," he said. "It is so peaceful here. There is always plenty of forage for our sheep and cattle. The stream below varies from a raging torrent to a quietly flowing stream to a dry wadi depending on the time of year and the weather conditions, but my well always has plenty of water for our needs."

The three of them were silent as they listened to the birds chirping and singing in the surrounding trees. They watched the stream and listened to it burbling over the rocks. "Living water," Sarah said. "Don't you love that expression? It describes the situation so perfectly. Still water eventually evaporates and dries up. Lakes turn to marshes. Marshes turn to mud. But running water replenishes the pools and lakes. Still water gets dirty from animals walking through it. Cisterns eventually get stagnant. But the running water in fountains and springs, rivers and streams flows clean and fresh from a higher source. Living water. From God."

Abraham nodded thoughtfully.

"Water is a valuable resource not to be wasted," he said. "In places it is so scarce that people must pay for it for their livestock or for use by a large group of people. Yet even in the desert no weary traveler is ever denied water. The first thing a nomad does when entertaining a stranger is offer him a drink. No one would think of demanding payment for a drink of water.

"Water is so valuable that we weave it into our everyday expressions. Adulterous actions are called 'stolen waters.'[66] Death is like water spilled on the ground, which cannot be recovered."[67]

Isaac said, "I guess that's why my friend said of his neighbor when he died, 'The old man kicked the bucket.'"

"Isaac! Don't be rude!" Sarah exclaimed.

"I didn't say it. I was just telling you what he said," Isaac replied defensively. "Besides, my friend heard it from someone else."

Sarah shook her head.

"The things people say! That has always struck me as an irreverent expression. But I can see how it fits with losing a valuable, unrecoverable resource. I remember the feeling of horror and loss during one especially dry season when someone tripped and inadvertently kicked over a bucket of water that had just been drawn up from a deep well. All that good water—gone!"

"There are even proverbs based on water," Abraham continued. "Adulterers are told, 'Drink water from your own cistern, running water from your own well.'[68] A wise man is considered a source of deep water and his words living water, so we have sayings like: 'The words of a man's mouth are deep waters, the fountain of wisdom is a bubbling brook.'[69] Or: 'Counsel in the heart of man is like water in a deep well, but a man of understanding draws it out.'[70] Meaning, if you are a man of understanding, you will draw wisdom from a wise man as we draw water from a well."

---

[66] Proverbs 9:17, KJV
[67] See 2 Samuel 14:14, NIV
[68] Proverbs 5:15
[69] Proverbs 18:4
[70] Proverbs 20:5, Amplified Bible

"That's why I listen to you, Father," Isaac said. "Your counsel is deep water."

Abraham wasn't sure whether his son was serious or mocking him, but he chose to accept the statement at face value.

"I've had a hundred more years of experience to draw from than you," he replied. "There is something wrong with me if I haven't gained wisdom over the years."

"I remember," Sarah commented, "that whenever Hagar recounted the story of her encounter with El Roi at Beer Lahai Roi, she used the word 'eye' for the spring. I had never heard that expression before, though I have heard some of our people use it on rare occasions since. In Hagar's case the choice of the word 'eye' seemed appropriate because she was talking about 'the Living One who sees me.' But I have often wondered how the expression got started. Why would you call a spring an 'eye'?"

"I wouldn't be surprised if Hagar herself coined the expression," Abraham said thoughtfully.

Sarah looked up at him in surprise.

"Think about it," Abraham reasoned. "There is nothing about a spring that looks like an eye. So the expression did not arise from a comparison or description. The expression had to come from someone's dramatic experience."

Sarah nodded as understanding dawned.

"Hagar's," she concluded. "I would like to ask her about her thought processes, but now that she is gone, I can only guess."

"I think I can guess," said Abraham. "There is something about running water—fountains, streams, rivers—living water—that makes me God-conscious. Look at us here. We stare at the stream and soon we are thinking and talking about God.

"I see in the living water God's provision for my needs. My livestock depend on me to provide them with food and water. How much more do we depend on God to provide our needs! Not just food and water, shelter and clothing, but our spiritual needs as well. When I see living water, I see that God sees me and my needs. I become conscious that he is the living, all-seeing, all-knowing, all-caring God.

"That's why Hagar called Yahweh 'El Roi', the God who sees. She could run away from her mistress, she could try to run from her troubles, but she could not run away from God. We didn't know where she was, but God found her in the desert. That's why she called the place Beer Lahai Roi. The well of the living God, who showed himself to her beside the living water. Who saw her need for water. Who saw her need for safety. Who saw her need for love and caring. Who saw her need for *hope*."

"God's eye on us is very personal," Sarah added. "I remember when Hagar told her story how she stressed the personal aspect. 'You are the God who sees *me*,'[71] she said to the angel messenger. He made Hagar feel like somebody. She was more than a slave. She was important enough in God's sight for him to send an angel to talk to her and bring her a message from God. She carried herself with more dignity after she returned from that encounter with God."

"Yes," said Abraham, "she spoke to the angel as if speaking directly to God himself. '*You* are the God who sees me,' she said, knowing that the angel would make sure that God got the message."

"The seeing was two-way," Sarah added. "I remember Hagar saying, 'I have now seen the One who sees me.' No wonder Hagar called the spring an 'eye'. She saw God, and God saw her. At the spring. At the place of living water."

Isaac had been silent during their discussion of Hagar. That event had happened before he was born. But he was intrigued by the story.

"I would like to see Beer Lahai Roi some day," he said.

"You will, Son," Abraham replied. "It is part of your inheritance—part of the land that Yahweh promised to give to me and my descendants."

Abraham's gaze wandered from his son back to the stream, then over to the well nearby. His son followed his gaze.

"What are you thinking, Father?"

"I was thinking of this stream and the well I dug nearby. I was thinking of Hagar's spring in the desert and the well, Beer Lahai Roi. The living water comes from God, but the well is man-made.

---

[71] Genesis 16:13

"There is a lesson here. I can satisfy my thirst temporarily by filling my hands at the stream and drinking. I can satisfy my thirst for a longer period by filling a skin with water and taking it with me. But I can satisfy the thirst of my entire people as well as all my flocks and herds by digging a well or building a cistern—like I did here. I can enlarge my capacity for water.

"I think there is a parallel there. Yahweh is my living water, but he wants me to enlarge my capacity for him."

"How do you do that?" Isaac asked.

"I'm not sure," Abraham replied. "Do any of you have suggestions?"

For some time Eliezer, Abraham's chief servant, had been standing quietly nearby, listening. Now he spoke up.

"I think we enlarge our capacity for God by the habits we establish. We have established the habit of not working on the Sabbath. That gives us time to meditate on God and his creation. Meditating is listening to God, actively thinking about him and expecting to learn from him. I have never heard Yahweh's voice with my ears, but I have often heard him whisper to my spirit."

"I *have* heard Yahweh's voice," Abraham said, "and his words must never be forgotten. On days like this I retell his words to my family and friends and whoever will listen. You must remember Yahweh's words, Isaac, and retell them to your children and your children's children. My forefathers told me about the creation and the great flood. About people like Enoch and Noah who lived godly lives. About the tower of Babel and Cain and others who did evil. We can learn from the good and the bad. Pass it on."

Isaac nodded solemnly.

Sarah added her thoughts. "Prayer also increases our capacity for God. The more we pray, the more we hear from God—if only we would listen. Prayer is, or should be, a two-way conversation with God."

Eliezer nodded in agreement. "Praising Yahweh is another habit we should cultivate. Yahweh showers us with so many wonderful gifts, yet too often people take those gifts for granted. Often they don't even recognize that the sunshine and the rain, the seasons and the crops come from him. When we praise Yahweh for his kindness and faithfulness, his strength and provision, he continues to shower us with blessings such as joy and peace."

"Let's take some time to identify Yahweh's gifts and thank him for them," said Abraham. "Open your eyes. Look around and really see what the living God has given you."

13

Child of Promise

Sitting by the well which Abraham had named Beersheba, Abraham and his household thanked Yahweh for his many gifts. Water topped the list. At first thirteen-year-old Isaac joined in, almost like a game, taking delight in naming little things that the adults had missed. Soon his interest in the game waned, and he got up and wandered toward the well.

Turning toward his father, he asked, "When did you dig this well?"

"I dug it not long after Abimelech said, 'My land is before you; live wherever you like' and a little while before you were conceived."

Isaac looked expectantly at his father, waiting for him to elaborate.

"Your mother bought a veil after the encounter with Abimelech, but she hated wearing it. When the rainy season began, we moved away from Gerar and the Philistines, following the river valley inland on a slow journey toward Hebron. As you know, Son, we stay in Hebron for part of every year. About half way to Hebron we stopped here—at Beersheba, though it wasn't called that at the time—on the eastern edge of Philistine territory.

"Pasture land was rich and water was abundant, but I knew the water wouldn't always be abundant, so I dug a well. Then no matter what time of year we returned here, water would always be available."

"One day Sarah woke up feeling nauseated. It continued to happen every morning when her stomach was empty. Hagar was the first to recognize the symptoms. 'You're pregnant,' she told an astonished Sarah."

At this point in the story Sarah spoke up to give her version of events. Several more servants had gathered quietly to listen. They loved hearing the miraculous story.

"I waited a few more days to be sure before saying anything to my husband," Sarah said. "When I was certain, I couldn't keep the news to myself. 'Good morning, Prophet Abraham,' I teased. 'Your prayer has been answered.'

"It took Abraham a few moments to figure out what I meant.

"'Abraham. Father of many,' I prompted him. 'Sarah. Mother of nations.'

"Then his jaw dropped and a big smile appeared on his face.

"'Really?' he asked, and I nodded.

"'Really!'

"Abraham's first reaction was to raise his hands to God.

"'Yahweh is so gracious!' he said. 'Yahweh did for Sarah what he promised in spite of our conniving and lack of faith from time to time!'

"We decided not to say anything until my pregnancy was obvious, but that didn't last long. Both Abraham and I had such big smiles on our faces that everyone asked what we were so happy about. Of course, we had to tell them that I was pregnant. Almighty God had made it possible. Every time we told it, we laughed and our hearers laughed with us. Yahweh is a promise-keeping God, we told them.

"My only request," said Sarah, "was that we be back in Hebron in time for the birth. Hebron was our favorite place, the place where Yahweh had said, 'I will surely return to you about this time next year, and Sarah will have a son.'

"The next few months went by quickly. And you, Son, were born right on time—exactly a year from the promise. We wondered if we would see Yahweh in some form, or see a messenger from him, because he had said, 'I will surely return to you about this time next year.' But the only one unusual we saw that day was a newborn baby.

"I guess you were evidence enough of Yahweh's presence," Sarah said, turning to Isaac.

"Your father named you Isaac, 'he laughs', just as Yahweh had instructed him. He also circumcised you when you were eight days old, just as Yahweh commanded, as a sign of the everlasting Covenant Yahweh made with him.

"Yes," Sarah said, trying to look solemn, "I bore Abraham a son in his old age." She looked around to make sure everybody got the joke. "In *his* old age," she repeated, and everybody laughed uproariously.

Then her expression changed to wonder, and she added quietly, almost as if speaking to herself, "Who would have said to Abraham that Sarah would nurse children?" The twinkle returned to her eye and the tease returned to her voice as she repeated, "Yet I bore him a son in his old age!"[72]

When Sarah was finished telling her story, Eliezer turned to Isaac. "I remember that day so vividly. "We all knew Abraham was a hundred years old, but it was hard for us to look at Sarah and think that she was ninety! Even today she doesn't look her age. A hundred and three! She hasn't stopped laughing since she discovered she was pregnant. I think all that laughter has kept her young."

---

[72] See Genesis 21:7

14

Ishmael Has To Go

"How did Hagar and Ishmael react when I was born?" Isaac wanted to know.

"Hagar was not a problem," Sarah replied. "Ever since she met 'the God who sees me', she was content to put her life into his hands. She did worry about Ishmael, though. She worried about the prophecy that his hand would be against everyone and everyone's hand would be against him.

"The first hint of trouble came when you were eight days old. Your father threw a big party to introduce you to his people. First he circumcised you. Then, while you were still squalling in pain, he held you up over his head for everyone to see.

"'Meet Isaac,' Abraham said. 'He laughs.'

"Everybody laughed because you were not laughing. You were crying your head off.

"'Meet the Son of the Promise, the Child of the Covenant.'

"All the people cheered. Ever since the time a year prior when all the males had been circumcised, they had anticipated with us the birth of a son from Sarah. Now they all cheered. Everyone, that is, except Ishmael.

"'This child,' Abraham continued, 'is proof that Yahweh is a promise-keeping God. He will establish his covenant as an everlasting covenant between me and this child and this child's descendants for the generations to come. He will be our God and the God of our descendants.

"'Yahweh promised us the whole land of Canaan as an everlasting possession for me and my descendants. That promise looks as impossible now as the promise of a child from Sarah did a year ago. But if Yahweh can give Sarah a child, he can give us the land of Canaan.'

"Again everybody cheered.

"'Yahweh is our God, our promise-keeping God. And Isaac has been circumcised as the sign of the Covenant, the everlasting Covenant from the promise-keeping God.'

"'You too have been circumcised,' Abraham told his servants, 'so you too will share in the blessings Yahweh promised to his people. You are part of the nation Yahweh has promised to bless.'

"The cheers grew louder. But Ishmael was still silent. Abraham didn't notice fourteen-year-old Ishmael standing nearby. His focus was entirely on his newborn son.

"One of Ishmael's playmates poked him in the ribs.

"'See!' he said. 'Now you're a nobody. You're just a slave woman's son like the rest of us.'

"Ishmael smashed his fist into the boy's face and gave him a bloody nose. Nobody called him a slave woman's son! He was Abraham's son. Soon they were in a full blown fight. Hagar rushed in and separated the boys, hopefully before Abraham would notice.

"Later that evening I found Hagar looking sad," Sarah continued. "When I asked what was wrong, she burst into tears.

"'It's starting to come true,' Hagar said. 'The prophecy. *His hand will be against everyone and everyone's hand will be against him.*[73] Ishmael is becoming a wild donkey.'

"What could I say to her? We had just been celebrating the fact that Yahweh is a promise-keeping God. Now God was again keeping his promise. Then I remembered what Yahweh had told Abraham.

---

[73] Genesis 16:12

"'You have good promises, too,' I reminded Hagar. 'Abraham asked Yahweh to bless Ishmael, and Yahweh said he would. He told Abraham, *"As for Ishmael, I have heard you: I will surely bless him; I will make him fruitful and will greatly increase his nation."*[74] When everybody turns against your son, remember that Yahweh still loves him. God will look after him and bless him.'

"Hagar smiled weakly and wiped her eyes.

"But things gradually deteriorated between Hagar and me after that day," Sarah said to Isaac.

"Abraham loved Ishmael and hoped that Ishmael would take an interest in you, his new half brother. Ishmael would pretend to be very brotherly one moment, then when he thought no one was looking, he would pinch you and make you cry. I tried to tell Abraham and Hagar, but neither of them had seen it happen. Ishmael, their son, would never do such a thing! Not to a defenseless baby!

"Both of them were in denial. Sometimes I wondered if I was imagining things.

"As time went on, Ishmael became very adept at concealing his meanness toward you," Sarah told her son Isaac. "As you grew old enough to walk and talk, Ishmael convinced you that life would be worse for you if you tattled on him. Many a time you came crying to me, but wouldn't tell me what was wrong.

"I had my suspicions, but seldom had any evidence, never enough evidence to prove anything against Ishmael. Sometimes I found bruises, but you would simply say that you had fallen or bumped into something."

"I don't remember any of that," Isaac said. "I just remember being afraid of Ishmael."

"You had reason to be afraid, Son," Sarah agreed. "Ishmael was a bully, and his teasing was always mean. I began to remember a prophecy that Yahweh had told Abraham before Ishmael was born, a prophecy I would rather forget. *'Know for certain,'* Yahweh had said, *'that your*

---

[74] Genesis 17:20

descendants will be strangers in a country not their own, and they will be enslaved and mistreated four hundred years.'[75]

"Now that I actually had a descendant, I began to think about it. How soon until my descendants were mistreated? How soon until my descendants were enslaved? Would the mistreatment be part of the slavery for a full four hundred years, or would mistreatment slowly escalate over the centuries and finally culminate in slavery?

"I could not stop that which Yahweh had prophesied—good or bad—but I determined to do what I could to postpone any mistreatment of my descendants.

"Things came to a head on your fifth birthday," Sarah told Isaac. "We were in Hebron again, as we were every year around that time. You were about to be weaned, and your father planned a great feast to celebrate. Weaning is a big deal, particularly for a boy. It marks the transfer of the child's training role from his mother to his father—a cutting of the apron strings, so to speak.

"For the next year you would spend half of every day with your father or with other men and boys, learning men's work. After that year you would spend all your work day with the men. Part of each day would be spent learning to read and write. The rest of the day would be spent with the sheep and cattle.

"The big celebration put Ishmael's nose out of joint. Abraham had not thrown a big party to celebrate Ishmael's weaning. He had just quietly taken him to work with him. He had also left much of Ishmael's training to other men, rather than do it himself.

"Abraham's servants noticed and whispered to themselves, 'It's because Ishmael is not a legitimate son.' Ishmael overheard and was deeply hurt.

"Abraham loved Ishmael deeply, but the long-ago promise of a son and the uncertainty as to whether Ishmael was that son kept him from openly treating Ishmael as his heir. Sometimes Ishmael was treated as Abraham's son, sometimes he was not.

---

[75] Genesis 15:13

"As a result, Ishmael was confused and angry. When Isaac was born, he was jealous," Sarah continued. "During the great feast Ishmael's jealousy and anger boiled to the surface and he could restrain his actions toward his half brother no longer. He mocked and tormented poor little Isaac until he ran to me in tears with Ishmael running right behind him.

"Only then did Ishmael realize that I was watching," said Sarah. "I had caught him red-handed. He gave me a defiant look, then quickly ducked into the crowd of celebrators, leaving me with a sobbing Isaac.

"I exploded with all the frustration that had been building for five years. I picked up Isaac, stormed over to Abraham, and demanded at the top of my voice, 'Get rid of that slave woman and her son! That slave woman's son will never share in the inheritance with my son Isaac!'

"Abraham tried to shush me up, but I wouldn't be shushed. I was furious!

"He tried to get me to at least use more polite language, but I kept calling her 'that slave woman' and Ishmael 'that slave woman's son.' It was the only way I knew to get Abraham to see how determined I was to be rid of Ishmael.

"In the middle of my ranting and Abraham's shushing, he suddenly stopped, frozen in space. He had a look on his face as though he was listening to someone I could not see," said Sarah. "I stopped talking, too, wondering what was happening. A few minutes later Abraham looked at me and said quietly, 'Alright.' Then he bent down, gently wiped away Isaac's tears, took him by the hand, and they walked away to join the party. With my mouth open, I watched them disappear into the crowd. I didn't have a chance to ask Abraham about it until bedtime.

"'What happened out there today?' I asked him.

"He told me that he heard the voice of Yahweh speaking to him. Abraham was greatly distressed when I insisted that we get rid of Ishmael and Hagar. He loved Ishmael, but Yahweh told him not to be distressed. *'To listen to your wife,'* he told Abraham, *'because it's through Isaac that your seed will be reckoned.'*[76]

---

[76] See Genesis 21:12

"I wasn't right to throw a tantrum at the weaning celebration," Sarah admitted to her son, "but I did have the right idea that it was time for Ishmael and Hagar to go. Abraham loved Ishmael. And I knew Abraham well enough to know that he would always be conflicted about treating Isaac as the firstborn as long as Ishmael was around. I also knew, because of Yahweh's prophecy, that Ishmael would never treat Isaac any better. If anything, he would treat him worse as time progressed.

"To make Abraham feel better about sending Ishmael and Hagar away, Yahweh reminded him of what he had promised when Abraham asked him to bless Ishmael. *'I will make the son of the maidservant into a nation also, because he is your offspring.'*[77]

"So early the next morning Abraham took some food and a skin of water and gave them to Hagar. He set them on her shoulders and then sent her off with her son. At 19 years of age Ishmael was a boy in a man's body—fully grown on the outside, but not yet ready to assume adult responsibilities. Abraham embraced Ishmael and both of them shed a few tears. Then he watched as mother and son started down the mountain."

"Did you ever see them again?" Isaac asked his mother.

"No, but we do receive word from Hagar occasionally. Abraham asked her to send news about Ishmael from time to time. Apparently the two almost died soon after leaving here. Hagar planned to return to her home in Egypt in the wilderness of Shur, but they almost didn't make it past Beersheba, where we are sitting now. Not only was it the dry season when they left, but the year had been unusually dry, so this area was desert.

"The travel was hot, so they used up their water faster than they had planned. Then Ishmael spotted a deer and started stalking it. He shot at it with his bow and arrow, but succeeded only in wounding it. He chased it for a long way, but eventually had to give up because of the heat. Ishmael finished off what little water was left in the skin, but it was not enough to slake his thirst.

77

"Hagar didn't know how to find water in the desert—that had never been her responsibility. And Ishmael was not yet skilled in finding water. When Ishmael's thirst became unbearable, he began to cry. His tears broke Hagar's heart. She tried to make him comfortable in the shade of a bush. Then she moved away, about as far as Ishmael could shoot an arrow, because she couldn't bear to watch him die. She sat down, put her head in her hands, and began to sob.

"'So much for the promise that Ishmael would become a great nation!' Hagar thought bitterly. 'God's promises might come true for Isaac, the son of the Covenant, but not for Ishmael, the son of a slave woman.'

"Ishmael was dying," Sarah continued. "That could have been the end of their story, but it wasn't. God heard the boy crying, and the most amazing thing happened! An angel of God called to Hagar from heaven and said to her, 'What is the matter, Hagar? Don't be afraid; God has heard the boy crying as he lies there. Lift the boy up and take him by the hand, for I will make him into a great nation.'[78]

"God had heard *Ishmael* cry! Hagar was reminded of another time when God had spoken to *her*. At that time she had called him 'the God who sees me.' Now he was the God who hears.

"But how was God going to keep Ishmael alive? she wondered. He needed water.

"Then God opened her eyes and she saw a well of water. It might have been this very well that Abraham had dug after leaving Abimelech. Hagar grabbed the empty skin, ran to the well and filled it with water. Then she ran to Ishmael.

"He was no longer crying. His eyes were closed. He lay so still that for a moment Hagar thought it was too late. Gently she shook her son.

"'God heard you,' she told Ishmael. 'God heard you cry! Look! Water!'

"She held the skin to his lips as Ishmael drank thirstily.

"'God heard you cry,' she said. 'You'll live, and you'll become a great nation some day. Yahweh keeps his promises.'"

---

[78] See Genesis 21:18

"I find it interesting that both times Yahweh spoke to Hagar he did so by a well," Isaac commented.

"Yes," Sarah replied. "He wants to remind us that he is the source of living water."

"Oh, I almost forgot to tell you," one of Abraham's servants said. "A man in a passing caravan gave me a message for Abraham."

He pulled a small scroll out of his tunic and passed it to Abraham. All eyes were on Abraham as he opened it. He read the scroll quickly, then shared the news.

"It's from Hagar," he announced. "Ishmael is living in the Desert of Paran. He makes his living as an archer. His mother recently got a wife for him from Egypt."[79]

The servant looked over at Abraham with a smile.

"Maybe in the next message you'll learn that you are a grandfather."

---

[79] See Genesis 21:20-21

15

Abimelech and Beersheba

Abraham, Sarah and Isaac were sitting outside their tent near a tamarisk tree in Beersheba watching the early evening sky change colors. Soon the sun would set, marking the end of the Sabbath, and Sarah would go inside to begin preparations for a late supper—nothing elaborate, something that could be prepared quickly because they were getting hungry.

"Yahweh is good," Abraham said. "He gives us a day of rest, then he paints a picture in the sky. Not to quench our thirst. Not to fill our stomachs. Not to fill any specific need. Simply for our pleasure. The sunset is his gift to us simply because he loves us."

The three watched in silence. Then Isaac had a question.

"Father, you said that this place wasn't always called Beersheba. Who named it? And why?"

"I named it Beersheba when you were five years old—not long after your weaning feast. The drought in this area where Ishmael had almost died of thirst was creeping up to Hebron. I decided to move back down to Philistine territory where pastures were always good. But I had to go through this area to get to the good pasture. When I reminded your mother to wear a veil in Philistine territory, she made a face at me, but she wore it.

"When I got to the eastern edge of Philistine territory and tried to water my livestock from the well I had dug with Abimelech's permission, I found that his servants had seized my well and would not give my servants access to it.

"I tried to explain that I and my servants had dug the well, therefore it belonged to us; but they refused to surrender the well to us. Without access to water, we couldn't stop there, but had to hurry on further down the valley where there was water and pasture. While we were there, Abimelech came with Phicol, the commander of his forces, to pay me a visit. I asked him how he and his family were doing, and he beamed.

"'You wouldn't believe how well we have been,' he exclaimed. 'Several of my wives had miscarriages in the short time that Sarah was under my roof, and one had a still-born baby. Since you prayed for my harem, not one of them has had a miscarriage or a still-born baby. We had a baby boom the year after you prayed for us. All of the children born since you prayed have been exceptionally healthy.'

"I proudly introduced them to my five-year-old son.

"'I heard about this miracle child,' Abimelech said, 'and wanted to meet him. God certainly has been with you in everything you do. We heard years ago about your putting the Babylonian armies on the run. And we heard about what your God did to Sodom and Gomorrah. And to Lot's wife. Now I see that your flocks and herds have increased greatly in the six years since I saw you. But this child! Is he really *Sarah's* child? Your ninety-year-old wife? Unbelievable!'

"Abimelech's wonder was soon replaced with a more serious tone.

"'I also heard about Hagar and Ishmael,' he said. 'You sent them away. Into the desert, where they almost died.'

"I was flabbergasted! What did Abimelech not hear! Abimelech shuffled his feet as if he wasn't quite sure how to say what was on his mind.

"'I brought Phicol, my commander-in-chief, because he wants to get a look at your army.' It was then that I noticed Abimelech's forces standing in the background.

"'I don't have much of an army,' I assured them. 'Even today I have less than four hundred trained fighters. It was El Shaddai, Almighty God, who won the victory for me.'

"I almost laughed, realizing that *they* were afraid of *me*! Abimelech was worried that the rich and powerful Abraham who had turned away his own son Ishmael might turn against him and his people! Abimelech was worried that in any dispute, with God on Abraham's side, he would come out the loser!

"Abimelech was determined to get what he came for.

"'I also brought Phicol to be my witness,' he said seriously.

"'Witness to what?' I asked, surprised and puzzled.

"'I want to make a treaty with you. I want Phicol as my witness.'

"'Why would you want to make a treaty with me? I have no intention of going to war against you. That would be folly. Besides, I have no reason to. You have treated me well. It was I who was at fault for not informing you that Sarah was my wife.'

"'Nevertheless, I want to make a treaty with you. As insurance. How do I know that a few years from now you won't be even more powerful and you might decide to take my land from me? Besides, I heard that you have plans to take over the whole land of Canaan—Philistia included.'

"I laughed and assured him that I had no such plans. Yes, Yahweh had promised me and my descendants the land. But I didn't have enough descendants yet to need a large territory. I had only one son, and he was only five years old. I assured him that the promise was future. Long into the future.

"'I will never be anything but an alien in this land,' I assured him. 'My permanent home is in Heaven, in a city whose architect and builder is God himself. We'll both be dead long before the promise is fulfilled.'

"'Nevertheless,' Abimelech insisted, 'swear to me here before God that you will not deal falsely with me or my children or my descendants. Show to me and the country where you are living as an alien the same kindness I have shown to you.'[80]

---

[80] Genesis 21:23

"'I swear it,' I said.

"As I spoke the words, I realized this was the perfect time to complain to him that his servants had seized my well. Abimelech couldn't believe it, so I took my chief servant Eliezer with me and walked with Abimelech and Phicol back up the valley a little way to where his servants were standing guard over my well. His servants expected to be commended for keeping aliens away from a well in Philistine territory. Instead, Abimelech was visibly upset.

"'Abraham isn't just any old alien,' Abimelech told his servants. Turning to me, he said, 'I don't know who would have given such an order. Certainly not me. I heard about this only today. Why didn't you tell me sooner?'

"I didn't bother explaining that we had just arrived. The important thing to me was getting Abimelech to acknowledge that I had dug the well, therefore it and the water were mine.

"Abimelech's invitation, given to me six years previously, to live wherever I liked on his land, did not include drawing water from a well that he had dug. Each of us has to dig his own wells. Otherwise he pays a big price for the water from someone else's well. That is an unwritten law for nomads using someone else's land.

"Digging my own well was also part of my determination to let no man claim that he had made Abraham rich. I had not taken undue advantage of Abimelech's agreement to let me roam peacefully within his territory. I had always been careful to pasture my livestock some distance away from other people's livestock. If they wanted to be where I was, I moved on. If I needed water, I dug my own well.

"When Abimelech agreed that I had dug the well, I wanted witnesses to that agreement; so I gave instructions to Eliezer to bring sheep and cattle and to bring a separate flock of seven ewe lambs."

"Did Abimelech give you any gifts in exchange?" Isaac asked.

"No."

"Why not?"

"Abimelech had already treated me with kindness. The sheep and cattle were merely a token gift, not an exchange representing land value. I wasn't buying his land. I was just agreeing to coexist peacefully in the land. Abimelech understood the initial gift of sheep and cattle as evidence that I accepted the treaty, but he was puzzled by the little flock of seven ewe lambs.

"'What's the meaning of these seven ewe lambs?' he asked, pointing to the little flock set apart from the other animals.

"'Accept these seven lambs as a witness that I dug this well,'[81] I said.

"I had another reason for bringing seven lambs, but I didn't explain it to him. That was between me and Yahweh. The fact that I wanted to extract a promise from him made him question whether I would keep my promise. I could see the doubts on his face. Then I had an idea.

"'Let's make a covenant,' I said.

"'What's a covenant?' Abimelech asked. It was my turn to be surprised.

"'Don't you make covenants in your culture? Other cultures that I have encountered—Hittites, Assyrians, Egyptians—all have some form of covenant. Don't the Philistines and Canaanites?'

"Abimelech shook his head.

"'We have already done part of it,' I explained. 'We have exchanged oaths and we have exchanged gifts. You gave me free use of your land; I gave you some sheep and cattle. You gave back my well; I gave you seven ewe lambs. Now to underline the solemnity of our oaths, we take an animal, cut it in half, lay the halves bloody side up, and walk between the pieces with your people standing on one side and my people standing on the other as witnesses. Finally we sit down together and share a meal. Whoever breaks the covenant will become like the animal on the ground with its carcass exposed to the scavengers. The witnesses will see to it.'

"Abimelech liked the idea, so we did it—we made a covenant. Abimelech accepted the seven ewe lambs as evidence that I had dug the well on his land with his permission. From that day forward, the place was called Beersheba, the well of seven. If the ownership of the well was ever in dispute again, I could appeal to Abimelech. After the covenant

---

[81] See Genesis 21:30

was made, Abimelech and Phicol returned to Philistia, satisfied that I was one less person to worry about.

"I heard one of my servants pronounce it Beershaba," Abraham continued. "I was about to correct him when I stopped to think about it. 'Shaba' means to swear or to take an oath. That's what Abimelech and I had done. We had each taken an oath. Well of seven, or well of the oath. Either name was appropriate."

"You said you had a special reason for bringing *seven* lambs," Isaac said. "What was the reason?"

"Let me ask you some questions and see if you can figure it out," his father replied. "Tell me. What is a day?"

"The time from one sunset to the next."

"What is a month?"

"The time from one new moon to the next."

"What is a year?"

"The time from one fall equinox to the next."

"Right. Now tell me, what is a week?"

"Seven days."

"Why *seven days*?"

"I don't know," Isaac replied.

"You defined other units of time in terms of the earth, sun and moon; but you can't define a week in those terms. If a week is to be defined at random, why not twelve days in a week? Or five, a number you can count on one hand? Or ten, which you can count on two hands? Why even define it in terms of *days*?"

"I don't know," Isaac responded, then a thought struck him. "What about creation week? God created for six days and rested on the seventh."

Abraham smiled.

"I was wondering when you would think of that, Son. Nothing except God's act of creation can account for the unit of time which we call a week. Creation explains both the 'seven' and the 'days'. Outside of that explanation, a week is completely artificial. Seven is a number that denotes something unprecedented, that has no greater cause than itself," Abraham explained. "Like God, a week is its own reason to exist."

"So you used seven lambs to seal your oath because it reminded you of Yahweh!" Isaac exclaimed.

"Yes," Abraham agreed, "for that reason and one other. Seven is the number of completeness, and I had finally arrived at the stage of complete faith in Yahweh's Covenant promises to me.

"When I left Haran and my father's household thirty years earlier, my faith was still young. My faith grew as I stepped out into the unknown, believing that Yahweh would show me where to go. My faith grew as I walked up and down in the land of Canaan, knowing it would some day belong to my descendants.

"My faith grew as I lived with insecurity, always living in tents, like a stranger in a foreign country. Though this land was promised to me, I never built a house on it. No house on earth is permanent enough for me.

"But it took longer for me to believe that with God *all* things are possible—that he could give me a child from my barren wife.

"When I let your mother talk me into sleeping with Hagar, I was inexperienced in faith. I had been walking the land for only ten years. I knew Yahweh had promised me a son from my own body, but I didn't yet understand that Yahweh wanted to give me a son from my barren wife.

"Finally, after Yahweh confirmed his Covenant with me, I received the faith to believe. At first I laughed. When Yahweh didn't strike me dead for laughing, but instead told me we would name our son 'he laughs', I began to believe that Yahweh would really do what he promised. When I took the step of obedience and was circumcised, my faith was strengthened, and I believed Yahweh's promise more fully.

"It took Sarah a little longer to believe that she was to be the mother of a great nation. But in time she too judged Yahweh faithful who had made the promise.[82] When she finally believed, she received the power to conceive. Almighty God waited until both of us had faith that he could do the impossible. Then he blew away the obstacles of barrenness and old age, and you were born!

---

[82] See Hebrews 11:11

"But I still struggled with wanting Ishmael to have some part in the Covenant. I still saw him as my firstborn for several years after you were born, Isaac. It wasn't until Sarah threw a tantrum and insisted that Ishmael and Hagar be sent away that my faith came to maturity.

"I think that I had clung to Ishmael as a backup in case Yahweh's promise failed. What if something happened to you, Son? If you got sick and died or were killed in an accident, I could always depend upon Ishmael as my offspring. But now, with Ishmael out of the picture, I have no plan but Yahweh himself. It is his responsibility to look after you and see that you survive to have children of your own.

"So Beersheba has special significance for me. I named it just a few days after sending Ishmael away. The well of seven. The well of the oath.

"Thirty is the age at which one is recognized by society as being an adult in the complete sense. Only then is one considered to have the experience and wisdom necessary to hold public office. Thirty years after leaving Haran and my father's household, I had finally grown up. Thirty years after leaving my father's household, I finally had complete faith in Yahweh's Covenant oath. Spiritually speaking, I was an adult."

16

Planting a Faith Garden

Abraham was in no hurry to leave Beersheba. A week later he and his family were still there. The Sabbath found them again sitting outside their tent in the shade of a tamarisk tree.

"What did you do after naming the well and after Abimelech left?" Isaac asked.

"What did I do? I did something predictable and something unpredictable."

"I bet I can guess what you did that was predictable," Isaac said. "You built an altar."

"Yes, Son, I built an altar. That's what I do in all my favorite places. Shechem. Bethel. Hebron. Now Beersheba. All special places. All marked with altars."

"What did you do that was unpredictable?"

"I planted a grove of trees, these tamarisk trees you see all around the well."[83]

"Really?"

Isaac observed the trees more closely.

"They're pretty," he said. "I like their feathery grey green leaves and smooth reddish brown bark."

---

[83] See Genesis 21:33

"If you think they are pretty now, Son, you should see them in winter. They grow beautiful little pink and white blossoms on spikes as long as the palm of your hand is wide. Each individual blossom is shaped like a miniature magnolia blossom. The tamarisk tree belongs to the same family. Tamarisks take lots of water to get started. Once they are properly rooted, they are extremely hardy. If you burn them down, they'll grow again."

"Really?" Isaac was skeptical.

"Look here. I'll show you," Abraham said.

He scraped the soil away from the base of the tree until he found what he was looking for.

"Look at this root, Son. See that little nodule? Here's another one. If the tree is burned down or cut down, it will grow again from those nodules. That's how I planted these trees. I found a tamarisk tree and dug up some of its roots with nodules on it. I planted them while my servants were digging the well. I buried the roots here, soaked the ground with water, and kept watering them until green shoots came up. By the time the well was finished, the plants were big enough to survive on their own. I drove a few protective stakes around them so they wouldn't get trampled by mistake and traveled on."

"I know you occasionally plant trees in your wanderings, Father," Isaac said. "Date palms for fruit, other trees for shade, so you can benefit from them when you return years later. But I got the impression from something you said earlier that these trees were special. Why did you plant trees on the occasion of making a covenant with Abimelech? And why tamarisk trees?"

"Abimelech and I had sworn oaths and made a covenant. But Yahweh had made an infinitely superior Covenant. He had promised me a son by Sarah. He had also promised that my seed would be uncountable. Like the dust of the earth. Like the stars in the heavens. Like the seeds of a tamarisk tree, I thought. Each tree has countless blossoms, and each blossom can produce thousands of tiny seeds. Uncountable. That's what Yahweh promised me, Son—that my descendants and yours would be uncountable."

Isaac went over to a tree to examine it more closely.

"What is this flaky white stuff along the branches?" he asked.

"Taste it," Abraham said.

Isaac moistened his finger, picked up a few flakes and put them into his mouth.

"Mmm. It's sweet. What is it?"

"Exactly. That's what the Bedouins call it," Abraham replied.

Isaac thought his father had misheard him.

"What is it?" he repeated.

"Exactly," Abraham said again with a twinkle in his eye.

Isaac looked to his father for an explanation.

"You just said '*manna*', meaning 'what is it'. That is exactly what the Bedouins call it. Insects puncture the bark to get at the sap. The sap oozes out and dries into this flaky substance."

"It tastes kind of like honey and . . . wafers," Isaac said.

"Yes, it tastes good, but I don't think you will find enough to fill your stomach."

Abraham wasn't finished talking about the tamarisk tree.

"See these little crystals on the leaves, Son?"

Isaac examined the leaves more closely.

"Yes, they sparkle in the sunshine."

"Taste them."

Isaac again moistened his finger to taste the crystals, not sure what he would find.

"Salty," he said. "It tastes like salt."

Abraham nodded.

"It is salt. That's another reason why I planted these trees near my well, Son. The trees survive harsh, dry conditions because they send down long roots that enable them to find water deep in the earth. At the same time the roots take up salt from deep ground water and accumulate it in their leaves. My well water will always be sweet because these trees will remove any salts from the water.

"Most trees don't provide shelter from blowing sand, but these trees are very dense at the base. They provide good shelter from wind and sandstorms. These trees are relatively young—only eight years since I planted them, and already they are well over my head. But they will continue to grow for a long time—longer than most other trees. They will eventually be 45 feet high.

"These trees will always be green. While other trees drop their leaves in winter when water is scarce, the tamarisk's deep roots ensure that they will be well supplied with water all year round."

"So now can you answer your own question, Son? Why did I plant tamarisk trees?"

"Let's see," Isaac said, trying to remember. "To provide shade. To protect us from the wind and blowing sand. To keep your well water sweet. And because they are pretty."

Abraham's look told Isaac he was expecting more answers.

"Beersheba," he prompted.

"To remind everybody that Abimelech acknowledged that you dug the well."

Abraham nodded. "Yes, but the name of the place would do that."

Abraham revised his prompt. "Beer*shaba*."

"Oh, yes. The oath. Because the countless seeds of the tamarisk tree remind you of the Covenant, God's oath. He promised that your descendants would be uncountable."

"Right."

Abraham leaned back from his sitting position and stared up into the tree above him. After a few moments Isaac did the same. It reminded him of the times in his childhood when they had stared up into the sky together, looking for pictures in the clouds.

"In what way is this tamarisk tree like me?" Abraham asked.

Isaac liked playing these games. His father often drew spiritual parallels from his surroundings.

"You were transplanted by the root," Isaac said. "The rest of your family tree was left behind in Ur and in Haran, but Yahweh brought a little piece—you and Mother—to Canaan and planted you here."

"Good answer, Son! What else?"

"You thrive in this climate."

Isaac struggled for a significant answer.

"You thrive in this climate because your roots go down deep. To streams of water deep in the ground. To Living Water. To Yahweh."

"Excellent!"

"You, like this tree, are long living," Isaac continued. The ideas flowed as he spoke. "You are already 113. And you are indestructible. If you are cut down, you will grow again from the root—me! And when I am cut down, my children will carry on, growing from the root."

"Maybe it would be more accurate to say that our family is like this tree, Son. We will always have descendants to receive the Covenant promises of God."

"Sometimes you produce manna," Isaac said.

"What do you mean, Son?"

"The way you live has something about it that raises people's curiosity. They ask, 'What is it? What is it that makes you different?' They want to know why you don't work on the Sabbath. Sometimes, when they see your altars, they ask about the God you worship."

"I hope I always have a ready answer when they ask," Abraham replied. "I want others to know and love Yahweh as I do."

After another silence, Abraham spoke again.

"Did you know these trees were the first trees I planted in Canaan?"

"Really?" said Isaac. "I have seen you plant trees a number of times."

"I plant trees more frequently now, Son, but these were the first; and it had to do with the oath. The oaths Abimelech and I swore to each other reminded me of Yahweh's oath to me—the Covenant oath. Now that you were born, I could see the beginning of the fulfillment of the promise that my descendants would be uncountable. But Yahweh had also promised to give me the whole land of Canaan. He had told me to walk the length and breadth of the land. He said he had brought me out of Ur so I could take possession of the land.

"So I began to think about what possessing the land meant for me. I knew it didn't mean fighting for it. Yahweh had promised to *give* it to me. Abimelech and I had just agreed to live peaceably with each other. Possessing the land meant making it my home. Tell me, Son, how do you make a place home?"

"Most people build a house," said Isaac.

"Yes," Abraham replied. "But I can't reconcile that with walking the length and breadth of the land. To do that, I must live a nomadic lifestyle. I must live in a tent. How else can I possess the land?"

"You can dig a well."

"Right. And I had already done that."

"You can . . . plant a garden!"

"Right! That was what I was starting to do—to beautify the place, to make practical improvements, to provide for the future. Planting the trees reminded me of something Shem had told my father Terah and me long ago about Noah. After the flood the first thing Noah wanted to do—after building an altar to Yahweh, of course—was return to his former occupation. Not ship-building, but farming. He was a man of the soil, so he planted a vineyard.

"I remember Shem telling us that his father Noah really enjoyed planting that vineyard. He had stepped out of the ark into a new world. All the wicked people were gone—destroyed by the flood. For the first time in his life Noah felt really at home in the world. The new world was a place where he could settle down and raise his family to know God. Sadly, not all his descendants followed in his righteous footsteps. Not all of them walked with God. But Noah wasn't the first person to plant a garden. Do you know who was?"

Isaac thought for a moment, then shook his head.

"I can't remember that far back," he quipped.

"Yahweh," Abraham answered, ignoring his son's attempt at humor. "Yahweh created the whole earth, but he planted a garden for Adam—a place for him to call home."

"The Garden of Eden," Isaac said.

"Right. But the garden didn't feel like home right away. Do you know why?"

Isaac shook his head.

"Because he was alone. He didn't have any family. Only after God created Eve did Adam feel at home in the garden.

"In Beersheba eight years ago, I realized that I was home. I was in the land Yahweh had showed to me and promised to me. It was mine for the claiming, so I went one step further and planted trees. I planted them as a testimony to my faith in the promise of Yahweh.

"I had a wife. I had a son. I had a well. Now I began planting a garden. But my garden isn't just this little piece of land in front of you. It's the whole land of Canaan. Everywhere I go now, I plant a little more of my garden. My descendants will benefit from the fruit trees and shade trees I plant. I am possessing my land. I am acting out my faith.

"As I thought about the Covenant, Yahweh's words came back to me. 'I will establish my covenant as an everlasting covenant between me and you and your descendants after you for the generations to come, to be your God and the God of your descendants after you. The whole land of Canaan, where you are now an alien, I will give as an everlasting possession to you and your descendants after you; and I will be their God.'[84] He also said of you, Isaac, 'I will establish my covenant with him as an everlasting covenant for his descendants after him.'[85]

"Listen to the words! Over and over again Yahweh said, 'for you and your descendants after you.' 'Everlasting covenant.' 'Everlasting possession.' He used the word '*olam,*' age-lasting. The Covenant is an *age-lasting* covenant. This whole land of Canaan is an *age-lasting* possession. Not just for my lifetime. Not just for your lifetime. *Age-lasting*!

"In Yahweh's mind, when did that age-lasting covenant begin? I wonder. When I was 99, when he spoke it to me? When I was 85, when Yahweh walked between the halves of the carcasses? When I was 75, when he first promised to make me a great nation? Or did it begin even earlier—when he conceived the plan? How long ago was that? And when does the age-lasting covenant end? The time we are living in is just one age. What about the ages to come?

"The more I thought about it, the more I became aware of the magnitude of the promise. For all eternity. Only an eternal God can make an eternal promise.

---

[84] Genesis 17:7-8
[85] Genesis 17:19

"And all that time he promised to be there with us. 'I will be your God and the God of your descendants after you.' Only an eternal God can be with us all the time. So I called him *El Olam*—the Eternal God.

"I was so excited and so blessed that I built an altar and worshiped Yahweh. This place became very special to me. Yahweh, as you so aptly put it, had planted me here.[86] Transplanted me from Ur. In turn, not only did I plant trees to claim the land, I also walked around in it. I sojourned in the land of the Philistines for a long time. And everywhere I went, I preached about Yahweh, *El Olam*, to anyone who would listen."[87]

---

[86] Compare Jeremiah 11:16, 17. "The Lord Almighty, who planted you . . . ." Compare also Jeremiah 2:21: "I had planted you like a choice vine of sound and reliable stock." And after the Fall of Jerusalem: "I will plant Israel in their own land, never again to be uprooted from the land I have given them" (Amos 9:15).

[87] See Genesis 21:33-34

PART TWO

Isaac's Faith Journey

17

Son of the Commandment

A few days after telling his son Isaac about the significance of Beersheba, Abraham and his family were still there in Beersheba. Abraham always lingered longer there than in other areas. It wasn't just that the conditions were good for grazing his livestock. It was the memories. It was the spiritual significance of the place.

Abraham was sitting alone under a tamarisk tree within sight of his well. Sarah was still cleaning up after supper, and Isaac was somewhere visiting with a friend.

Out of nowhere Abraham heard a voice.

"Abraham!"

Abraham hadn't heard that voice for a while, but he recognized it instantly, and his heart leaped with the delight of hearing it again.

It was Yahweh. The Oath Maker. The Promise Keeper.

Abraham looked around, but saw no one.

"Here I am," he replied into the early evening dusk.

Whatever Yahweh wanted, he would do. But nothing could have prepared Abraham for what he heard next.

"Take your son, your only son," God said, "yes, Isaac, whom you love so much—and go to the land of Moriah. Go and sacrifice him as a burnt offering on one of the mountains, which I will show you."[88]

---

[88] See Genesis 22:2

The night was warm, but suddenly Abraham felt cold. Never had he gone from so high to so low so quickly. He clutched at his heart as if he had been stabbed. He wanted to scream, but no sound would come from his mouth. He had never been wounded so deeply.

"Maybe I didn't hear God right," Abraham thought. "Did he say I was to sacrifice my *son*? My *only* son? That's too much to ask."

This was not the request of Abraham's friend Yahweh. This was the request of God. *El Elyon.* God Most High. The Supreme Commander of the universe. The One who will tolerate no other gods before him.

Had Abraham made Isaac his god, he wondered?

He searched his heart and felt that he could honestly say no. Yes, he loved Isaac, loved him enough to die for him. But he had a reverential fear of God that was greater than his love for his own son.

Abraham knew he had to obey. Tears ran down his face as he lifted his hands in silent surrender to God.

Just then Isaac returned. Abraham was glad that the increasing darkness hid his tears. He rose and hugged his son tightly before sending him to bed.

Now he had to talk to Sarah. How would she respond when she heard God's command? Would she throw a tantrum and yell as she had when she wanted Hagar and Ishmael sent away? Abraham called her outside, so they could talk where Isaac would not hear them.

"I heard God's voice today," Abraham began.

"Oh!" Sarah said with excitement. "What did he say?"

There was a long silence before Abraham continued. Sarah realized it was not good news. Then, word for word, Abraham repeated what God had said.

Abraham waited for the tantrum or the scream, but it never came. For a long time Sarah was so still that Abraham began to wonder if she had even heard him. Then she reached over and took his hand in both of hers.

"If God has spoken to you, he has spoken to both of us," she said quietly. "We are husband and wife. We are one."

Abraham was a little surprised and very much relieved at her reaction. They had grown much closer since Hagar and Ishmael had left. They were closer now than at any time since Abraham first slept with Hagar, probably the closest they had ever been.

In the past they had not always agreed in their faith walk with God, but now they were one in faith as well. Now whenever one wavered in faith, the other was there for support and encouragement, and they were soon both on track with Yahweh.

"When God gives a command, it is not open for discussion—only obedience," Sarah reminded Abraham.

"I plan to obey, but I wonder how Yahweh is going to do it? He will have to do another miracle. He will have to raise Isaac from the dead. He promised to establish his everlasting Covenant with Isaac."

"No one has ever come back from the dead before," Sarah said, "but then, no woman past child-bearing age—not to mention barren all her life—has given birth before either. Not until Isaac was born. Yahweh has already proved he is Almighty God."

"I will leave first thing in the morning," Abraham said. "If I delay, I may convince myself that God didn't speak to me—that I don't have to do it. My biggest concern right now is what to say to Isaac."

"Tell him the truth. When you tell your child the truth, something inside him will agree with it."

"I sure hope so," Abraham said solemnly. "Isaac has grown big and strong. He's already as tall as you are and still growing. I'm not strong enough to put Isaac on the altar without his consent and help."

Abraham didn't get much sleep that night. Both he and Sarah tossed and turned, wrestling with their thoughts. How could Yahweh ask Abraham to sacrifice his own son? What was he trying to prove?

"*I am God Almighty.*" The words came back to Abraham, words God had spoken when he confirmed his Covenant. Mentally Abraham reviewed the promises of Yahweh.

"*To your seed I will give this land.*" He had said it not once, but four times. When Abraham first arrived in Canaan at the age of 75. When he parted company with Lot. When Abraham was 85, and Yahweh walked between the bloody carcasses to make the Covenant with him. And when Abraham was 99, when Yahweh confirmed his Covenant.

> *"I will make you into a great nation*
> * and I will bless you;*
> *I will make your name great,*
> * and you will be a blessing.*
> *I will bless those who bless you,*
> * and whoever curses you I will curse;*
> *and all people on earth*
> * will be blessed through you."*[89]

Yahweh had promised his Covenant would be an *everlasting* Covenant. He had used the word 'everlasting' at least four times.

Was God going to fulfill his promise through Ishmael?

No. That couldn't be. Yahweh had promised Sarah that *she* would be the mother of nations. "*I will establish my Covenant with Isaac,*" he had said, and repeated it.[90]

"*Count the stars—if indeed you can. So shall your seed be.*"[91]

God. *Elohim*. The Creator. If he could create, he could recreate. If he could make Adam from the dust of the earth and breathe into dust the breath of life, he could breathe life into Isaac's lifeless body.

"*I am God Almighty.*"

Those were the words Abraham clung to.

God Almighty. *El Shaddai*. He could do anything. He could start with two sons of Abraham and send one away. Then he could whittle that one down to zero and start all over again—with a resurrected Isaac. There was no other possibility.

With that thought, Abraham finally drifted off to sleep.

When a rooster crowed, Abraham was wide awake. It was time to obey. Quietly he rose and dressed, then gently shook his sleeping son. While Sarah prepared breakfast, Abraham went out to instruct two of his servants to get ready for a week's journey for four people. It would take three days to reach their destination.

---

[89] Genesis 12:2-3
[90] See Genesis 17:19, 21
[91] See Genesis 15:5

During breakfast Isaac, to his father's relief, was not awake enough to make conversation. Abraham and Sarah said little, though much was on their minds. When Abraham went out to saddle his donkey, Isaac followed.

"Where are you going?" he asked.

"*We're* going," Abraham corrected him. "God spoke to me again last night."

Now Isaac was all ears.

"He told me to take you and go to the region of Moriah and sacrifice a burnt offering on one of the mountains. He will tell me which one when we get there."

"I wish I had heard him speak. If he wanted me to go, why didn't he also talk to me? I hope I hear Yahweh tell us which mountain."

Abraham was glad his son hadn't heard the whole message. Not this time.

"Yahweh will talk to you some day, Son. You will hear his voice. Now help me cut the wood for the burnt offering."

While they were cutting the wood, the two servants arrived, each leading a donkey loaded with food, water, and supplies for the journey. While they were adding the wood to the donkeys' loads, Sarah came out to see them off.

She hugged Isaac long and hard, then kissed him tenderly. Isaac wondered why she had tears in her eyes. *Just a sentimental mother who can't stand being parted from her son for a few days*, he supposed.

Abraham hugged his wife goodbye and whispered in her ear, "We'll be back."

Sarah nodded silently, wiped her eyes, and tried to smile as she watched Abraham carefully strap a fire pan containing hot coals to one of the loads, and mount his donkey. Then the little procession headed north with Isaac in the front leading his father's donkey and the two servants leading the other two donkeys.

Sarah watched the little procession until it disappeared out of sight.

Will I ever see Isaac again? she wondered.

As quickly as the thought came, she dismissed it. Yahweh had promised that she would be the mother of nations, that he would establish his Covenant with Isaac. She would review Yahweh's promises over and over again until her husband and son returned.

Meanwhile Abraham had other things on his mind. He felt the sheath containing his knife and felt a chill. How could he raise his knife against his son? How could he harm his son—even for a moment?

Then his thoughts turned to more practical aspects. How could he—a hundred years older than Isaac—get his strong young son onto the altar? Abraham wasn't even strong enough to walk for three days in difficult terrain. He had to ride a donkey. He would have to convince Isaac to cooperate. Abraham had his work cut out for himself for the next day or two.

Up until now, this faith journey to Canaan had been Abraham's faith journey. The time had come for Isaac to join him in his faith journey. Isaac would have to choose faith in Yahweh for himself. Abraham would do his best to help Isaac make that choice.

If this was a test of Abraham's faith, it would also be a test of Isaac's faith. Abraham was glad for the long walk ahead. It would give him time. Time to think. Time to talk to Isaac.

"You have an altar in Beersheba and another one in Hebron," Isaac observed. "We'll be there by nightfall. Why did Yahweh ask us to go all the way to Moriah to make a sacrifice?"

"I don't know, Son, any more than I know why he asked me to leave Ur; though I have some theories as to why he had me leave Ur. All I know is that Yahweh said, '*I am God Almighty; walk before me and be blameless.*'[92] Part of being blameless is obeying him implicitly. Completely. Unreservedly. Unquestioningly. He knows why, I don't. He knows the end from the beginning, I don't.

"Another part of being blameless is having faith. Do you know what faith is, Son?"

"Believing."

"It's more than just believing something in your head or agreeing that something is so," his father replied. "Faith is putting what you say you believe into action. Faith is being sure of what you hope for,

---

[92] Genesis 17:1

being certain of what you don't see. Without faith it's impossible to please God.

"Faith starts with believing the evidence written in the sky. Even before I knew much about Yahweh, way back in Ur where the people worshiped the moon as if it were a god, I knew that someone greater than the moon had made it. By faith I understood that the universe was formed at God's command. I knew it even before I knew his name."

As they journeyed, Abraham talked to Isaac about what he had come to believe of God from creation. Together they discussed the evidence and the implications for their lives. Then the conversation turned toward people who had lived before them and how they had responded to what they knew of God.

They talked about Cain and Abel. Cain, a farmer, had brought an offering from his crops. Abel, a shepherd, had brought an offering from his flocks.

"Why was Abel's offering accepted and Cain's not?" Isaac asked. "Was Abel just lucky because he happened to be a shepherd?"

"No, Son. Adam and Eve had taught their children that God required a blood sacrifice. Sin requires the death penalty. Bringing a blood sacrifice indicates faith in God's solution. It indicates that you acknowledge that you are sinful and deserve death. It indicates your belief that God will accept the death of an innocent one who dies in our place. God's way to Heaven is not earned but is provided by a substitute who pays your death penalty. Someone in the future will pay the penalty once for all, but until then we offer blood sacrifices on a regular basis. Offering a blood sacrifice is faith in action, Son, faith in God's way."

Abraham and Isaac came to the conclusion that Cain had tried to do things his own way rather than God's way. Cain had tried to impress God with good works, with an offering from his crops. His actions showed that he didn't believe that he was a sinner, and he didn't believe a blood sacrifice was necessary. The fact that he didn't have any livestock was not an excuse. He could have bartered some of his produce for a sheep from Abel.

Abel, on the other hand, was not simply lucky to be a shepherd. He, too, could have side-stepped God's requirement. He could have shorn his sheep and offered the wool or something made from wool. Instead he killed some of the firstborn of his flock and brought the best portions as an offering to God.

Abraham summed up Abel's case.

"Abel believed that a perfectly holy God demanded that anyone who was less than perfect be put to death. Abel also believed that man could escape God's harsh punishment for missing God's target of perfection by offering blood sacrifices as per Yahweh's instruction. Abel knew that the death of an animal was not an adequate substitute for the death of the offender. He believed that some day Yahweh will provide a complete sacrifice for sin. In the mean time, Abel offered a lamb to acknowledge that he had offended God and to demonstrate his faith that Yahweh will provide the perfect substitute. Abel's actions demonstrated his faith in substitutionary death as the only way to please God."

They talked about Enoch.

"He believed in coming judgment," Abraham said. "He warned the ungodly saying, 'Listen! Yahweh is coming with countless thousands of his holy angels to execute judgment on the people of the world. He will convict every person of all the ungodly things they have done and for all the insults that ungodly sinners have spoken against him.'[93] Enoch also named his son 'Methuselah' as a warning of coming judgment. Methuselah in one sense means 'man of the javelin,' but in another sense it means 'when he is dead, it (that javelin) shall be sent.' In other words, when Methuselah dies, judgment will come! Methuselah lived longer than any other man—969 years—which shows God's mercy in postponing judgment; but the same year that Methuselah died, the Great Flood came. Judgment fell."

"Did Enoch predict one judgment or two?" asked Isaac.

"Why do you ask that?" asked Abraham.

"Well," responded Isaac, "Methuselah's name pointed to the judgment in Noah's time, but I am not aware that God sent his holy angels during the Flood. There are plenty of wicked people in the world today. Maybe there is another judgment coming."

---

[93] See Jude 1:14-15

They went on together in silence. The climb made conversation difficult for the older man. When they reached the place God had told him about, Abraham noticed a flat spot.

"Right here!" Again Abraham felt that quiet sense that God was directing him. He stopped to catch his breath and then helped Isaac take off his load of wood. Together they built an altar and arranged the wood on it.

"So where's the lamb?" Isaac asked.

Abraham didn't answer the question immediately.

"We have been discussing faith these last few days, Son. I have done my best to teach you to walk by faith. I have tried to demonstrate my faith with my life. But at some point in your life, you will have to declare what you believe. You are thirteen. Old enough to know right from wrong. Old enough to have your own faith. You can't rely on my faith to make you acceptable before God."

"I believe everything you believe, Father," Isaac said.

"Saying it is good, Son, but it's not enough. Faith is more than words. Faith requires action. I have been trying to obey Yahweh's commandments and laws—whether spoken by him or written on my heart—ever since I left Ur. When Almighty God confirmed his Covenant with me, he commanded, '*Walk before me and be blameless.*' God also commanded me to circumcise all the males in my household. I was old enough to choose to be circumcised. That day I became a Son of the Commandment—*bar mitzvah*. But you were only eight days old when I circumcised you. Circumcising you was *my* act of faith, not yours. Now you must demonstrate *your* faith. You, too, must become a Son of the Commandment."

"So how do I demonstrate my faith?" Isaac asked. "I honor the Sabbath. And I have already placed my hand on the head of a lamb before it was sacrificed and told Yahweh I was sorry for my sin."

"Do you believe all the Covenant promises that Yahweh made to me?"

Yes."

"Do you believe Yahweh will establish his everlasting Covenant with *you*?"

"Yes."

"That it is through you—Isaac—that my seed will be reckoned?"

"Yes."

"That *your* descendants will be as the dust of the earth, as the stars in the sky—too numerous to count?"

"Yes."

"That God is almighty?"

"Yes."

"That he can do anything?"

"Yes."

"Even raise the dead?"

"No one has ever been raised from the dead!"

"But do you believe Almighty God could do it?"

"Why are you asking me all these questions?" Isaac wanted to know.

"Because, Son, I want to obey God, and I cannot obey him without your consent."

"I have nothing to do with whether or not you obey God!"

"Oh yes, you do, Son," Abraham insisted.

"How? What do you mean?"

"When God asked me to come here and make a burnt offering, he asked me to offer you as a sacrifice. You are the lamb."

There. Abraham had finally said it.

Isaac was stunned.

"I can't do that unless you allow me to," Abraham continued. "If you run away, I can't catch you. If you struggle, I can't tie your hands and feet. And you are too heavy for me to lift onto the altar. I couldn't even carry the load of wood for the sacrifice."

Tears started falling down Abraham's face.

"But God has promised that he will establish his Covenant with *you*. He can't do that if you are dead. So the only way I can obey him and he can keep his promise is if I kill you and he brings you back to life again. Do you believe he can do it?"

Isaac covered his face with his hands. For a long while neither of them said a word. Finally Abraham spoke up.

"So what is your decision, Son," he asked softly. "Will you become a Son of the Commandment? Will you demonstrate your faith by your actions?"

When Isaac finally looked up at his father, his face was wet with tears. He reached his hands toward his father and clasped them together, signifying that he was willing to be bound.

Abraham hugged his son and Isaac hugged him back. After a long embrace, they walked slowly toward the altar. With Isaac's cooperation, Abraham managed to get his son on the altar on top of the wood. Then Abraham bound Isaac's hands and feet.

Isaac squeezed his eyes tightly.

"Make it quick, Father," he pleaded.

Abraham reached into his sheath for the knife and raised it high to slay his son. Just as he was looking for the target that would make the deed quick and painless, the angel of Yahweh called to him from Heaven.

"Abraham! Abraham!"

Abraham stopped with his knife in mid air.

"Here I am."

"Don't lay a hand on the boy," the angel said. "Don't do anything to him. Now I know that you fear God, because you have not withheld from me your son. Your only son."[95]

Abraham dropped his knife and slumped against the altar. Words can't express his relief. Some moments later he came to his senses when he heard Isaac stirring on the altar.

"Help!" Isaac cried. "Help me down."

Abraham used his knife to slit Isaac's bonds. As he looked up, there in a nearby acacia thicket he saw a ram caught by its horns. Its struggle to get free had left it torn and bloody. Long acacia thorns encircled its head.

"I told you so," Abraham said, turning to Isaac with a smile. "I told you God would provide a lamb."

"And you told me I would hear God's voice some day," Isaac countered.

---

[95] See Genesis 22:12

Together they untangled the ram from the thicket. Before Abraham sacrificed it on the altar, Isaac laid his hands on the head of the ram. Now he really understood what substitution meant!

"I thought I knew what it meant when I placed my hands on a sacrifice before," Isaac said as they watched the hot coals ignite the wood, "but now I really know! Every time I sacrifice a burnt offering in the future, I will remember this moment. I was sentenced to die, but the ram died in my place."

His father agreed. Together they watched the fire consume the sacrifice then burn down to a few smoldering coals.

"*Yahweh yireh*," Abraham said. "That's what I will call this place. 'Yahweh provides.' I will teach my people to say, 'On the mountain of Yahweh it will be provided.'"

As the last few embers died out, the angel of Yahweh called from Heaven a second time.

"I am taking an oath on my own name, declares Yahweh, that because you have done this and have not withheld your son, your only son, I will certainly bless you. I will multiply your descendants beyond number, like the stars in the sky and the sand on the seashore. Your descendants will take possession of the cities of their enemies. Through your seed all nations on earth will be blessed—all because you have obeyed me."[96]

For a while father and son were each lost in their own thoughts. Then Isaac spoke up.

"He did it, didn't he?"

"What are you talking about?"

"Yahweh redirected your steps."

Abraham still didn't follow Isaac's train of thought so Isaac continued.

"You once said, 'If your heart is right, but your steps are wrong, Yahweh will redirect you.' Your heart was right when you raised your knife to kill me, but that wasn't what Yahweh meant by 'sacrifice', so he redirected your steps."

"So he did, Son. I'm glad he did."

---

[96] See Genesis 22:15-18

In half the time it had taken to climb the mountain, Abraham and Isaac descended to where the servants were waiting for them. The servants were amazed to hear what had transpired on the mountain.

All the way back to Beersheba, the four of them tried to understand what had happened. They all agreed that it was a test of faith, but it also had a greater meaning—something related to a future sacrifice.

When they came in sight of their tents, Sarah came running out to meet them. Throwing her arms around Isaac, she hugged him long and hard.

They stayed in Beersheba longer than usual that year. Abraham often sat under his tamarisk tree when his work was done, looking toward his well and pondering the Covenant promises of Yahweh. Often Isaac and Sarah joined him, and the discussion went well into the evening.

When the seasonal drought finally forced them to look for greener pastures, they headed north toward Bethel and Shechem.

18

The Death of Sarah

A sharp, shrill, ear-piercing shriek rent the air, announcing her death to the whole camp. Soon others picked up the lament with prolonged wails.

Following a brief illness, Sarah was dead at the age of 127. Her family and friends, indeed, all of Abraham's camp, would fast until she was buried later that day.

Thirty-seven-year-old Isaac was heart-broken.

"Alas, my mother!" he moaned tearfully over and over, hugging his knees, and rocking back and forth.

He had watched his mother's strength deteriorate steadily over the last few months. When it was obvious that Sarah was dying, Abraham had brought her to Hebron, Sarah's favorite place. From here they could survey the land that Yahweh had promised to them. Since Isaac's birth, Sarah had enjoyed Hebron even more. She often looked out at the view, dreaming of the nations—people born of her—that would live within sight of Hebron.

Isaac's father was in their tent now, mourning for Sarah and weeping over her.

"O my wife Sarah, my sister, my wife! O Sarah, my wife, my beloved!"

Abraham could hardly remember life before her. Now he couldn't imagine life without her. Finally Abraham rose from kneeling beside his wife's body. He wiped his tears on his sleeve.

"No more walking the land for her," he said to Isaac while trying to smile. "No more wandering. She's finally home—in the Heavenly City."

Then the conversation turned to practical matters. They would have to bury Sarah before nightfall. Abraham didn't want to bury her in the ground like a common person. Sarah was a princess. Yahweh had named her Princess. A princess needed a royal burial. In a tomb.

But Abraham had not prepared to bury his wife. He had no tomb. He didn't even own land on which to build one.

"Yahweh hasn't given any land to me yet. I'll have to buy a burial site," he said to Isaac. "Come with me."

Before going out, Abraham made sure that, as a sign of respect, Sarah's body would not be left unattended at any time during the day. Then the grieving father and son threw ashes over their hair and garments and smeared ashes on their faces. Their tears carved little streaks through the ashes.

Abraham decided to inquire first of his friend and neighbor, Mamre, for a burial site.

"I heard the death wail and knew she was gone," Mamre said sympathetically. "I don't have a tomb, but I do have an idea."

He took Abraham to a nearby field with trees all around its border. At the end of the field almost hidden by the trees was a large cave.

"It's perfect!" Abraham exclaimed. "The cave is big enough for several bodies. This field could become a cemetery in the future. How much do you want for it?"

"It's not mine," Mamre said. "It belongs to Ephron son of Zohar, a Hittite who lives in the city—Kiriath Arba."

So Abraham and Isaac went to the city and respectfully squatted down facing the elders who were sitting at the gate. Isaac listened as his father negotiated.

"I am an alien and a stranger among you," Abraham said. "Sell me some property for a burial site here so I can bury my dead."[97]

---

[97] Genesis 23:4

The Hittite elders brushed aside his humble introduction.

"You are no stranger," one of them spoke for all. "You are a mighty prince among us. Bury your dead in the choicest of our tombs. None of us will refuse you his tomb for burying your dead."

Abraham was pleased to learn that he was respected and that he wouldn't face opposition in obtaining a burial site. He wasn't interested, however, in burying his wife in a borrowed tomb amongst people who didn't serve Yahweh. Furthermore, he wanted something that could be used not just for his wife, but for generations to come. He had no guarantee that the good relations he enjoyed with his neighbors now would be extended to his descendants, so he rose to press his case. Bowing before the elders, he explained his specific request.

"Please intercede with Ephron son of Zohar on my behalf," he pleaded, "so he will sell me the cave of Machpelah, which belongs to him and is in the end of his field. I'm not asking for a bargain. Ask him to sell it to me for the full price."

One of the elders spoke up.

"I'm Ephron son of Zohar," he said. "You don't need to buy the place. I *give* you the field, and I give you the cave that is in it. I give it to you in the presence of my people," Ephron said, waving his arm in a sweeping motion toward the elders seated at the gate as well as toward any bystanders. "Bury your dead."

Isaac was happy that the solution was so simple. He rose to leave with his father. But Abraham was not satisfied. Respectfully he bowed again.

"Hear what I'm saying," he begged. "My request is not just for today. I will pay the full price of the field. Please accept it from me so I can bury my dead there."

Ephron replied, "*You* hear what *I'm* saying. The land is worth four hundred shekels of silver, but what is that between me and you? I *give* it to you. Bury your dead."[98]

Abraham reached for his money pouch, walked over to the stall of a merchant, and starting putting silver coins onto his scale. When he

---

[98] See Genesis 23:15

had weighed out four hundred shekels' worth, he put that silver into a separate pouch.

Then he walked over to the scribe who was sitting at a small table beside the city elders. On the table were a small pile of parchment papers, a jar of ink, several quills, and a knife to sharpen them with. The scribe was there to record the decisions of the elders and important events. He also recorded land transactions.

"Please write me a receipt," Abraham requested the scribe, "for the field of Ephron son of Zohar the Hittite in Machpelah near Mamre. For the cave in it, and all the trees within the borders of the field. Payment in full—four hundred shekels of silver."

He spoke so all the Hittites in the vicinity of the city gate could hear. When the receipt was written, Abraham signed it, gave the money to Ephron, and motioned to him to sign the receipt. Two other elders also signed as witnesses to the transaction. Carefully, Abraham rolled up the receipt and tucked it into his robe.

"Thank you," he said, bowing toward the elders once again. Then he took Isaac's arm and headed for home.

"Why didn't you take Ephron up on his offer?" Isaac asked when they were out of earshot of the Hittites. "You could have had the land for free."

"Yahweh said *he* would give me the land," Abraham replied. "Somehow I didn't feel that Ephron was offering it on Yahweh's behalf. Besides, in time the Hittites may forget what Ephron said, or twist his words to say he just meant I could use the cave for Sarah, not for the rest of my family. If they do, you can show them the receipt."

Abraham pulled the receipt out of his robe and handed it to Isaac. "Guard it carefully, Son."

* * *

Father and son arrived back in Hebron to find that Sarah's handmaids had finished preparing Sarah's body for burial. They had sprinkled her body liberally with spices and wrapped her in white linen. Only Sarah's face was visible.

Even in death Abraham could see the beauty that had first started his heart racing. A handmaid handed Abraham a napkin. Abraham gently placed it over his wife's face. At the thought of never seeing her face again, Abraham again wept.

Sarah's body was lifted onto a bier. Then four servants carried her out to the cave of Machpelah, followed only by Abraham and Isaac.

A host of mourners watched from near Sarah's tent as her body was carried out to the cave, but they didn't follow, respectfully giving the immediate family their space to grieve alone. The mourners' wails rose to a crescendo as the tiny procession disappeared in the direction of the cave.

"Ah, our lady! Our princess!" they exclaimed. "Ah, her beauty!"

"We'll miss her laughter," others mourned.

After Sarah was laid lovingly in the cave, Abraham spoke a few words of remembrance over her, then committed her to Yahweh. Isaac was too broken with grief to speak.

Husband and son sat by Sarah's body until almost sunset. Isaac was numb with grief. Alternately Abraham wept and talked to his wife as if she could hear him.

"Here you are, sweetheart," he whispered. "You are home. This cave is ours. This field is ours. Isaac has the receipt. Our address is the Field of Machpelah, near Mamre, in Hebron, in the land of Canaan. This little piece of land is just the tiny beginning of the fulfillment of Yahweh's promise to give us the whole land of Canaan."

Abraham listened to Isaac's sobs, then continued talking to his wife.

"Your body is home in Canaan, but your spirit and soul are with Yahweh. The real 'you' is in the Heavenly City. You are truly home!" Reluctantly Abraham motioned for his servants to roll a large stone over the mouth of the cave.

After the cave was sealed, Abraham and Isaac returned to Sarah's tent, where they were offered bread and wine as a comforting refreshment. This mourning 'feast' was a signal to the rest of the camp that they could break their mourning fast.

For the next seven days Abraham and Isaac sat in Sarah's tent and received their friends' and neighbors' condolence calls. Isaac sat cross-legged on the floor, while his father sat on a low stool. Both sat shoeless in the same ash-covered clothes they had worn the day of Sarah's death. Neither of them washed his face, bathed or shaved for the entire week.

When the guests first arrived, they sat in silence, allowing the bereaved to initiate the conversations. The guests were careful not to divert the conversation from talking about the deceased. Talking about Sarah seemed to ease the pain for Abraham and Isaac.

Upon leaving the tent of mourning, the callers bowed respectfully and said, "May Yahweh comfort you." Even Canaanite callers who didn't worship Yahweh said, "May Yahweh comfort you," such was their respect for Abraham.

Abraham was aware of the profound grief his son Isaac was experiencing, and wondered what affect that might have on his faith. He was pleased on the first day after Sarah's death, when their guests numbered a quorum of ten men, to see Isaac stand up and publicly express his love of God and acceptance of God's will, even while feeling great loss and sorrow over the death of his mother.

Isaac continued to do this, not only during the week of mourning, but for months following her death. Rather than losing faith in God or crying out against him for taking his mother, Isaac found his faith and hope in Yahweh strengthened through the experience.

Isaac quoted an ancient Aramaic poem that he had learned from his father, and closed with his own conclusion in Hebrew.

> Glorified and sanctified be God's great name
> throughout the world
> which He has created
> according to His will—
> and say, Amen.
> May He establish His kingdom
> in our lifetime,
> during our days,
> and within the life of our descendants,
> speedily and soon—
> and say, Amen.

May His great name be blessed
   forever
      and to all eternity—
         and say, Amen.
Blessed and praised,
   glorified and exalted,
      extolled and honored,
         adored and lauded
            be the name of the Holy One,
               blessed be He—
                  and say, Amen.[99]

Dominion and awe belong to God;
   He establishes order and peace in the heights of heaven[100]—
      and say, Amen.
May He create peace for us and for our descendants—
   and say, Amen!

---

[99] Adapted from Kaddish, the Jewish mourners' prayer, www.ou.org/yerushalayim/kadish.htm

[100] Adapted from Job 25:2

19

Lot Pays a Visit

Three years after Sarah died, Abraham received a surprise visit from Lot. Since the destruction of Sodom and Gomorrah they had not seen each other, though they had kept in touch by sending the occasional message with a passing caravan.

Abraham welcomed him with open arms, but he was surprised at how old and frail his nephew looked. Though Lot was only a dozen years older than Abraham, their difference in age appeared to be much greater.

While servants unsaddled Lot's donkey and gave it hay and water, Abraham himself poured water for Lot to wash his hands and feet. He instructed his servants to prepare a feast, then ushered Lot into his tent, poured him a cup of wine, and settled down to talk.

"We haven't had a long talk since you moved to the plain decades ago," Abraham said. "How are you doing?

Just then Lot looked up and saw Isaac, who had been standing at the entrance to the tent waiting for an introduction.

"This must be the miracle child," Lot said, rising to take Isaac's hand. "Son of the Promise. I've heard so much about you."

"Yes, this is Isaac, my pride and joy," Abraham said to Lot. Turning to Isaac, he said, "Come in and join us, Son. Meet my nephew Lot."

Isaac came in and sat down.

"I heard that Sarah had died," Lot said. "Knowing how much she meant to you, I came to express my condolences in person. She felt like *my* sister too. After my father Haran died, Grandfather Terah took me in and treated me like another son. I felt as if you and Nahor were my brothers, not my uncles. After all, I am older than both of you."

"It's so good to see you! I appreciate your thoughtfulness in coming to visit," Abraham responded. "How is your family doing?"

"I bring greetings from my sister Milcah," Lot said. "She has eight fine sons, most of whom now live in Aram Naharaim, the country between two rivers—the Habor and the Euphrates.

"The country was originally settled by Aram, son of Shem. He was a godly man, and his influence still permeates the region. Haran, the largest city in Aram Naharaim, being at the crossroads of two major caravan routes, has been influenced by other cultures. Now most of the people in Haran follow the moon god Sin, a variation of the moon god Nannar in Ur. But you already know that, having lived in both Haran and Ur. The people in Haran have, for the most part, lost their knowledge of Yahweh, but in the countryside Yahweh is still known and worshiped.

"My sister Milcah is doing well, though life has been more difficult for her since her husband, your brother Nahor, took a concubine. Reumah gave Nahor four more sons."[101]

Abraham shook his head sadly.

"I know by experience the grief that can bring to a household," Abraham said sympathetically. "I hope Milcah and Reumah don't fight the way Sarah and Hagar did."

"The names Reumah gave her sons suggest that her life is not happy," Lot said. "How sad!" Abraham said. "I didn't have a good relationship with either my wife or my concubine after Hagar got pregnant. When the squabbling carried over to Ishmael and Isaac, I finally agreed to send Hagar away. Concubines really complicate a marriage.

---

[101] See Genesis 22:20-24

"Enough about my wife and my concubine," Abraham said, changing the subject. "Tell me about Milcah's sons."

"You would be very interested in two of them, Abraham. They have decided to live all out for Yahweh, and have changed their names to reflect that. Milcah's third son now calls himself Kemuel, meaning 'God stands' or 'God rises'. He really sees Yahweh as his protector, the One who stands by him in all situations, the One who rises up to protect him.

"Kemuel named one of his sons Aram, in honor of their godly ancestor; and Aram seems to be walking in his forefather's footsteps."

"Very good," Abraham said, nodding in approval at the news.

"Aram also considers himself to be named after you, Abraham. After all, that was your original name—before the people of Ur added the title 'Ab' to it. And before Yahweh changed it again."

Abraham looked surprised.

"Oh, don't be surprised, brother," Lot said. "You made an impression on many when you lived in Haran. And your reputation has increased with your rescue of me and my family from Kedorlaomer and the Babylonians.

"Milcah's youngest son now calls himself Bethuel, meaning 'abode of God' or 'dweller in God'. His name says it all. It is very evident that he dwells in God and God in him."

"I'm so pleased to hear that," Abraham said. "Living in Canaan, it is easy to think that nobody else knows and loves Yahweh."

"That's exactly how I felt in Sodom," Lot replied.

For a while they made small talk, then Lot turned to his host.

"I noticed your altar outside," Lot said. "That's how I found your place. I expected that you would be in Hebron this time of year. When I asked for directions at Kiriath Arba, they pointed me in this direction. I asked directions again when I got a few miles down the road. A fellow named Mamre told me to look for the altar."

"Mamre's a good friend," Abraham said. "I've known him for years. In fact, he and his brothers came with me to rescue you from Kedorlaomer."

"So that's why his name sounded familiar!" Lot exclaimed.

"I built the altar right after we went our separate ways and you moved into the plain near Sodom."

"Those were good days when we were traveling together," Lot said wistfully.

"Don't apologize for leaving," Abraham said. "It was the right thing to do. Yahweh had told me to leave my country and my people and my father's household, and you were the last of my people that I still had close contact with. Besides, our herdsmen were starting to quarrel over pastures and access to water."

"Sorry to disillusion you, brother," Lot said, "but our herdsmen disagreed over more than land and water. The friction between them was partly religious."

Abraham looked at him in surprise.

"You didn't allow the worship of other gods among your servants," Lot continued. "Your requirement for employment was a willingness to quit idol worship and at least listen about Yahweh. Your herdsmen objected when my herdsmen worshiped idols. Didn't you notice?"

Abraham shook his head.

"*I* did," Lot said. "The quarreling began after we returned from Egypt right after we came back to Bethel. At Bethel we found the altar you had built when we first arrived in Canaan. The first thing you wanted to do was worship Yahweh. When you made sacrifices and called on the name of Yahweh, my herdsmen didn't participate. They couldn't fathom making a sacrifice without having an image of their god present. They thought you were crazy. They were glad when I moved away to the plain of Jordan."

"Lot, didn't you build an altar to Yahweh in Sodom?"

Lot shook his head.

"Didn't you tell your servants and herdsmen about Yahweh?" Abraham asked.

Lot was slow to reply.

"I thought I would just let my life speak for itself," he said lamely.

"We both know the end result of that," Abraham said. "Tell me. What happened when God destroyed Sodom? How did you escape?"

"I will never forget that day as long as I live," Lot began. "I was sitting at the city gate as usual. It was getting late in the day when two strangers approached the city. I always cringed inwardly when travelers were forced to stay overnight in Sodom. The elders at the gate were always friendly. Too friendly. Too quick to suggest a home where they could stay for the night. Sometimes I heard whispers about how they were treated. The very thought of what was common practice in Sodom tormented me day after day.[102] Mostly I didn't want to know.

"But these two strangers seemed different from ordinary men. I knew instinctively that they were decent and wholesome, so I made sure that I was the first to greet them. Respectfully I bowed and invited them to stay at my house for the night.

"At first they declined my invitation. They were content to spend the night in the city square, as is the custom of travelers who can't afford a room in the inn. But I knew they wouldn't be safe in the square in Sodom, so I insisted. Finally they gave in and came with me. My wife wasn't surprised when I brought the visitors home for the night. It happened regularly. We fed them well, showed them to the spare room on the roof, and were about to go to bed ourselves, when we heard a commotion outside.

"I looked out the front window and saw men all around. My wife looked out the back. There were more men there. Our house was surrounded. Young men, old men, men from every part of the city of Sodom surrounded us. Men whose faces I recognized. Men whose reputations made me shudder. I could hear them shouting, 'Lot! Where are the men who came to you tonight? Bring them out to us so that we can have sex with them.'[103]

"'I was afraid this would happen,' I said to my wife and daughters, who didn't seem as distressed as I was. 'What can we do?'

"My daughters whispered together, then looked at their mother as if looking for permission to speak. My wife quietly nodded back.

---

[102] See 2 Peter 2:7-8
[103] Genesis 19:5

"'What if we went out to them, Father?' the older one said, indicating her sister and herself. 'That might pacify the mob.'

"'No!'

"I was horrified that they would suggest such a thing! All my life I had done my best to protect my daughters from sexual predators and lecherous men. They hardly went anywhere without a chaperone. I was even more horrified to see that my daughters seemed disappointed at my answer. I realized I had been foolish to think that I could raise my family to love Yahweh in that wicked city. The surrounding influences were just too overwhelming.

"I stepped outside and shut the door behind me—partly to protect my family from the mob, partly to shut out the pain of what I had just seen and heard inside. I tried to dissuade the mob from their wicked intentions. But they wouldn't be dissuaded. I told them that as host I was obligated to protect the guests under my roof. But they wouldn't be dissuaded.

"Finally, hating myself even before I spoke the words, I offered my two virgin daughters for their sport. But they weren't interested. They wanted men—the two strangers, my guests! The men of Sodom started pushing and shoving, trying to get past me. They insulted and threatened me.

"'This fellow came here as an alien,' somebody shouted, 'and now he wants to play the judge!'[104]

"'We'll treat you worse than them!' somebody else threatened.

"I struggled to push back the crowd as they moved forward to break down the door. Suddenly the door behind me opened, and my guests pulled me back into the house and shut the door.

"'Yahweh sent us here to see if the people of Sodom and Gomorrah were really as wicked as we had heard,' my guests said. 'They are all that—and worse! Yahweh plans to destroy Sodom and Gomorrah and all the cities in the plain of Jordan. We have come to get you out, Lot, before that happens.'

---

[104] Genesis 19:9

"I expected to hear the mob outside banging on the door, but things were strangely quiet. Puzzled, I looked out the window. It was almost full moon. In the bright moonlight I could see the men waving their arms around as if they were feeling their way in the dark. I turned to my guests for an explanation and saw that they seemed amused.

"'The men outside are blind,' they told me. 'Stone blind!'

"That's when I understood that my guests were angels. They had struck the men of Sodom blind. Yet even in their blindness, the men kept feeling for my door!

"Then the angels got serious again.

"'You're safe from the mob,' my guests said, 'but not from the disaster Yahweh plans to bring on this place tonight.'

"'Tonight!'

"'Yes, tonight.'

"My first thought was for my family. I was beginning to understand that the angels were there to rescue me only. They planned to leave my family behind.

"'Please!' I begged them. 'Let my family come with me.'

"They weren't quick to agree.

"'You, Lot, are the only righteous person in the whole area. We noticed how eager your young daughters were to experience life on the wild side. And your wife seemed to think throwing them to the wolves out there was a reasonable remedy. Even *you* stooped to suggest it to the mob. Yahweh told us you were righteous!'

"'Please forgive me!' I begged again, falling on my knees and grasping their feet. 'I was desperate. I didn't know how else to protect you. Have mercy on us! Have mercy on *me*! Life would not be worth living without my family. Please let me take my loved ones with me. If not, let me stay here and die with my family.'

"'Yahweh won't destroy you with the wicked people of Sodom. That would be unthinkable!' one angel exclaimed. 'Yahweh wouldn't kill the righteous with the wicked as if there were no difference between them! The Judge of all the earth will do what is *right*!

"'So we will grant your request. For your sake we will give you a chance to save your family. But you'll have to hurry. How big is your family anyway? Do you have anyone else besides the ones here in your house? Sons-in-law, sons or daughters or anyone else in the city who belongs to you?'

"I told him that I had no sons, but I did have two married daughters.

"'Get them out of here,' they urged. 'Tell them we are going to destroy this place. The outcry to Yahweh against this people is so great that he has sent us to destroy it.'[105]

"So I hurried out to my married daughter's house—the one who lived closest to me. Her husband answered the door.

"'Hurry and get out of this place,' I said, 'because Yahweh is about to destroy the city!'

"He thought I was joking.

"'Do you think blindness is a joke?' I asked him. 'Look out in the streets. See those men feeling their way? They should be able to see in this bright moonlight. But they are blind! The angels blinded them because of their wickedness. They want to have sex with the men visiting in my house. Worse judgment is coming on the whole city. We have to get out!'

"He wasn't convinced. He thought there must be some other explanation for his neighbors' strange behavior. I asked to talk to my daughter, but he said she was asleep and he wasn't about to wake her up for some crazy joke.

"I ran to my other daughter's house, but the same thing happened. Nobody would believe me! I talked till I was blue in the face, but they only laughed at me. Finally I returned home empty-handed.

"The angels were waiting impatiently for me. It was still dark, but a faint light was starting to show at the eastern edge of the sky.

"'Hurry!' they said to me. 'Take your wife and your two daughters who are here, or you will be swept away when the city is punished.'[106]

"I hesitated. I wanted to return to my married daughters' houses later in the morning when they were awake. Maybe my daughters, if not my sons-in-law, could be persuaded to come with us. My wife wanted

---

[105] See Genesis 19:13
[106] Genesis 19:15

to pack some of her clothes and jewelry. But the angels wouldn't wait. One of them grasped my hand and the hand of my wife. The other angel grabbed my two virgin daughters by the hand.

"As they dragged us out of the city, they described what Yahweh was about to do. At sunrise Yahweh was going to rain down burning sulfur from the sky on Sodom and Gomorrah. We could hardly believe our ears, but they did succeed in convincing us that we were in imminent danger.

"As soon as we were outside the city gates, one angel said, 'This is as far as we can take you. You are on your own now. Flee for your lives! Don't look back! And don't stop anywhere in the plain! Yahweh plans to wipe out the whole plain and all the cities in it. Flee to the mountains or you will be swept away! But hurry! The sun will soon be up.'[107]

"I thanked the angels for saving our lives, but I was afraid that we wouldn't make it to the mountains in time. I was well over a hundred years old and not able to run fast or long, and I was already tired from not having slept during the night. I begged for permission to flee for refuge to a little town just on the edge of the plain.

"'It's a very small town,' I pleaded. 'You won't be sparing very many more lives. And they aren't as bad as the people in Sodom and Gomorrah. By shortening the distance we have to flee, you will be sparing my life.'

"'Very well,' one of them said. 'I will grant this request too. I won't overthrow the town you speak of. But flee there quickly, because I can't do anything until you reach it.[108] And remember. Whatever you do, don't look back!'

"We ran as fast as we could for a while, then slowed to catch our breath. We weren't used to long distance running, but we couldn't rest for long. I kept one eye on the eastern sky. Fearing we wouldn't get to Zoar before sunrise, I urged my family to hurry. They didn't seem to sense the urgency as much as I did.

---

[107] See Genesis 19:17
[108] See Genesis 19:21-22

"'I wish I were at home in my own warm bed,' my wife complained, 'not out here in the dark on some wild goose chase.'

"By the time the sun peeked over the horizon, Zoar was visible in the distance. Behind us we heard a rumble, like thunder only more steady, and the earth shook beneath our feet. Fear energized us for the final dash into town.

"We ran past a barn and headed for the nearest house.

"'Stop!' I called to my wife and daughters. 'We can't barge into the house. They're still sleeping. We'll scare them out of their wits!'

"Opening the barn door, I ushered them inside, shut the door and leaned against it, panting hard. Several hens, startled from their nests by our rude entrance, flapped their wings and clucked excitedly. The cow gave a startled moo. A sow that had been sleeping in the corner with her little piglets nestled against her flank stood up quickly to protect her litter. With squeaky little oinks the piglets objected to being dumped in a heap.

"My wife sat down on a milking stool and my daughters collapsed on a pile of hay. I sat down beside them. My daughters were so exhausted that they soon fell asleep, but my wife wanted to know what was going on.

"'Our daughters! Our house! Our beautiful furniture!' she wailed. 'We can't leave all that. I didn't even have time to grab my jewelry!'

"She moved toward the door.

"'You can't go outside,' I told her. 'The angel said, "Don't look back!"'

"'Do you really think Yahweh is destroying Sodom and Gomorrah?' she asked skeptically. 'Maybe it's just a thunderstorm.'

"With that she stepped outside.

"The barn was facing Zoar, so I knew we would be safe as long as we kept the barn between ourselves and Sodom. I scrambled quickly to grab my wife before she could look toward Sodom.

"'Don't!' I yelled.

"She ignored me, went past the edge of the barn, and turned toward Sodom. Just then a ball of fire fell from the sky directly over her head.

I heard a strangled gasp. I was close enough to feel the scorching heat. The acrid sulfurous fumes made me cough.

"When I finished coughing, I looked for my wife. All I could see was a smoking charred statue of a woman where my wife had been. Black as coal. I smelled the unmistakable smell of burning flesh. Then the reality struck me. That statue was my wife! Fried to a crisp! Instantly mummified!

"'No!' I screamed, and ran back into the barn. My daughters awoke and wanted to see what had happened, but I wouldn't let them look for fear they, too, would be destroyed.

"The sky turned dark, darker than a thunderstorm. The rumbling sound continued, punctuated by distant booms. A strong wind came up, filling the air with ash and smoke.

"My daughters and I huddled together in fear. Then everything went quiet. The silence was more ominous than the smoke.

"About mid day we ventured outside to get food and water. The whole world around us was white. Or pale gray. The trees were covered with what looked like a fine dusting of snow. I stooped to touch the mysterious substance around my feet and discovered to my surprise that it was gritty. Ashes! The ashes weren't loose, as in a fireplace, but sticky. They clung to everything.

"Looking where I had last seen my wife, I gasped. She was no longer black as coal. She too was a grayish white, and she sparkled in the sunshine.

"Just then the door of the house opened, and a woman came out.

"'Why have you erected a statue in my yard?' she asked. 'Who gave you permission to do so?'

"'That's not a statue,' I replied through my tears. 'That's my wife!'

"My daughters weren't quite convinced that that was their mother. For one thing the statue was much thinner than their mother. And how could she still be standing? I looked again, noticing that she was indeed very thin. That's when I noticed that her flesh had melted in a lump around her feet, securing her to the ground.

"'She's been turned to salt!' the Zoarite woman exclaimed.

"My daughters, by now convinced that it was their mother, also thought she had been turned to salt.

"It dawned on me that she was not made of salt, but completely covered in fine ash. The wind had driven the ash into every pore of her being and it had stuck there as if with glue. My wife was mummified and totally encrusted in ash—the ash from the destruction of Sodom and Gomorrah!

"My daughters began crying hysterically at the sight of their mother. I wrapped my arms around them and tried to comfort them. All I could say in explanation was, 'She looked back. The angels told her not to, but she looked back. I reminded her not to, but she looked back.'

"Word about what had happened to my wife spread through the little town like wild fire. Everybody came to see the strange statue that had been alive the day before. They preferred my daughters' version of the story: She had been turned to salt.

"Why? they wanted to know.

"So I told them the whole story, starting with the wickedness of the cities in the plain. Their wicked reputation had reached Heaven, I told them, so Yahweh sent his angels to check out the report. If it was true, they were to destroy the cities and rescue me. I told them how shamefully the men of Sodom had behaved.

"Then I told them what had happened to my family. Some of my family didn't believe that Yahweh would judge them for their wickedness. Those family members never got out of the city. My wife and I and two of our daughters escaped the city, but we were warned that we were not to look back. Doing so would indicate that we sympathized with Sodom rather than agreeing with the justice of Yahweh. As for my wife, well, the statue spoke for itself.

"When I told the people of Zoar that they were originally slated for destruction, too, they became very serious. It was only because I didn't have time to reach the mountains before disaster hit, I told them, that I had obtained permission to find refuge in Zoar. The Zoarites solemnly swore that they would change their ways and not behave like the people of Sodom ever again.

"Then the townspeople told me what they had seen and heard that morning. Noise like thunder had attracted their attention in the direction of Sodom and Gomorrah. All over the plain of Jordan there were fountains of fire. At times balls of fire flew high into the air as if propelled from a giant underground catapult. Following each flash of flying fire, they heard a loud boom—like thunder following lightning. The people in the cities must have thought the fire fell directly from heaven. Soon everything combustible was on fire. Dense smoke rose from the land like smoke from a furnace. I didn't dare look, but the townspeople told me that Sodom was still smoking.

"Forty years later it is still as vivid in my memory as if it were yesterday."

Lot paused at the end of his story. Abraham and Isaac were listening with rapt attention. It was the first time they had heard the story in full detail.

"That's what I remember seeing," Abraham said, as he nodded in agreement. "Dense smoke rising from the land, like smoke from a furnace. But I don't remember a town called Zoar."

"You would have known it as Bela," Lot told Abraham. "The townspeople changed the name to Zoar, meaning 'small', after they learned that I was able to convince the angels to spare it because it was so small."

"What happened after that?" Isaac asked.

"My daughters and I had nothing except the clothes on our back. I went from riches to rags. From owning houses, servants, and lots of sheep and cattle to having absolutely nothing. From being an elder in a prosperous city to being a nobody.

"The people of Zoar knew me by name and reputation. I became famous, Abram, after you rescued me and the rest of Sodom and Gomorrah from King Kedorlaomer and his Babylonian confederacy. Many of them knew me by sight because they often did business in Sodom."

"My name is Abraham now," Abraham reminded him.

"Sorry, Abra*ham*. Your name change came after we parted company, and I have trouble getting used to it. Anyway," Lot continued, "the townspeople were so grateful that I had interceded on their behalf that they welcomed us with open arms and offered us a place to stay. They showered us with food, clothes and household goods to replace some of what we had lost. They gave us a donkey and two pairs of goats to restart a herd. They even invited me to join their town council. Having escaped the kidnapping and this new disaster, I was 'twice lucky', they said. They believed my presence in town would bring them good luck.

"But I wasn't interested in staying. I remembered that Yahweh's original plan was to destroy the whole Valley of Siddim—including Zoar. I didn't plan to be around if and when he decided to finish the job.

"When I declined the invitation to stay in Zoar, the townspeople wanted to know why, so I told them. Then they *begged* me to stay, fearing that they might be in danger if I left the town. But I wouldn't be persuaded. My daughters and I packed up our new possessions and left. Reluctantly the townspeople said goodbye. Again and again, they assured me that they would change their ways.

"I didn't plan to stop until we were well into the mountains southeast of the Salt Sea. We followed a caravan route that circled through the valley until it came to the Zered River, where it flows into the Salt Sea. Then we left the caravan route and followed the river eastward up the valley into the mountains.

"My daughters, having been raised in the plain, weren't used to walking in steep terrain. I found the climb difficult, too. It was a long time since I had climbed mountains, and I was more than a hundred years old. My daughters wanted to stop, but I was afraid to. My fear was contagious. We were all exhausted, but fear drove us on.

"Late in the afternoon of the second day of hard climbing, we found a large cave. From the ridge we were on, we could see west to the Salt Sea and east to the King's Highway, which snaked through the valley below. The caravan route we had followed from Zoar joined the King's Highway a little farther north of us. We had climbed about as high as we could go.

"The cave, I decided, would be our home. There we were safe. Safe from fire and brimstone falling from the sky. Safe from the contaminating influence of pagan societies.

"My daughters felt safe there, too. They planted a garden and a vineyard on the mountain slope and diverted water from the river to irrigate it. Our goats supplied us with milk and cheese. At first we set out snares to catch the occasional wild animal for meat. After our goats multiplied, on special occasions we had goat meat. I'm quite proud of the way my city-raised girls adjusted to life in a cave."

"They're not girls any more," Abraham observed. "Are you still living in a cave? After all these years?" Abraham exclaimed incredulously.

"Yes," Lot replied. "My descendants live on the plain just north of us, but my daughters and I still live in the cave. They don't feel safe outside of it, so they never wander too far away. Sometimes we go down to the King's Highway to buy goods from a passing caravan, but mostly we are self sufficient where we are.

"I had to be mother and father to them—a task I found burdensome. How does a father teach his girls to be women? That is their mother's job."

Abraham was puzzled.

"You have grandchildren, Lot. You mentioned descendants. So where are your daughters' husbands? Why are your daughters still living with you?"

Lot looked uncomfortable.

"They have no husbands," he said simply.

"You mean they are widowed?"

Lot shook his head.

"Divorced?"

Lot shook his head again.

"Then how on earth—?" Abraham didn't finish the question.

Lot blushed deeply. The explanation was painful.

"After living in the cave for a few years, my daughters started talking about wanting children. To find husbands for them, we would have had to move down into the valley. But I was afraid to leave the protection of the cave and so were my daughters. So we stopped talking about children. I didn't know until later that my daughters never stopped *thinking* about having children.

"Every year we enjoyed making wine from the grapes in our vineyard. One evening instead of giving me the usual cup or two of wine, my older daughter kept refilling my cup. I should have paid more attention to what she was doing, but I just kept drinking. The next thing I knew, it was morning and I had a terrible hangover. That evening my daughters again kept my wine cup full, and again I got drunk and woke to a terrible hangover.

"The third evening I was ready for them. I scolded them for getting me drunk and told them not to do it again. They looked at each other and giggled and swore that they wouldn't do it again.

"Everything seemed fine for a few months. Then I noticed that my daughters were starting to gain weight. It wasn't much longer until I realized that they were both pregnant! I demanded an explanation. I hadn't seen any men around, and we hadn't visited the valley for ages.

"Sheepishly my daughters admitted that they had deliberately gotten me drunk, then slept with me while I was in a drunken stupor. They were carrying my offspring! When I expressed my horror, they were defensive.

"'What did you expect us to do?' they asked. 'There aren't any other men around here to sleep with. Everybody on earth does it!'

"'Not with their own father!' I shouted at them. I was concerned for my reputation.

"'What reputation?' they taunted me. 'Everybody who knew you when you lived in Sodom is dead. Here nobody sees us. Nobody knows us.'

"'Yahweh sees,' I said. 'He knows.' "They rolled their eyes. Yahweh again!

"They didn't care. They had what they wanted—babies on the way—and there was nothing I could do about it. It was too late. The damage was done.

"That was when I realized how far from Yahweh my daughters had strayed. They didn't love him. And they didn't care two figs what Yahweh thought about them.

"I had tried to teach them about Yahweh, but they didn't want to hear about him. He had destroyed everything they cherished—their mother, their married sisters, their friends, their home, their belongings.

Even the boys they had a crush on! They were afraid of Yahweh. Scared to death of him.

"I eventually stopped talking about Yahweh. I didn't know how to answer their fears. I too was afraid of Yahweh. That's why we were living in a cave.

"What my daughters had done was a wake-up call to me. I hadn't seen this disaster coming, but I realized that my selfish choices had inevitably led them to their evil choices. When I found out my daughters were pregnant, I tried to remedy things by suggesting that we move down into the valley, where we could start a new life. There they could find a midwife and there they could get married. But my daughters wouldn't hear of it. They preferred the safety of the cave.

"When it came time for the births, I was the midwife. I didn't know what to do, but my older daughter gave me instructions. She had attended at the birth of a neighbor's child in Sodom and had helped the midwife. They both went into labor on the same day. Somehow we muddled through, and each of my daughters gave birth to a son."

Just then the servants announced that dinner was ready.

As the servants brought in the food, Abraham, Isaac and Lot reclined around the table, though they had little appetite after hearing Lot's story. Before they ate, Abraham thanked Yahweh for the food and for Lot's safe arrival.

"It's good to hear you pray, Abraham," Lot said. "I haven't heard anyone pray to Yahweh for years."

"Didn't you and your daughters ever pray together?"

"No. I used to say a prayer of thanks at meal time, but my daughters resented even that. So I stopped. How could I be thankful to Yahweh, they asked, when he had destroyed everything they loved and owned? They saw Yahweh as a cruel judge, someone to be feared. What was there to be thankful for?"

"Lots of things!" Abraham exclaimed. "Be thankful that you are alive, that Yahweh spared you and your daughters, that he gave you a second chance. The very fact that Yahweh spared you shows that he had a purpose for your life. If he wanted to destroy you, he would have done it back in Sodom without warning. Being away from Sodom and its influences, you had the chance to influence your daughters for Yahweh, to build an altar and worship him. You and your daughters need to praise him for saving you rather than cringing in fear that he might destroy you!"

Abraham stopped at the look on Lot's face.

"Didn't you build an altar there?" he guessed.

Lot shook his head.

"You never built an altar to Yahweh?" Abraham asked. "Not in Sodom, nor on the mountain where you live?"

"No."

"Why not? What kind of spiritual heritage have you left for your daughters? How did you expect to teach your daughters to love Yahweh if you didn't build an altar? How did you expect to show the people of Sodom how to live if you didn't build an altar? Did you ever talk to them about Yahweh? Did you ever take a public stand in Sodom for him?"

Lot looked uncomfortable.

"I didn't know how to bring up the topic of Yahweh in Sodom," he said lamely. "They bragged about their sexual exploits, but I hoped my righteous living would influence them for good."

"Did people ever talk to you about being rescued from Kedorlaomer?"

"Oh, yes! Frequently."

"And what did you say?"

"That my uncle rescued me," Lot said proudly. "Abram and his army. You were famous!"

"And that made you famous too, I suppose," Abraham replied. "Reflected glory. It wasn't me that rescued you, Lot. My 'army' consisted of only 318 men. Entire nations fell to the Babylonians. If their armies couldn't withstand the vast Babylonian armies, how could I withstand them? But one little alien and his handful of men were able to rescue you. How could that possibly happen? If you had asked that simple question, there was only one possible answer: Almighty God. Yahweh!

"If you had given Yahweh the glory, rather than try to claim the glory for me and for yourself as my nephew, who knows how many people you could have turned to Yahweh!"

Abraham paused. Lot looked ready to weep again.

"I know how you feel, Lot. I know what it is like to fail miserably. I failed miserably in Egypt, but I came back to Yahweh. He gave me a second chance just like he gave you a second chance to raise your daughters for him.

"After I failed Yahweh so miserably in Egypt, I made things right with him at Bethel. That was where our ways parted, Lot. Up to then your life and mine, materially and spiritually, were on the same path. But from that point onward we went our separate ways in more than one sense. I shared my faith with my household and with everyone who worked for me and with everyone who met me. You hid your light under a bushel. Yes, you are a righteous man, but that is not enough. You hid your light under a bushel—and look what happened!

"Did you know that if there had been as few as ten righteous people in Sodom, Yahweh would have spared it? Surely you could have influenced ten people for God if you had opened your mouth!

"When Yahweh told me he was about to destroy Sodom and Gomorrah, I tried to persuade him to spare them. He agreed to spare the city of Sodom for the sake of fifty righteous people there, but there weren't fifty. I negotiated with him to spare the city for the sake of 45 people, then forty, thirty and twenty. Finally I got Yahweh to agree to spare the city for the sake of ten righteous people.

"Ten! Sodom wasn't destroyed because of the thousands of evildoers in its midst. It was destroyed simply because it lacked ten good people in its society. Yahweh is merciful. He would rather have saved the city than destroy it. A few good people would have made all the difference to the fate of Sodom.

"You sat with the city elders day after day, Lot. There were ten of you. If you had influenced them for Yahweh, Sodom would still be standing today. And what about your family? They should have been the easiest to influence. Your wife should have been your *soul* mate. You, your wife, your four daughters and two sons-in-law make eight. With them and only two more the city would have been spared."

Lot's face showed his misery.

"But Yahweh has given you a second chance," Abraham continued gently. "You failed in Sodom, but Yahweh has given you a second chance with your daughters. Start over again with them and with their sons.

"Teach them to be thankful," Abraham advised him. "Teach them to thank Yahweh for his mercy. The very fact that Yahweh rescued you is evidence of his mercy. Teach your family that Yahweh is just. The things that went on in Sodom and Gomorrah were not just abhorrent to Yahweh, they were also abhorrent to the nations around them! Some people think that because Yahweh promised never again to destroy the earth by flood that he would never again judge them, that they could get away with anything. But Yahweh is just, and justice demands that evil be punished. Evil was punished in Noah's day. Evil was punished in Sodom and Gomorrah, and evil will continue to be punished. Just because punishment is delayed doesn't mean it won't happen.

"But you didn't come here for me to scold you, Lot," Abraham said, changing the subject. "Tell me about your boys. I suppose they are men by now."

"I have never been close to those boys," Lot admitted. "I never know whether to think of them as my sons or as my grandsons. I prefer to call them my grandsons.

"When it came to naming their sons, my daughters had no shame. I thought they might try to hide the incest, but they bragged about it! Nothing phases my daughters. Adultery. Homosexuality. Incest. Group sex. Child molestation. They heard about it all in Sodom. They think it's normal!

"My older daughter named her son Moab. 'Who's your daddy?' she asks him with a smirk. My younger daughter named her son Ben-Ammi—'son of my people.' The boys are just like their mothers. Ben-Ammi was unhappy that his name wasn't explicit enough. When he got older, he started calling himself Ammon—'inbred'!

Lot buried his face in his hands and wept.

"Every time I hear their names, I am reminded of how they were conceived, and I'm ashamed. People will know the instant they hear my grandsons' names that they are the children of incest."

Abraham and Isaac were silent. They didn't know what to say.

"It gets worse," Lot said.

Then he poured out more heartbreak than Abraham and Isaac had ever heard. Haltingly Lot told his story with frequent outbursts of tears.

"My daughters haven't just rejected Yahweh. They have created a religion of their own. The traumatic experience of escaping Sodom by the skin of their teeth, then having their city destroyed by burning sulfur from out of the sky and having their mother turned into a pillar of salt, gave them a love/hate fascination with fire. They incorporated the sexual immorality that they had learned in Sodom with the fire of God's wrath, and came up with a religion whose god could be appeased with sex and fire. This religion is more abhorrent than any religion dreamed up by the notoriously pagan Canaanites.

"Worse, they have taught this to their sons. When their sons grew up, they left the cave and moved into the plain north of the river Zered. They live a promiscuous lifestyle and have fathered many children.

"Moab and Ammon have each come up with their own version of their mothers' religion. Moab calls his god Chemosh, meaning 'fire' or 'hearth.' Ammon calls his god Molech, a variation of 'melek', meaning 'king' or 'counselor.' They have set up huge idols in front of their homes.

"Moab and Ammon seem to delight in inventing more and more bizarre rituals for worshiping their gods. Moab came up with the idea of sacrificing children and burning them on the altar to Chemosh.

"Not to be outdone, Ammon came up with a more maniacal idea. He swears his counselor, Molech, suggested it. Instead of killing the children first, he makes them walk barefoot through fire. If they come out unscathed, he says, their life will be spared. If they suffer burns in the process, they will be tied alive onto the altar to finish the job. Of course, none of the children are ever spared.

"When I heard that Moab had sacrificed one of his own children to Chemosh, I clapped my hands over my ears. I didn't want to hear any more. That very day I packed up a few belongings and left. I didn't know where to go, so I came here."

By the time Lot finished his story, they were all weeping.

"So you see why I came here, don't you?" Lot said. "I had to get away from my family. I have no influence over them. I never did have. I can't take it any more! I came here to die. But I have one last request."

"What is it, brother? We'll do anything we can for you."

"Please, take me to Bethel, the house of God. When I was last there, I didn't join with those of you who made things right with God. I didn't think I needed to. Abraham, I thought you were the only one who had messed up in Egypt, but I was wrong. It was in Egypt that I became attached to prosperity. That's why I chose to live in the well-watered plain near Sodom. I want to return to Bethel one more time and do what I should have done long ago. I want to repent, confess my sins, and get right with Yahweh. Then I can die in peace."

"We'll do that first thing tomorrow," Abraham said. "Isaac and I will go with you."

* * *

The next day they started on their journey from Hebron to Bethel, the two old men on donkeys, led by Isaac on foot. One servant led a sheep for the sacrifice; another servant led a donkey carrying wood and other supplies. They reached Bethel on the afternoon of the second day and repaired the altar, which was somewhat weather-beaten.

Tearfully Lot laid his hands on the head of the sheep while confessing his sins to God, then he slit the sheep's throat and sprinkled its blood on four sides of the altar. Silently they watched the fat and the inner parts burn on the altar as the meat roasted on a separate fire.

After they had eaten, Lot leaned back against the trunk of a tree.

"I felt Yahweh's presence with us during the meal," Lot said. "I sensed that fellowship with him is restored. Now I am ready to die. Please bury me here at Bethel."

That night Lot died peacefully in his sleep, and Abraham and Isaac buried him at Bethel, the house of God.

20

Lessons from Lot

Not long after Lot's death, Abraham and Isaac were relaxing in their tent after their day's work.

"I can't help but think about you and Lot, Father. You had so much in common. You shared the same occupation. You were both raised in idolatry, yet you both came to know Yahweh. You were both righteous men. You left Ur together, stayed in Haran together, then came to Canaan together, where you were both considered aliens.

"Yet you were very different. Though you were an alien—though your ancestors had not lived there, though you spoke a different language, and though you worshiped a different God—you, Father, were always respected. Lot, on the other hand, at least in the latter part of his life, was disrespected. You are a great success. Lot started successfully, but ended up as a terrible tragedy. What made the difference?"

Abraham paused before he answered.

"I have been pondering that, too, Son. And I think the answer is tied up in our understanding of Yahweh. Lot saw him as someone to be feared. I saw Yahweh as my friend. Lot loved Yahweh as much as anyone with his concept of Yahweh can. But he never knew the joy that comes from knowing Yahweh as a friend. He never danced under the stars in Yahweh's presence, as Sarah and I often did. He never danced in the rain. He never reveled in the beauty of nature as Yahweh's gifts to him personally.

"With the exception of my wife Sarah and a few of my forefathers—like Shem, Shelah and Eber—Lot was as righteous as anyone I know. Yet Lot never felt that God accepted him just for being Lot. He tried to please Yahweh with hard work and upright living. He never saw Yahweh as his friend. He never sensed Yahweh's approval.

"While Sarah and I often laughed with the pleasure of feeling Yahweh's presence even when we didn't hear his voice, Lot was more serious. He saw Yahweh as the Supreme Judge, waiting to hand down a severe sentence on evil doers. Did you notice, Son, how the men of Sodom picked up on that? They resented Lot as the alien in their midst, not because he was an alien, but because he was so judgmental. 'Now he wants to play the judge!' they said. The destruction of Sodom and Gomorrah served only to confirm Lot's opinion.

"Our perception of God affects our choices in life. Lot chose success so he could win Yahweh's approval. Consequently, he succeeded materially and politically. I didn't choose either riches or success. I chose to walk with Yahweh.

"That's why I built altars in so many places. Those altars were a place to worship Yahweh, but they were also a visible testimony of my faith. They provided an opportunity to witness for Yahweh. People who worship multiple gods, as most Canaanites do, are always curious to know what god others worship. They are surprised that I worship only one God, and that gives me an opening to tell them about the one true God, Yahweh.

"Lot sought to exert his influence through politics. I sought to exert my influence through my faith. When Lot and I parted company, he chose prosperity. I chose peace."

"It looks as if your choice to walk with Yahweh made all the difference in your influence, Father," Isaac said. "You've been able to influence all your household and all your servants to follow Yahweh. The greatest proof of that is that you were able to convince all the males in your employ to be circumcised. Not very many grown men outside of our camp would agree to that!"

Abraham nodded in agreement.

"But Lot didn't influence even one! I can't speak for Lot's efforts to tell others about Yahweh, but if he tried, he didn't succeed."

"Not even with his daughters," Isaac said. "But you influenced *your* sons, Father. I have faith in Yahweh, and from what I understand, Ishmael does too."

"What surprises me most, Son, is that Lot didn't even succeed in convincing his wife to follow Yahweh. She should have been his soul mate—his spiritual equal. From what I knew of her, she seemed like a good woman. But she must not have been a true follower of Yahweh, or she would not have looked back toward Sodom. By contrast, not only did my wife Sarah love Yahweh, but she influenced Hagar, her handmaid, to have faith in Yahweh too."

"I still marvel that Yahweh spoke to Hagar, Father. A woman! He spoke to her twice! But he hasn't spoken to me yet."

"You heard his voice on Mount Moriah, Son."

"Yes, Father, but he was talking to you."

"Have patience, Son. You will hear Yahweh's voice speaking to you someday."

Isaac pondered that thought, wondering how long he would have to wait.

"You know, Son, Yahweh did what he did in Sodom as a lesson for you and me and for our descendants. He told me so. He said, 'I shouldn't hide what I am going to do from Abraham. After all, Abraham is going to become a great and mighty nation and through him all the nations of the earth will be blessed. I have chosen him so that he will direct his children and his family after him to keep the way of Yahweh by doing what is right and just.'[109]

"Doing what is right and just has a consequence. Teaching my descendants to do what is right and just has a consequence. Can you guess what that consequence is, Son?"

Isaac waited for his father to answer.

---

[109] See Genesis 18:17-19

"'*So that Yahweh will bring about for Abraham what he has promised him.*'[110] Yahweh wants us to be worthy of his promises. He wants us to walk before him and be blameless. Not perfect—that's impossible—but blameless.

"So tell me, Son, what lessons have you learned from Sodom?"

"That wickedness will be punished. That homosexuality is sin. Yahweh's judgment against Sodom and Gomorrah should provide proof of that. It should also be incentive for godly living and be a warning against sexual immorality and perversion."

"Good. Did you know, Son, that some people in Sodom thought they could get away with their sexual immorality and perversions because God had promised never again to destroy the whole world with a flood?"

Isaac shook his head.

"It's true. Some of them even painted rainbows in their houses as a reminder. It was as if they were taunting God with his own promise. 'Ha, ha! You can't judge me because you promised not to!'"

Isaac was horrified at this distortion of Yahweh's words.

"But there are other ways for Yahweh to judge sin," Isaac objected. "The flood was only one weapon in his arsenal. As Yahweh showed at Sodom, he can use fire. He could have used an earthquake. Or pestilence. Or an epidemic disease. Or any other means."

"And he can judge selectively," Abraham added. "Yahweh doesn't have to judge the whole world at once. In Noah's time he judged the whole world. But Yahweh could still flood a whole city and not be breaking his promise. Yahweh destroyed Sodom and the surrounding area without destroying the whole world. Yahweh destroyed Lot's wife without destroying Lot and his daughters. Have you learned anything else from Sodom, Son?"

"Yes," Isaac replied. "I learned that God will ultimately save the righteous when he destroys the wicked. He won't treat them alike. God's wrath won't fall unrestrained until the righteous people are gone. This is a repeat of the lesson of Noah and the Flood. I learned from Sodom that

---

[110] See Genesis 18:19

a few good men really matter. Sodom was destroyed not just because of its wickedness, but because of its dearth of godly citizens. I learned that the few are often right. The majority of people in Sodom thought their way of life was acceptable. Maybe even normal. But righteous men, like you and Lot, who were in the minority, were proven correct. The behavior and opinions of the many were proven to be wrong—and even dangerous."

"What have you learned from Lot, Son?"

"That being righteous can be lonely," Isaac responded. "Lot felt isolated in Sodom. Going against the grain of society isn't easy. That is where we have an advantage, Father, being nomads. We don't feel the pressures of society as keenly as Lot did.

"I also learned that we influence people more by what we do than by what we say. If there is a disconnect between our words and our actions, our actions have the greater influence. Lot railed against the evils in Sodom, yet he chose to live there. Lot chose wealth in the well-watered plain of Jordan and political influence as a city elder in Sodom while holding his nose about the spiritual and moral depravity there. That choice cancelled out any spiritual influence he might have had."

Abraham nodded in agreement.

"Lot had enough authority over his daughters to control their actions for a while," Isaac said, "but not enough influence to control their hearts. He was able to make sure that they were virgins in Sodom, but obviously the girls themselves were not concerned about sexual purity, as their later actions reveal. Moab and Ammon turned out the way they did because their mothers lived what they believed—evil as that was. Lot could have had more influence if he had been more genuine."

"What else did you learn about Lot, Son?"

"That he didn't know Yahweh very well. Lot seems not to have known God well enough to give his daughters a proper perspective on what had happened in Sodom and Gomorrah. Lot should have stressed that God was right to judge evil. That he is merciful to those who love him and live for him. Sometimes he is merciful to those who *don't* love him for the sake of those who *do* love him. For example, he spared Lot's daughters, and he spared Lot's wife until she looked back.

"Lot claimed to have faith in Yahweh, but his actions spoke otherwise. He believed *in* God, but he didn't believe *God*. He feared him. Unbelief disguised as fear kept him from experiencing God's best for him. Faith would have believed the angels when they said they would spare Zoar.

"Faith would have believed that God's wrath was satisfied when he destroyed Sodom and Gomorrah. But after escaping the destruction of Sodom, Lot seems to have spent the rest of his life in a cave figuratively holding his hands over his head in case God came back and dropped more fire from heaven!"

"Faith and fear are not entirely incompatible, Son. Having faith does not guarantee you will never fear. But faith moves ahead in spite of fear. Fear is only a problem when it keeps us from doing what God wants us to do.

"Have you ever watched a mother eagle teach her eaglets to fly, Son? The nest is a safe place for the eaglets, but nature never intended that they stay there forever living off the parent eagles. When the eagles build their nest, they put pebbles, sticks and sharp objects like bits of broken pottery into the nest, then they line it with soft feathers before laying their eggs. When it's time for the eaglets to learn to fly, the mother stirs up the nest so the prickly things come to the surface. She creates discomfort for the little eaglets so they will want to leave, so they will learn to fly and soar. If they are afraid to leave, she will push the eaglets out of the nest.

"Yahweh did that for Lot. His torment over the sins of Sodom was God's way of prodding to get him out of the nest. But Lot chose the comfort of city life over the safety of obeying God, so he missed God's best for his life. Though I have never heard Lot accused of any offence worse than allowing his daughters to get him drunk, his sins of omission were enormous. He could have done so many things differently. He could have been an outspoken witness for Yahweh in Sodom. He could have moved away from Sodom. He could have sent someone back to his former home in Aram Naharaim to find suitable godly husbands for his daughters. But he didn't. His mistakes came back to haunt him.

"The saddest part of Lot's story is not about those who died in Sodom, but about those who survived. His daughters lived a very tragic life. As a result, Moab and Ammon were born and turned out to be even worse. Who knows where their story will end? On the other hand, Son, we can't be too hard on Lot. He wasn't perfect, but he was better than anybody else in Sodom. His daughters chose to follow the way of Sodom rather than the example of their father. They are responsible for their own choices.

"It's easy to put the blame on our parents. But even the most perfect parents can't guarantee that their children will make the right choices. Look at Adam and Eve. Their 'parent' was God himself, yet they made the wrong choice. They disobeyed him."

Isaac nodded solemnly.

"It's getting late," Abraham said after a moment of silence. He got up to blow out the lamp and get ready for bed, then, on second thought, stepped outside the tent. When his eyes adjusted to the darkness, he was impressed with the sky overhead.

Calling back to Isaac, he said, "Come, Son. Dance with me under the stars. I haven't done it since your mother died. Let's celebrate Yahweh's promise, *Like the stars in the sky. So shall your seed be.*"

From his nearby tent, Eliezer, Abraham's chief and most trusted servant, was watching with interest.

"Come quickly," he called to his wife. "You have to see this!"

Together, arm in arm, Eliezer and his wife watched as Abraham and Isaac expressed with their whole beings the joy of their faith.

"Who would guess," Eliezer's wife remarked, "that our master is 140 years old!"

"It was times like this," Eliezer said, "seeing Abraham live out his faith so joyfully, that convinced me to leave Damascus and work for Abraham, to leave my gods and follow Yahweh!"

21

A Wife for Isaac

Lot's visit set Abraham to thinking. So much of Lot's downward spiral was due to his lack of thankfulness. Had Lot praised Yahweh for rescuing him from Sodom rather than fearing that more judgment was to come, the end of his life might have been very different. Abraham determined to glorify Yahweh as God and always be thankful.

As Abraham looked back on his life, he could see that Yahweh had blessed him in every way. Yahweh had blessed him materially and made him very rich. He had blessed him with the respect of everyone he met. He had blessed him with a beautiful wife who had walked his faith journey with him. He had blessed him with the miraculous birth of a wonderful son, and there were more promises still to be fulfilled.

Yahweh had blessed Abraham with long life and the good health to enjoy it. While others around him seldom lived past 120 years of age, Abraham was 140 and still relatively strong. Sure, he rode a donkey while younger men walked, but he could still put in a full day's work. Recently he had even surprised himself by taking an interest in beautiful women. He had thought that no one could replace his beloved Sarah, but now he wanted someone to share his twilight years with him.

What concerned him was his son. Isaac still grieved for his mother and refused to be comforted.

For the last three years Abraham and Isaac had dragged Sarah's tent from place to place as they moved their flocks and herds. Mostly they left it rolled up. Occasionally, when Isaac was particularly missing his mother, he would set up her tent carefully. Then he would sit in the tent where he had been born and raised and openly grieve for his mother. Abraham dreaded the anniversary of Sarah's death.

Maybe if Abraham found a wife for Isaac, he would stop grieving. Maybe if Isaac could see that Yahweh was fulfilling promises, not just to his father but to him personally, he would begin to heal from the grief of losing his mother.

Abraham had been keeping an eye out for many years for a wife for Isaac, but he couldn't find a woman of high enough character to be matched with his son. If all nations were to be blessed through Abraham and Isaac's descendants, Isaac must have an exceptional wife. A great nation must have not only a great father but a great mother.

Sarah's death had placed even greater urgency on the task of finding a wife for Isaac. Abraham would miss being able to consult with her on the issue. She had been a good judge of character. She had also been a woman of great faith. If only Abraham could find for Isaac a woman of similar faith!

Lot's visit had impressed Abraham with the impossibility of finding a godly wife in Canaan. Talk about his relatives in Aram Naharaim had set him thinking. Surely he could find a godly wife there!

But there were obstacles.

Yahweh had commanded Abraham to leave Ur and later to leave Haran, then Yahweh had shown him the way. But Abraham had no sense that Yahweh was asking him to leave Canaan to find a wife for Isaac. Besides, Abraham was an old man. A journey to Aram Naharaim and back would take a long time—not to mention the time necessary to scout around, find a suitable wife, and then convince her to leave home to marry an unknown man and live in an unknown country. Abraham could not imagine embarking on such a long journey at his age.

Someone else would have to go.

One possibility was Isaac himself. But Abraham rejected that idea almost as quickly as it crossed his mind. It was not appropriate for Isaac to choose his own wife. Too much was at stake. He might be dazzled by first impressions and not be able to see beyond them to assure the woman was of solid character. Sometimes the best wives are not the women who attract attention to themselves.

And what if Isaac fell in love with a woman who refused to move to Canaan? Would Isaac be able to walk away from her, or would he stay in Aram Naharaim? Yahweh had promised Canaan to Abraham's descendants. Abraham could not entertain the slightest risk that Isaac might live elsewhere.

Who would understand the importance of finding not just a wife for Isaac, but a mother for a nation unlike any other nation—a nation that would bless all peoples on earth? Whom could Abraham entrust with such a weighty task?

The first name that came to mind was Eliezer.

On his way from Haran to Canaan almost 65 years ago, by the road to Damascus, Abraham had found Eliezer starving and beaten half to death. Abraham took him into his care and discovered that Eliezer was a runaway slave. He had run away from his master in Damascus, not because he was unwilling to work, but because his master mistreated him cruelly. After Abraham nursed the slave back to health, he told the runaway that he was free to leave. But Eliezer, who felt he was born to serve, vowed never to leave Abraham. At last he had found a worthy master.

Young Eliezer soon proved to be indispensable. He had been Abraham's right hand man ever since. Abraham at one time had even chosen him to be his heir. That was long ago, before either Ishmael or Isaac was born.

Now Eliezer was Abraham's oldest servant. He was also the most trusted servant in his household, the one in charge of all that he had.

The bonus was that Eliezer was a godly man. His loyalty to Abraham had soon resulted in loyalty to Abraham's God. Eliezer was an ardent follower of Yahweh.

The more Abraham thought about Eliezer, the more he liked him as the one to fulfill the task. But how could he possibly convey to him the enormity of the task—a task with eternal consequences?

Suddenly, Abraham was struck with an idea, an idea which seemed to come from outside of himself. At first Abraham rejected the idea as too bizarre. Then the more he thought about it, the more it made sense. Eliezer—and only Eliezer—would understand what he was about to ask. Had the idea come from Yahweh?

Abraham was sitting cross-legged on the floor when he made his request.

"Eliezer, I want you to promise me something."

"Oh course, master, I will do anything you ask."

"Isaac needs a wife," Abraham began. "I have given up finding a wife for him in Canaan. The nearest place I can think of to find a suitable wife is in Aram Naharaim. My relatives there are followers of Yahweh. But my wife is dead and I am too old for such a journey, so I need someone to take as much care in selecting a wife for Isaac as his parents would."

"I would be honored to do that, my lord," Eliezer replied.

"I also need someone to be the 'friend of the bridegroom,' to negotiate with the family of the bride on my behalf."

"Again, I would be honored to do that, master."

"But I want more."

Abraham's eyes pleaded with Eliezer to understand him.

"I want you to swear on my family jewels."[111]

---

[111] Author's note: As people today avoid using explicit terms when recounting certain details in polite company, so did the writers of the Hebrew Bible. Rather than name sexual organs and bodily functions, the writers used euphemisms.

For example, the Bible speaks of Jacob's descendants as "coming out of his____". Here the writer used the Hebrew word *yarek*, meaning thigh. (See Young's Literal Translation of Genesis 46:26.) We all know children do not come from a man's thigh! The same euphemism was used in Genesis 24:2 when Abraham asked his servant to "put your hand under my____".

Jacob later asked Joseph to swear in the same manner when he asked Joseph to bury him in Canaan, not in Egypt (Genesis 47:28-30).

Jews today refer to a solemn oath sworn in this manner as a *"yarek* oath." In keeping with the spirit of this tradition, I have also used a euphemism, but have chosen one more likely to be understood by my readers.

Eliezer was startled by the request. What was Abraham asking? Had he taken leave of his senses? Was he turning into the proverbial dirty old man?

"Put your hand under them," Abraham continued. "Hold them as you swear. Swear by Yahweh, the God of heaven and earth, that you will not allow my son to marry one of these local Canaanite women. Go instead to my homeland, to my relatives, and find a wife there for my son Isaac."

Eliezer now understood why Abraham had requested him to swear in such a strange manner. Abraham was invoking the Covenant and all that it entailed. Eliezer knew the Covenant promises as thoroughly as Abraham did. No one other than Abraham himself was more anxious to see the promises fulfilled.

The sign of the Covenant was circumcision. Eliezer would never forget the day that Abraham and all the males in his entire household were circumcised. He was the one that 99-year-old Abraham had entrusted with the knife when it was his turn to be circumcised. That scene was deeply etched in Eliezer's memory.

Instantly Eliezer knew he would comply with his master's request.

But he was a practical man. He needed to understand his master's priorities.

"What if the woman doesn't want to come back to this land with me?" Eliezer asked. "Should I take your son back to the country you came from?"[112]

"Absolutely not!" Abraham replied vehemently. "Make sure that you don't take my son back there. Yahweh, the God of Heaven, who brought me out of my father's household and my native land and who spoke to me and promised me on oath, saying, 'To your *seed* I will give this land'—he will send his angel before you to get a wife for my son. If the woman is unwilling to come back with you, then you will be released from this oath of mine. Under no circumstances are you to take my son back there!"[113]

---

[112] See Genesis 24:

[113] See Genesis 24:6-8

So Eliezer did as he was asked. Kneeling before his master, he swore an oath to do as his master requested.

As he did so, images, feelings and words from the past flashed though his brain.

Promises: "I will make you into a great nation. I will bless you. I will make your name great. I will bless those who bless you and curse those who curse you. All peoples on earth will be blessed through you."

"Count the stars. So shall your *seed* be."

"To your *seed* I will give this land."

Images: Being circumcised. Circumcising his master. Barrenness blown away by the power of Yahweh. An 89-year-old pregnant woman. A miracle baby with a 90-year-old mother and a 100-year-old father.

Feelings: Hope. Laughter. Joy! Awe.

In all his Covenant promises Yahweh had consistently used the word 'seed' or 'sperm' to denote Abraham's offspring. It hadn't been a mistake. He had used the word deliberately even before he gave the sign of circumcision, knowing that the connection would be obvious some day.

As Eliezer held the 'jewels' that Almighty God had empowered to fulfill the promises thus far, he was impressed with the very weighty responsibility of doing his part to see that the promises continued to be fulfilled in the manner that God had intended.

* * *

The next few days were full of preparations for the long journey to Aram Naharaim. A dowry was assembled. Costly gifts for the bride's family. Gold and silver jewelry and clothes for the bride. Gifts worthy of a queen—the mother of a nation-to-be.

It took ten camels to carry all the good things from his master! And a team of servants to take care of the camels. Abraham gathered Eliezer and his team together and prayed for them before they left. He prayed that Yahweh would go before them and give them success in finding a wife for his son Isaac.

Eliezer looked forward to this journey. He would have time along the way to plan each step and to pray for guidance. The routine of caring for the camels would give him opportunity to focus on his main duty.

It took twenty travel days for his caravan of fully loaded camels to reach Aram Naharaim. They traveled seven or eight hours a day, stopping overnight at the stations which were situated one camel journey apart all along the major travel routes. At these stations he could purchase water and feed for his camels. In the driest stretches the camel stations consisted of nothing more than bales of hay strewn across the sand, with a place for travelers to leave money for the fodder used. The camels could go up to a week without water if necessary. Thankfully, on this journey Eliezer's camels never had to go without water for more than two days in a row.

Once Eliezer reached Aram Naharaim, he went to the town of Nahor, Abraham's brother. He needed to find a way of observing women without their knowing that they were being evaluated as a potential wife. He clung to Abraham's words, "Yahweh will send his angel before you to get a wife for my son."

When he reached the town of Nahor, Eliezer found a natural spring just outside the town gates. A well had been dug nearby to assure that the townspeople would have water even in the dry season. Near the well was a trough where animals could be watered without contaminating the spring.

But the town was not a caravan station; there was no prearranged setup for watering and feeding camels. They couldn't just help themselves to the water in the spring. They would need permission to water the camels.

Eliezer had devised a plan, and he explained it now to his servants. Right here at the spring they would start their search for Isaac's bride.

Normally, permission to draw large quantities of water from the town's water source would be obtained from the elders at the town gate. After obtaining permission, Eliezer's servants could draw water for their camels. But Eliezer planned something completely different. He had asked for a sign from Yahweh—something so unlikely that only a woman prompted by God would do it. He asked that God's choice of wife for Isaac would offer to water his camels!

The servants at first were skeptical. No woman would do that. The pottery jars the women typically brought to the well held ten litres.[114] A thirsty camel could drink up to ten of those. They had ten camels. So God's special woman would have to fill her jar, carry it to the trough, and empty it a hundred times!

The servants agreed that if a woman did make such an offer, she would have to be Yahweh's choice for Isaac.

The thirsty camels could smell the water and moved about impatiently, but the servants made the camels kneel down near the well and wait. The camels moaned and bawled as they struggled to kneel under their heavy loads, much like a weight-lifter grunting under his load. Eliezer and his men settled down to wait.

The time of their arrival was good. It was toward evening, the time when the women go out to draw water. So, they wouldn't have to wait long for water, and at the same time they would have a great opportunity to observe and compare the women in this area.

As they waited, Eliezer again prayed in his heart as he had all along his journey.

"O Yahweh, God of my master Abraham," Eliezer prayed, "please give me success today. Treat my master Abraham well! As the young women of the town come out to the spring to get water, I will ask for a drink. Let the woman you have picked out for your servant Isaac not only give me a drink, but offer to water my camels also. Then I'll know that you're working graciously behind the scenes for my master."[115]

Before he had finished praying, a girl came out of the town with her jar on her shoulder. Eliezer was struck first with her graceful movements. As she got closer, he was impressed with her beauty.

"*Eiza yofi!*"[116] he exclaimed under his breath. "Wow!"

He heard a quiet whistle come from one of his men.

---

[114] About 2½ US gallons
[115] See Genesis 24:12-14
[116] Literally, "Very beautiful!" Colloquially, "Wow!"

The girl's beauty reminded Eliezer of Sarah in her younger days. He watched with interest as she went down to the spring, filled her jar and came up again.

"Wouldn't it be amazing," Eliezer whispered to one of his servants, "if someone this beautiful turned out to have the character necessary to be Isaac's wife!"

He hurried out to meet her and asked for a drink.

"Drink, my lord," she said politely, and quickly lowered the jar from her shoulder to her hands and gave him a drink. After she had given him a drink, she uttered the words Eliezer had hardly dared to hope for.

"I'll draw water for your camels too," she offered.

Quickly she emptied her jar into the watering trough and ran back to the well to draw more water. The servants got the camels to their feet. They didn't need much urging. The girl continued back and forth between the well and the watering trough.

Eliezer watched her without saying a word. Who was this remarkable girl? Would she quit before the task was done?

Seven camels were watered. The girl wasn't running any more, but she was working steadily and purposefully.

Eight camels. With graceful strides she covered the ground between the well and the trough. With strong arms she lifted her jar to her shoulders at the well, then lowered it later at the trough.

Nine. One more camel to go. Ten more trips to the well and back to the trough. Eliezer reached inside his cloak and felt the pouch containing the betrothal jewelry.

He didn't know the girl's name. He didn't know anything about her. But one thing he did know. She was Yahweh's choice for Isaac.

As the girl made her last trip to the well, Eliezer knew that Yahweh had made his journey successful. He pulled out the pouch containing the betrothal jewelry.

As the girl poured the last jar of water into the trough, Eliezer called out to her, "What is your name?"

"Rebekah," she said, as she picked up her empty jar and approached Eliezer.

"Rebekah." Eliezer rolled the name on his tongue. "That means something like rope, or noose, or rope with a noose, doesn't it?"

"Yes. My father picked the name. It comes from the concept of tying up cattle. For their own protection. To keep them from wandering off. To lead them home."

"How fitting!" Eliezer replied as he held out to her his hands, fists facing down, with the betrothal jewelry hidden inside.

"What is the meaning of this?" Rebekah asked, not knowing how to respond.

"I've come to lead you home," Eliezer said, turning his hands upward and revealing their contents.

Rebekah stared in astonishment at the gold nose ring and two gold bracelets he held out to her. The gold was so yellow that she knew it was pure gold, not diluted with cheaper metals. Jewelry of that size and quality could mean only one thing. A marriage proposal!

Who was this stranger? Rebekah wondered. He was too old to be the groom. He must be the friend of the bridegroom—the one authorized to negotiate with the bride's family. Who was the bridegroom? Where did he live? Why had this stranger proposed to her without knowing anything about her?

To Eliezer's relief Rebekah didn't reject his proposal outright. Now he needed to negotiate with her family.

"Whose daughter are you?" he asked. "Please tell me, is there room in your father's house for us to spend the night?"[117]

Rebekah smiled at Eliezer's reference to his men and his camels as "us." Caravan drivers tended to look upon their camels as part of their family.

"I am the daughter of Bethuel, the son that Milcah bore to Nahor. We have plenty of straw and fodder for the camels," she assured him, "as well as room for you to spend the night."[118]

Upon learning that Rebekah was a relative, Eliezer immediately fell to his knees and bowed his head in worship.

---

[117] Genesis 24:23
[118] Genesis 24:24-25

"Praise be to Yahweh!" he said. "Praise be to the God of my master Abraham. He has shown unfailing love and faithfulness to my master. Yahweh led me right to the door of my master's relatives."[119]

"Amen!" came the hearty chorus from Eliezer's men. "Hallelujah!"

Listening to his prayer, Rebekah was pleased to learn that this camel driver was a follower of Yahweh. She was awed to learn that he was negotiating on behalf of Abraham. His name was well known in Aram Naharaim. Many people remembered him from the days he had lived in Haran. Others knew him by reputation because of the stories that had filtered back from Canaan. Stories of rescuing Lot and putting the Babylonian armies on the run. Stories of the destruction of Sodom and Gomorrah. Stories of a miracle baby born to elderly parents—to a woman who had been barren all her life.

This camel driver was asking her to marry the miracle baby, who was now a man! Of course she would say yes!

When Eliezer finished his prayer and again extended the betrothal jewelry to Rebekah, she accepted.

As she put on the jewelry, she said to Eliezer, "There is more to my name than I told you. Rebekah means more than 'a rope with a noose'. My name, as my grandmother Milcah explained to me, also carries the notion that two individuals are brought together by someone higher and smarter than they. Yahweh works behind the scenes in mysterious ways to perform his wonders. He 'ties the knot'!

"'One day, daughter of mine,' my mother keeps telling me, 'Yahweh will bring a special man for you. Our relative Abraham had to wait for his special son. You may have to wait for your special husband.'

"I must go and tell her that Yahweh is about to tie the knot. Won't she be surprised to find out who the man is!"

Forgetting her water jar in her excitement, Rebekah left Eliezer standing by the well and ran all the way home to tell her mother the good news.

"What took you so long at the well? And where is the water?" her mother asked. "I need it to finish preparing supper."

---

[119] See Genesis 24:27

The water was soon forgotten again as Rebekah's brother Laban noticed her nose ring and the giant bracelets on her arms. Rebekah's words tumbled over each other as she told her story. All her family members' mouths fell open as they heard it. Laban was the first to recover.

"Where is this man, this friend of the bridegroom?" he asked.

"He must still be by the spring," Rebekah answered. "That's where I left him."

Rebekah's father Bethuel immediately stepped in to negotiate for the betrothal of his daughter in the traditional manner.

"Laban, I appoint you as my deputy to represent me to the friend of the bridegroom. Bring him here at once!"

Laban hurried out to find Eliezer.

"Don't forget the water jar!" his mother called after him.

Bethuel shouted orders to the servants to prepare for guests.

Eliezer was still standing with his camels near the spring when Laban arrived. He had filled Rebekah's water jar, expecting that she would soon return for it.

Laban welcomed him warmly in the flowery tradition of negotiating a bride price.

"Come with me, you who are blessed of Yahweh! Why are you standing out here? I've got the house ready for you; and there's also a place for your camels."[120]

Eliezer went with him to the house; his men followed with the camels. The camels were unloaded and given straw and feed. Water was brought to bathe the feet of Eliezer and his men, then Laban brought out food.

Coffee was offered to Eliezer, but he refused to drink or eat until his mission was accomplished.

"I won't eat until I have told you what I have to say,"[121] Eliezer said.

That was the signal for negotiations to begin in earnest.

"Go ahead; tell us," Laban replied.

---

[120] See Genesis 24:31
[121] See Genesis 24:33

The two deputies, Laban and Eliezer, sat down facing each other. They would do all the talking. Behind Laban sat Bethuel. Behind Eliezer sat his men.

The women—Rebekah, her mother, her nurse and her maids—stayed out of sight in the next room. But not out of earshot!

Eliezer introduced himself and explained his mission.

"I'm Abraham's servant. Yahweh has blessed my master abundantly, and he has become wealthy. Yahweh has given him sheep and cattle, silver and gold, servants and maidservants, camels and donkeys. Sarah, my master's wife, gave him a son in her old age and he has passed everything on to his son.

"My master made me promise, 'Don't allow my son to marry one of these local Canaanites. Instead, go to my father's home, back to my family, and get a wife for my son there.'

"I said to my master, 'But what if the woman won't come with me?'

"He said, 'Yahweh, before whom I have walked faithfully, will send his angel with you and he'll make things work out so that you'll bring back a wife for my son from my family, from the house of my father. Then you'll be free from the oath. If you go to my family and they won't give her to you, you will also be free from the oath.'[122]

Then Eliezer recounted how he had picked Rebekah as the future bride. He had asked Yahweh for a very improbable sign—that the woman of Yahweh's choice would not only give him a drink, but offer to water his camels. Before he had even finished praying, Rebekah appeared, gave him a drink at his request, then offered to water the camels. Only after the camels were watered did he discover that Rebekah was a relative of Abraham.

"Then I put the ring in her nose and the bracelets on her arms," Eliezer said, "and I bowed down and worshiped Yahweh. I praised Yahweh, the God of my master Abraham, who had led me on the right road to get the granddaughter of my master's brother for his son."

Eliezer paused at the end of his story. Now it was decision time for the bride's father. Eliezer needed a definitive answer.

---

[122] See Genesis 24:34-41

"Now, tell me what you are going to do. If you plan to respond with a generous *yes*, tell me. But if not, tell me plainly so I can figure out what to do next."

Bethuel was so impressed with Eliezer's story that he forgot to keep silent until the negotiations were over.

"This is obviously from Yahweh," Laban and Bethuel both agreed. "We can't haggle over the bride price."[123]

Without even looking at the gifts Eliezer had brought on his camels, they agreed to the marriage proposal.

Rising to his feet, Bethuel called the women to come from the next room. He put his arm around his daughter and presented her to Eliezer.

"Here's Rebekah! Take her and go, and let her become the wife of your master's son, as Yahweh has directed."[124]

For the second time that day Eliezer fell to his knees, bowing right to the ground and worshiping Yahweh, who had found for Isaac a godly wife.

Then he motioned to his servants to bring in the dowry. More jewelry for Rebekah. Articles of gold and silver. Articles of clothing. Costly gifts for the bride's family—especially for her mother and brother—those who would be most affected by the loss of Rebekah in their household.

Everybody 'oo'ed and 'ah'ed as each item was brought out and presented to the bride and her family. After the last gift was brought out for display, Laban called out, "Bring on the coffee!"

Congratulations were exchanged all around, coffee was brought in, and they all drank as a seal of the covenant that had just been entered into.

With the formal negotiations over, they settled down to eat. The feasting and excitement lasted well into the night. Finally Eliezer stood to his feet.

"Normally at this time, the groom would make an announcement," Eliezer said. "As the groom is not here, I will make it for him." He held

---

[123] Genesis 24:50. "We cannot speak to you either bad or good" (NKJV) refers to the practice of the seller pointing out the good features and the buyer pointing out the flaws when haggling over a purchase.

[124] See Genesis 24:51

up Rebekah's arms laden with bracelets. "See, by this ring," he said pointing to her nose ring, "and these bracelets, you are set apart for my master's son Isaac!"

Everybody cheered. The evening's celebration was done. Rebekah and Isaac were officially betrothed.

* * *

Eliezer awoke the next morning knowing that his duties as friend of the bridegroom were not finished.

Normally a whole year or more elapsed between the betrothal and the wedding. Adjustments, decisions and preparations had to be made when a daughter left the family. Who would take over her duties? What would the father give his daughter as her personal dowry? Who would be invited as guests? And preparations had to be made for the wedding itself.

But Eliezer did not have the luxury of time. It had taken three weeks to get here, and it would take just as long to return. This was not a journey he wanted to repeat next year. Besides, Abraham wanted to see his son married before he died. He was already 140. Though he was currently in good health, he had no guarantee how much longer he would live. Eliezer would have to convince the bride's family to let Rebekah return with him now.

Eliezer spoke to Laban, who discussed the situation with his mother. They both agreed that, considering the distance between their home and the home of the groom, waiting a year was not practical.

"Let the girl stay with us ten days or so," they suggested. "After that she may return with you."

But Eliezer was not satisfied with that answer. He wanted to return immediately to his master Abraham.

"Don't delay me," he pleaded. "Yahweh has made my mission successful. Send me on my way so I may return to my master."[125]

"Let's let Rebekah herself make the decision," Laban and his mother suggested. So they called Rebekah and asked her, "Will you go with this man? Today?"

---

[125] See Genesis 24:56

Rebekah didn't need time to deliberate. She was already convinced that Yahweh had been working behind the scenes to choose a husband for her. Even more exciting to her was the fact that the husband Yahweh had chosen for her was the son of Abraham—the miracle Son of Promise!

"I will go," she said.

Rebekah's father Bethuel quickly decided that her personal dowry would consist of several maid servants and Rebekah's nurse, Deborah. Deborah was like a second mother to her. She was the midwife who had attended at Rebekah's birth, and had looked after her ever since. Rebekah would be happy to have a nurse and midwife around when she had children of her own.

Rebekah and her maids got ready as quickly as they could and packed their belongings onto the camels for the return journey.

Meanwhile the family was preparing to stage an impromptu wedding sendoff for the bride. On short notice they would try to do what usually took a year of preparation. They chose the most elaborate gown and veil from the gifts Abraham had sent, as well as the bridal jewelry. While some servants ran to the neighbors to announce the wedding, other servants braided jewelry into Rebekah's hair and dressed her in her wedding gown. Once she was fully adorned and perfumed, they covered her with a veil.

Eliezer, standing in for the groom, took Rebekah by the hand and led her on a circuitous route from her home through the streets of town and out to the spring where he had first laid eyes on her. Family members, friends and neighbors followed them in a grand procession, proclaiming marriage blessings with flowery words.

"Our sister, may you increase to thousands upon thousands; may your offspring possess the gate of their enemies,"[126] they chanted and sang.

Well-wishers scattered ears of parched grain to the children along the way. The children plucked the kernels and threw them in the path of the bride, occasionally nibbling a few kernels themselves. Some people played on flutes or drums or strummed lyres while others danced to the accompaniment. The air was filled with gladness and rejoicing.

---

[126] Genesis 24:60

At the spring Eliezer helped Rebekah onto a camel, while his servants helped her maids and Deborah mount the other camels. Then Eliezer and his men led them on the long journey to Canaan.

The family and wedding guests watched until the caravan disappeared out of sight, then they returned to Bethuel's house to continue the wedding feast without the bride or groom.

* * *

What a difference a day made! Yesterday at this time Rebekah was a virgin with not a thought about marriage. Now she was not only betrothed, but in the process of being married. She was dressed in bridal finery. She had left her parents' household, and was on her way to live with her husband, whom she knew only by reputation.

From now until her marriage was complete, she would not unveil her face in public. For the next three weeks her maids would be quick to notify her when strangers were near and would remind her to cover her face if she forgot.

* * *

Meanwhile Isaac was living in the Negev. He had instructed Eliezer to meet him there—somewhere in the triangle between Beersheba, Kadesh and Beer Lahai Roi—upon his return journey.

Isaac had grown up to be a quiet, thoughtful man. He didn't have the charismatic character that attracted so many to his father, but he shared his father's deep faith. He loved to return to places his father had been and contemplate the stories his father had told him of what had happened there.

Isaac wanted to walk in his father's footsteps of faith while avoiding his father's mistakes.

While waiting for Eliezer to return with a wife for him, Isaac had gone to Beer Lahai Roi. This was where Hagar had ended up when fleeing from Sarah's heavy-handed treatment of her. That grief had been caused by Abraham's taking a concubine to 'help' Yahweh fulfill his promise of a son.

Isaac loved to go off by himself at the end of his work day and converse with Yahweh. God had never spoken to him audibly, but Isaac would talk to him out loud, then listen for God's voice in his spirit. Often he would 'hear' Yahweh repeat things he had said audibly to his father Abraham.

In Beer Lahai Roi Isaac heard Yahweh repeat to him what he had said here to Hagar and elsewhere to Abraham: "I will so increase your descendants that they will be too numerous to count."

"Yes, but I need a wife first," Isaac replied.

"I saw Hagar's circumstances and met her needs," Yahweh whispered into Isaac's spirit. "I see your needs, too. And I will keep my promises to your father and to you."

* * *

Isaac's people lived in tents made of goat hair. The goat hair fabric was very heavy and served as a good protection from the cold winds of winter. In the summer the sides of the tent could be lifted up on poles to provide shade without holding in the heat. Cords were tied to the tent fabric and fastened to the ground with tent pegs.

Desert dwellers and nomads seldom made new tents. When the roof got old and worn and started to leak, the women would take clippings of goat hair which they had been accumulating for a year or so and weave it into a coarse fabric. This fabric would be used to replace a section of the roof, while the former roof material would be recycled as a side curtain and used a little longer. The new fabric was porous, but that didn't matter. For a day or so, when it first rained on the new roof, everybody would move to a section of the tent under the old roof. After the first rain the new fabric would shrink together and become waterproof.

Inside each tent, rugs covered the ground, and people usually sat cross-legged on the floor. Abraham and Isaac, who were rich enough to have camels, used the camel saddles as furniture for sitting on inside the tent. Bedding was rolled out at night for sleeping, and rolled up during the day to provide additional places to sit.

In cold or wet weather a hole was dug inside the tent and stones were put around it to create a hearth. A fire was built inside the hole and cooking pots sat on the stones. In warm weather the hearth was built outside the tent.

As families grew, the tent was enlarged. A new section was added to the roof and three new side curtains were added, creating a separate apartment. The original tent became the men's apartment and also served as the place for receiving guests. The side apartment was for women and children. Sometimes servants lived in a separate side apartment.

Each year new strips of fabric replaced old ones, and the "house of hair" was handed down from father to son without its being completely new or completely old at any one time. A new tent was created only when a young groom and his bride set up housekeeping for themselves or when a man took a new wife. If he had several wives and many children, each wife would live in a separate tent with her children and the man would have a tent of his own.

For years Abraham's tent had had a side apartment for Sarah and another apartment for Hagar. When Sarah finally got pregnant, a new tent had been made for her. Isaac had been born in and had grown up in that tent. On his thirteenth birthday Isaac had moved into the apartment of his father's tent that had once been occupied by Hagar and Ishmael.

While Eliezer was away searching for a wife for Isaac, Abraham brought up the topic of accommodations for the new couple.

"Son, what have you been doing about preparing a place for your bride?"

"I have been fixing up my apartment, Father. Haven't you noticed? I have gotten some maidservants to replace the worn curtains with new fabric. The roof is still good after last year's repairs."

"Don't you think you should live in a tent totally separate from me?" Abraham asked. "Why don't you live in your mother's tent?"

Isaac could hardly bare to consider the thought. How could he desecrate his mother's memory by bringing another woman into her tent? How could a woman he had never set eyes on ever replace his mother?

"What's wrong with living beside you?" Isaac objected. "When you die, this will be my tent."

"Don't rush me into the grave before my time, Son. I am still perfectly healthy."

"I'm sorry, Father. I didn't mean any disrespect, but I am comfortable here with you."

"What if I'm not comfortable with having you here? What if I take another wife? Then you would have to move anyway."

Isaac had never considered that possibility.

"Are you getting married again?" he asked in a shocked voice.

"Not right now, Son. But don't rule out the possibility of it happening some time down the road."

That possibility had never occurred to Isaac. He was stunned into silence.

Abraham understood his son's reluctance to use his mother's tent, but life goes on.

* * *

The next day Isaac again left for Beer Lahai Roi. That was the place where he did his best thinking. He sat down beside the spring where God had talked to Hagar, and wept.

"O God Who Sees Me," he cried, "El Roi, what should I do? My mother is dead. My father is withdrawing from me emotionally. I will soon have to share my life with a woman I have never met. How can I take her into my mother's tent?"

"Isaac," God whispered into his spirit, "I see you. I see your pain. I see your grief. I see your need for a wife. I am not only El Roi. I am Yahweh Yireh. I will provide for all your needs—physically, spiritually and emotionally. Trust me. Trust me to provide. Don't worry that you don't know anything about your wife-to-be. I have picked her specially.

Just for you. You won't be disappointed. Now wipe your tears and go back. Unfurl your mother's tent and prepare it for your bride."

* * *

For the next few days Isaac busied himself with preparing his mother's tent for his bride. Finally he was satisfied that everything was ready.

At that moment Isaac looked up and saw camels approaching. As they got closer, Isaac recognized Eliezer leading the caravan. And there were women on the camels! Eliezer's journey to Aram Naharaim must have been successful!

Isaac hurried across the field to meet the caravan.

At the same time Rebekah looked up and saw Isaac. She didn't know him, but his purposeful strides suggested that this must be her new husband.

Immediately she called to Eliezer to lower her camel to its knees. She got off quickly, turned her back to the stranger, and asked Eliezer, "Who is that man in the field coming to meet us?"[127]

"He's my master."

So Rebekah rearranged her veil to cover her face before Isaac was close enough to get a good look at her.

Isaac was eager to hear how Eliezer had come to choose this particular woman as his wife, and Eliezer was just as eager to fill in all the details. Both of them praised Yahweh for his very obvious leading. Isaac and Eliezer could hardly wait to tell the story to Abraham, and Isaac looked forward to getting to know the remarkable woman Yahweh had chosen for him.

Rebekah was introduced to Isaac, who took her back to his father's tent and introduced her to Abraham. All the while, Rebekah had her head and face covered.

There in Abraham's tent, in the apartment which had once been Sarah's, Rebekah's maids quickly helped her change out of her travel

---

[127] Genesis 24:65

clothes and into her wedding gown. They again wove jewels into her hair, anointed her with costly perfume, and replaced her veil over her head.

Then came the most important moment of the entire marriage festivity.

Rebekah was led to her place under a canopy that had been set up in front of her new home—Sarah's tent. Isaac stood beside her, dressed in his finest clothes and wearing a crown on his head. He looked like a king. A crown was placed on Rebekah's head, and Abraham spoke words of benediction over the couple.

Then the feasting began. Eliezer, his role as friend of the bridegroom accomplished, now stepped into the role of ruler of the feast. He gave thanks at the beginning of the dinner, then rose at various times throughout the day to pronounce other benedictions. When wine was served, he blessed the wine.

At the end of the day Isaac's closest friends escorted him and Rebekah into Sarah's tent—now Rebekah's tent—where the marriage was to be consummated. Isaac was dying of curiosity to see what his new bride looked like. Eliezer had assured him she was beautiful. Now, finally, he had the chance to see her.

He lifted Rebekah's veil and his heart almost stopped. Then it started beating like a hammer. She was so beautiful! He hadn't dared to hope for a bride so beautiful. One look into her eyes and his heart was hers. It was love at first sight!

For a whole week weddings guests and friends came and went. They were expected to praise the bride and pronounce blessings over the bridal couple. There was nobody from the bride's family in attendance and nobody other than her nurse and maids who knew her well, but the story of how she had offered to water Eliezer's camels quickly spread and was repeated over and over in praise of the bride.

* * *

So Isaac married Rebekah. She became his wife, and he loved her. O, how he loved her! And Isaac was comforted after his mother's death.[128]

---

[128] See Genesis 24:67

22

Yahweh Speaks to Rebekah

Isaac fell madly in love with the wife Yahweh had chosen for him. Not only was she incredibly beautiful, but she also had a wealth of skills to bring to the family. Isaac loved sharing with her the details of Yahweh's promises to his father Abraham and now to him. And Rebekah embraced those promises wholeheartedly.

Rebekah complemented Isaac's personality. She was aggressive, but knew when to give in. He tended to be passive, but wouldn't budge on matters of principle. She was outgoing. He was quiet.

Rebekah put the laughter back into Isaac's life. She was perfect for him in every way. Except one. Rebekah, like Abraham's wife, was barren.

But Isaac determined not to do what his father had done. He would not take a concubine to help Yahweh solve the problem. He knew that Yahweh had chosen Rebekah for him. So some day—maybe soon, maybe years down the road—Almighty God, El Shaddai, would do a miracle for her as he had for his mother Sarah.

Meanwhile he would pray and he would cling to the promises.

"Yahweh, you promised my father that his descendants would be as the dust of the earth, as the stars in the sky, as the sand on the seashore. You said you would fulfill that promise through me. So far there is only one descendant in the line of promise, but I believe your promise. I pray that you will give my wife a son."

Year after year, when Isaac and Rebekah were walking down a dusty road, one would kick up the dust and say to the other, "As the dust of the earth!"

On a dark starry night they would say to each other, "As the stars in the sky!"

When they were on the western coast of Canaan, they would dig their toes into the sand and say, "As the sand on the seashore!"

When they were in Hebron, they would stand on the ridge surveying the land of Canaan in all directions, and say, "To your offspring will I give this land."

When they returned to Beer Lahai Roi, one of Isaac's favorite places, they would talk to El Roi, the God Who Sees Me, and remind him of their need for a son.

Isaac hoped he wouldn't have to wait until he was a hundred years old, like his father had, to become a father. But if Yahweh chose to do it that way, so be it.

All around him, people were obeying God's command to be fruitful and multiply and fill the earth. After Isaac's marriage, Abraham married again and had six more sons. Ishmael, by now in his seventies, had twelve sons. And still Isaac and Rebekah had none.

Isaac continued to pray for his wife.

Finally, after nineteen years of marriage, Yahweh answered his prayer and Rebekah became pregnant. What a celebration when they discovered the news! Isaac, at the age of 60, would become a father. Abraham, at the age of 160, would become a grandfather.

It wasn't long until Rebekah could feel activity in her womb. She had heard of babies moving around, kicking and poking, but this was ridiculous!

"Why is this happening to me?" she asked Isaac. But he knew nothing about babies.

"Why is this happening to me?" she asked her nurse Deborah. Deborah tried to assure her that movement in the womb was normal.

Rebekah had no previous pregnancy to compare things to, but she was sure her baby was unusually active. Finally Rebekah asked the one who did know.

"Why is this happening to me?"[129] she asked Yahweh.

The answer she received came as a happy surprise. She was expecting twins!

Yahweh spoke to her in the form of a poem. It sounded like a riddle, good news and bad.

> *"Two nations are in your womb,*
> *and two peoples from within your bowels will be separated;*
> *one people will be stronger than the other,*
> *and the older will serve the younger."*[130]

Yahweh's choice of the word 'bowels' told Rebekah that she was in for a wild emotional ride, like being in a small boat during a rough storm. Bowels were considered to be the seat of a person's emotions.

Rebekah ran to find Isaac and tell him the news.

"Isaac, we are going to have twins!" she exclaimed breathlessly.

"How do you know?"

"Yahweh told me."

"What do you mean, Yahweh told you?" Isaac asked. "How do you know it was he?"

"I asked Yahweh a question, and I heard his answer. It's like you and Abraham have always told me," Rebekah replied, upset that Isaac would doubt her. "When he speaks, you just know it's Yahweh."

Isaac was stunned. All his life he had wanted to hear Yahweh speak to him. Now, when there was news for him, Yahweh had spoken to his wife. To a woman! Surely if the message was from Yahweh, he would have told the father-to-be, he would have told the man of the household!

Rebekah was annoyed by Isaac's silence.

"Don't you want to know what Yahweh said?" Rebekah asked.

---

[129] Genesis 25:22
[130] Genesis 25:23. Compare NIV and KJV.

"Oh, alright," Isaac replied, coming out of his reverie. He knew his wife would tell him whether he wanted to know or not. He still wasn't convinced the voice had been Yahweh. Maybe Rebekah had been dreaming or hallucinating.

So Rebekah repeated what Yahweh had said to her. But Isaac was skeptical.

* * *

As time went on, it became obvious that Rebekah was carrying more than one baby. Then Deborah detected two separate heartbeats. Rebekah *was* carrying twins.

"See!" Rebekah said to Isaac. "Yahweh was right. We are going to have twins. And they must be boys, because Yahweh said 'two *nations* are in your womb.'"

Isaac conceded that his wife was right about twins, but wasn't yet willing to embrace the rest of the prophecy.

"And the older will serve the younger," she added thoughtfully.

There was silence between them for a while, then Rebekah spoke again.

"What do you think that means, Isaac?"

"Hm?" Isaac's thoughts were elsewhere. "What are you talking about?"

"*The older will serve the younger.* What do you think that means for us? If Yahweh has made the younger one stronger and decided that the older will serve the younger, don't you think that should affect how we treat the boys?"

"You're sure they are boys, aren't you?" Isaac said, ignoring Rebekah's question.

"Yes. They have to be."

Silence fell between them again, but Rebekah wasn't ready to change the subject.

"Don't you think we should do something to show that we believe Yahweh?" Rebekah asked.

"Like what?"

"Like treat the younger as the firstborn. That would be an act of faith."

"Rebekah, dear," Isaac said, trying to hide his annoyance, "I wish you would drop this notion that Yahweh has spoken to you. If he had something to say to us, he would have said it to me."

"So you don't or won't believe a message is from Yahweh unless you hear his voice? Is that what you are saying?"

"Well . . . . I guess so. Yes."

"How about: 'I will bless you'?"

"I heard Yahweh say that to my father when we were on Mount Moriah."

"How about: 'I will make your descendants as the stars in the sky'?"

"I heard him say that too."

"As the sand on the seashore?"

"That too."

"As the dust of the earth?"

"Yahweh said that to my father."

"But not to you?"

"No."

"But you still believe it?"

"Of course!"

"So you *do* believe messages from Yahweh even when you don't hear his voice," Rebekah said triumphantly.

"Of course," Isaac replied. "I believe everything Yahweh said to my father Abraham. And to my forefathers."

"But not what he said to your *wife*!"

"Rebekah, Yahweh didn't tell my mother to leave Ur. He told my father, and Mother came along. Yahweh didn't tell Noah's wife to build the ark. He told Noah."

"So you are telling me that Yahweh doesn't talk to women? He doesn't care about women?"

"Of course, he cares!" Isaac retorted. "Don't twist my words! But he treats the man and wife as one, and he speaks to the man. When Yahweh announced my birth to my mother Sarah, he didn't talk to her directly. He talked to my father Abraham. Mother was inside the tent listening. Yahweh knew she would be listening."

"And she laughed," Rebekah reminded her husband. "She didn't believe him. Yahweh knew she wouldn't believe him. He knew she would laugh. Maybe that's why Yahweh didn't tell her to her face. Maybe that's why Yahweh didn't talk to you. Maybe he knew you would laugh. Maybe that's why he named you Isaac—he laughs!"

Her words stung. Isaac got up and stomped away angrily.

"I'm sorry!" Rebekah called after him. "I didn't mean to be mean. I got carried away. I just didn't know how to convince you that Yahweh really spoke to me."

Rebekah resolved not to bring up the subject again until after the children were born. This should be a happy time in their lives, not a time for fighting. But Rebekah couldn't shake the conviction that Yahweh's prophecy had some implications for her and Isaac's actions toward their children.

* * *

"Isaac," Rebekah said, "what do you think we should name our sons? They will be born any day now."

"Why name them ahead of time?" he replied. He still wasn't sure the twins would both be boys. He wanted boys, but was realistic enough not to count on it. They could be a boy and a girl. Or both girls. But he didn't feel like arguing that point.

"You were named before you were born," Rebekah reminded him.

"Yes, but that was different. Yahweh named me. He told my father what to call me. Most people don't name their children before they are born. Sometimes circumstances at the time of birth suggest a name. Sometimes the name is indicative of the parents' aspirations for their child. Like my father, who was originally named Aram—'exalted'. Grandfather Terah wanted his son to be respected by others. Sometimes the parents pick a name suggested by the child's appearance or character. They may wait for months or even years to pick the right name—a name that really fits."

"And meanwhile they call the child 'Hey, you'?" Rebekah asked.

"No, silly! They call the child 'baby' or 'little sister' or 'little brother.' There is no rush to find a suitable name. And if they get it wrong, the name can be changed later. As you know, my father had his name changed twice. The people of Ur, out of their respect for him, changed it from Aram, 'exalted', to Abram, 'exalted father.' Later Yahweh changed it from Abram to Abraham, 'father of many.' Some names stick. My grandfather was called 'the little wanderer' as a toddler when he showed no fear in straying from his parents and exploring his surroundings. So they called him Terah, 'wanderer', and he grew up to explore the world."

"But we have two babies coming," Rebekah said. "We can't call them 'baby one' and 'baby two' for the first few years of their lives!"

"Don't worry about it," Isaac advised her. He was the easy-going one. "At the right time they will be born and they will be named."

23

Twins!

When Rebekah went into labor, Deborah took charge and gave instructions to Rebekah's maids to boil water and get all the supplies ready. Isaac was not allowed into the tent. He would be notified when it was all over.

Soon a tiny cry rang out.

"It's a boy!" Deborah exclaimed. "Look how red and hairy he is!"

Before the umbilical cord could be cut, the next baby was on its way. Deborah turned her full attention to the delivery of the second baby.

"Another boy!" she exclaimed joyfully. "And look! He's holding onto his brother's heel!"

The maids all crowded around to see. Sure enough, one baby was tightly clutching the other's heel. Deborah tried to pull his tiny hand away and was amazed at the little one's grip.

"He won't let go!" she laughed.

"He's continuing the fight that started in the womb!" Rebekah replied, exhausted but happy.

The women busied themselves with caring for the mother and the new babies. After the umbilical cords were cut and tied, the babies were washed and rubbed with salt. Then swaddling strips of soft Egyptian cotton were wound tightly around each baby. Starting with the legs, the babies were wrapped from toe to head with their arms at their sides, with only their faces showing. Then they were placed in their mother's arms.

"They're perfect," Deborah announced happily.

"They look like little mummies!" Rebekah laughed. "Bring in Isaac. Announce the good news. He is the father of two healthy boys!"

Isaac thought he would burst with love and pride at the sight of his little family. Rebekah glowed. He thought she had never looked more beautiful than now in motherhood. And he had not one but *two* sons! Yahweh was good.

Even though the babies were wrapped like mummies, Isaac could see that the babies were not identical. One had a very red face and had a lot more hair than the other. Isaac commented on it.

"You should see the rest of him," Rebekah replied. "His whole body is red. And he's hairy all over, as if he's already dressed in a furry garment! Deborah has delivered many babies in her lifetime, but she has never seen anything like this!"

"Maybe we should call him Edom—red," Isaac suggested.

"I don't think so," Rebekah replied. "His redness will probably fade in a little while."

"How about Seir—hairy?"

"Absolutely not! You might as well call him Horny!"

"I wasn't thinking of it in that sense," Isaac objected. "I was thinking of it in the sense of 'male goat.' Goats are more alert than sheep. If I want to know whether there is any danger approaching my flocks, I watch the goats, not the sheep. The goat is my early warning system. In my mind Seir connotes intense awareness, with undertones of fear or reverence and the wish for self-preservation. The people of Javan[131] have chosen the hairy he-goat as their symbol, and from what I hear, they have some great philosophers and mathematicians."

"Yes, and the people of that country are also renowned for their sexual orgies," Rebekah countered. "Besides, Seir sounds too much like the word for storm, tempest or rage. It suggests to me a person of violence. Metaphorically it suggests out-of-control human passions.

---

[131] now Greece

Rather than alertness, I still think the stronger connotations of Seir are the negative ones. To call someone a hairy old goat is to suggest that he isn't too bright and he has nothing but sex on his mind."

"You made your point, dear," Isaac replied. "We won't call him Seir. By the way, which one is the firstborn?"

This was a very important question. A question that had implications for a lifetime.

"The red, hairy one," Rebekah answered, cringing at using the words 'edom' and 'seir', but not knowing how else to indicate the unnamed baby.

"So he *was* like the goat," Isaac remarked. "He was aware that it was time to be born. He wanted the privileges of the firstborn, so he acted. He came out first."

Rebekah laughed.

"Maybe that's what all the kicking in the womb was about," she said. "Maybe they were fighting for supremacy, for the rights of the firstborn. When the contractions started, the little red hairy one was the first one out the door. He acted. He got the job done."

"So let's call him Esau—doer," Isaac suggested. "That indirectly implies alertness without all the negative connotations."

"Esau, it is," Rebekah agreed. "If we don't name him quickly, he will be called Edom or Seir by default."

"What about our other son?"

"He came out right behind his brother, hanging onto Esau's heel."

"So let's call him Jacob—'he grasps the heel.' "Agreed."

Isaac was pleased that that decision was so easy.

"We'll announce their names when they're circumcised at eight days of age."

It wasn't until later that Isaac and Rebekah thought about the negative connotations of Jacob's name. Abraham thought of it when he heard the name Jacob, but he wasn't about to dampen the joy of the proud new parents.

* * *

Right from the beginning it was obvious that the twins were not identical. Esau's redness soon faded, as his mother predicted it would. But he remained remarkably hairy. Jacob was as smooth as Esau was hairy.

Esau was rightly named. He was a doer. As soon as he could crawl, he was exploring his surroundings and beyond. Jacob was less daring. But wherever little Esau went, little Jacob was not far behind. He didn't want to be outdone by his brother.

Watching them crawl on the floor of the tent with Esau in front, Isaac commented, "There goes our little doer."

"Yes," Rebekah replied, "and Jacob is right behind him, trying to keep up, trying to grasp his heel, trying to get ahead of Esau."

* * *

As the twins grew, their differences became more evident.

Esau's proclivity to act reminded Isaac of Rebekah's quick offer to water Eliezer's camels. His interest in exploring things further from home reminded Isaac of Rebekah's quickness to agree to leave her home and move to Canaan to marry a man she had never met.

Esau loved the open country and soon showed signs that he would grow up to be a skillful hunter. Esau was barely thirteen when he proudly brought home a deer he had shot with his bow and arrow. Isaac had been brought up on beef and lamb and goat meat, but when Esau started bringing home wild game, Isaac soon developed a taste for it. Because Esau was so much like his mother, Isaac was drawn to him.

Jacob was not as adventurous as his brother Esau. So he spent more of his time close to home inside the great semicircle of tents formed by his father's and grandfather's people. As a child, Jacob loved to sit on his grandfather Abraham's lap and listen to him tell stories and talk about Yahweh. As a young boy, Jacob enjoyed spending his days with the flocks and learning about animal husbandry.

Jacob took special interest in the Covenant Yahweh had made with Abraham. Esau, unlike Jacob, usually wandered out to play or hunt when the topic of Yahweh or the Covenant came up. He was bored by his grandfather Abraham's stories.

Isaac loved both his sons dearly, but he had to admit that Esau was his favorite. He looked forward to the extra time he would have to spend with his firstborn son in order to teach him more about Yahweh and the Covenant. He would need to invest a lot of time in the one through whom Yahweh's promises would be fulfilled.

* * *

When the twins were thirteen, Abraham started talking to Isaac about the need for the boys to take a stand for Yahweh.

"Do you remember what happened when you were thirteen?" Abraham asked Isaac.

"Remember! How could I forget?"

"Even though you had been taught about Yahweh all your life," Abraham reminded his son, "you needed to declare your personal faith. You had to demonstrate to God and to the world that you believed the Covenant promises. Against all logic, you let me bind you on the altar as I prepared to sacrifice you at Yahweh's command. You and I both believed that God could raise you from the dead if that's what it took for him to fulfill the Promise through you.

"Now your sons are old enough to choose to follow Yahweh," Abraham told Isaac. "They are old enough to declare that they love Yahweh with all their heart and with all their soul and with all their strength. They are old enough to be Sons of the Commandment."

"What do you propose, Father?" Isaac asked. "Yahweh hasn't told me to sacrifice my sons."

Abraham chuckled. "I know. And I don't expect you to tie them to an altar! But you could organize a ceremony in front of all our people to acknowledge that your faith and mine is being passed to the next generation. I'm 173 years old, and all my contemporaries are dead. I don't expect to live forever. I would take great pleasure in seeing that before I die."

Isaac hesitated. He knew Jacob would jump at the idea, but he wasn't so sure that Esau was ready to make such a declaration.

"I'll talk to the boys," Abraham offered. "I'll tell them our story once more."

To Isaac's surprise and pleasure, both boys agreed to the ceremony. Abraham coached them as to what he expected of them. He outlined in general what they should say, but stressed that it should be in their own words and spoken from the heart.

Abraham opened the ceremony by addressing all his household.

"Hear, O my people: Yahweh our God, Yahweh is one. Love Yahweh your God with all your heart and with all your soul and with all your strength. This commandment is to be upon your hearts. Impress it on your children. Talk about it when you sit at home and when you walk along the road, when you lie down and when you get up. Write it on the entrance to your tent.[132] My grandsons are sons of this commandment. Listen to their declarations."

As the boys spoke, everybody listened attentively. Abraham, Isaac and Rebekah beamed with pride at their speeches. Then Abraham led his grandsons in their vows.

"I, Esau," Abraham prompted.

"I, Esau, with God's help, resolve to love Yahweh my God with all my heart, with all my soul, and with all my strength. On this day, in the presence of these witnesses, I declare myself to be a Son of the Commandment."

Then it was Jacob's turn. Afterwards, Abraham led his household in a vow.

"We solemnly pledge before God to pray for Esau and Jacob, and to encourage them in their walk with God," they said in unison.

Later that night Isaac and Rebekah discussed the ceremony. Isaac had nothing but praise for the events of the day. Rebekah had reservations.

"Did you notice that Jacob sounded as though he meant it, while Esau did not?" she asked.

---

[132] Adapted from Deuteronomy 6:4-9

"Oh, Rebekah!" Isaac said in exasperation. "Why do you have to spoil a wonderful day by criticizing Esau? Just because his speech was shorter doesn't mean he didn't mean it. I do have to admit, though, that Jacob surprised me with his passionate delivery."

24

The Death of Abraham

Though Abraham always took a keen interest in the welfare of his livestock, eventually he grew too old to follow the annual migration of his flocks. Putting his servants in charge of his herds and flocks, Abraham retired with his wife Keturah to Hebron. From there he could survey most of the land of Canaan and dream of the day when his descendants would settle there in permanent dwellings and fill the land.

Jacob was not happy to see his grandfather Abraham grow weaker, but he was delighted to have the opportunity to spend more time with him. Jacob, like his father Isaac, was fascinated by the stories Abraham told about hearing Yahweh's voice and about the Covenant promises and blessings.

"As a son of Isaac," Abraham told Jacob one day, "you will live under the general blessing of Yahweh, but the everlasting Covenant promises and future blessings to 'all peoples on earth' will be passed on to the firstborn—your brother Esau."

"That's not fair!" Jacob objected. "Esau doesn't even care about the Covenant promises."

"Nevertheless," Abraham replied, "that is the way it works. Yahweh promised that I will be the father of kings, the father of many nations. But only one of those nations will possess the land of Canaan. Anybody can live under Yahweh's blessing simply by choosing to follow him in faith. But the everlasting Covenant and its specific promises cannot apply to everybody. Only one line will produce the future One through whom all peoples on earth will be blessed."

Jacob wasn't satisfied with that answer. He had never wanted his brother to get the better of him. When they were little, he openly competed with Esau. As they grew, he learned to compete in more subtle ways. Now in his early teens, Jacob desperately wanted both Esau's birthright, which included the Covenant promises, and the blessing due to the firstborn.

* * *

In his old age, Abraham talked increasingly to his family about "his people." Isaac, Rebekah and Jacob spent hours in his company, but Esau usually wandered away to join his friends in more active pursuits.

"When Yahweh first spoke to me," Abraham told the three who were interested, "he told me to leave my people. I left my relatives in Ur, then I left my father and brother in Haran, then I parted from Lot, who moved to Sodom. I have come to realize that Yahweh took me away from my former people in order to give me a new people. In Canaan, my people included not just my immediate family, Sarah and Ishmael, but all my servants, whether they were bought with my money or born into my household.

"When he established his Covenant with me, Yahweh said that any male born in my household or bought with my money who was uncircumcised would be 'cut off from *his* people.'[133] That was when I realized that Yahweh's people and my people may not be exactly the same thing. All of my people are Yahweh's people, but Yahweh's people are more than the men in my household who have been circumcised and the female members of their families."

"So Yahweh's people," said Isaac, "are not defined purely by circumcision?"

---

[133] Genesis 17:14

"No," responded Abraham, thinking carefully as he spoke. "Circumcision is neither a guarantee nor a requisite for being included in Yahweh's people. Yahweh's people are all who love and obey him. I feel a kinship with all who love Yahweh. My beloved Sarah. My father Terah. Ancestors like Shem and Shelah and Eber who taught me about Yahweh. Even people I never met—like Noah, Methuselah, Enoch, Seth and Abel. None of them was circumcised, yet they all loved Yahweh and put their faith in him. I want to embrace all of Yahweh's people as my people. When I reach the Heavenly City, I will truly be gathered to my people."

"Now my earthly pilgrimage is almost over," said Abraham. "I'm tired of walking as an alien in a foreign country. I'm tired of moving my tent from place to place. I'm going Home."

"Don't you feel any attachment to Canaan?" Isaac asked in surprise. "After all, you have walked up and down through it for a hundred years, and Yahweh said he would give it to you."

"Canaan is my land in promise but not yet in fact," replied Abraham, "Legally I own almost none of it. Just the tomb here in Hebron that I bought for my beloved wife Sarah, and another tomb in Shechem that I bought from the sons of Hamor.[134] You may wonder why I purchased tombs for the dead but no land for the living."

"I was about to ask that," said Isaac.

"Because it will be many generations before my descendants possess Canaan and settle in it."

"How do you know that?" asked Rebekah.

"Long ago, before Ishmael was born, Yahweh told me that my descendants will be strangers in a country not their own and that they will be enslaved and mistreated for four hundred years.[135] Yahweh told me I would die in peace at a good old age, then he said, 'In the fourth generation your descendants will return here to this land.'"[136]

"So if your descendants will be away from this land for four generations, there is no point in buying property," concluded Isaac.

---

[134] See Acts 7:16
[135] See Genesis 15:13
[136] See Genesis 15:16

"Right," said Abraham. "In the mean time, who knows how many of my descendants will die here? Hence the tombs. Yahweh knew that I needed to learn to live with the insecurity of not belonging to any country so that I could look forward to his country—Heaven. There I will live one day soon. There I will finally meet the rest of my people."

Isaac, Rebekah and Jacob were silent for a while. They could not imagine life without Abraham.

* * *

When Jacob was fifteen, his grandfather Abraham took a turn for the worse. Sensing that his remaining time on earth was short, Abraham gathered his entire family around him for final instructions. He announced that Isaac would be the sole heir of his estate. Then he made sure that Hagar and his wife Keturah were well cared for financially, gave generous gifts to Ishmael and to Keturah's six sons, and sent them all eastward, away from Isaac.[137]

Isaac, Rebekah and Jacob spent as much time as they could at Abraham's bedside. Esau, uncomfortable with the thought of death, stayed only long enough to be respectful. A few days later Abraham breathed his last and was gathered to his people. He was 175.[138]

Isaac did his best to notify his half brothers of their father's death. He had no idea where Keturah's sons had gone, but he had a hunch where he might find Ishmael—and it wasn't east.

Beer Lahai Roi was in the neighborhood of Kadesh, on the border between Canaan and Egypt. Here Ishmael would technically be out of the land of Canaan, the land God had promised to Abraham's descendants, but still in familiar territory. Here his mother Hagar, pregnant and running away from her mistress Sarai, had met the angel of Yahweh, who saw Hagar's misery. He had told her she was carrying a son whom she was to name Ishmael and promised to give her descendants too numerous to count.

---

[137] See Genesis 25:1-6
[138] See Genesis 25:7-8

Here, at the age of thirteen, Ishmael began to comprehend what it would mean to him when Sarah gave birth. He would no longer be considered Abraham's number one son. Ishmael began to resent Isaac even before he was born.

Six years later, during a party for Isaac's fifth birthday, Sarah threw a tantrum because Ishmael was pestering Isaac. When Sarah insisted that Ishmael and Hagar be sent away, Abraham was distressed. But Yahweh assured him that this was part of his plan to make sure that Isaac was the son of the Promise. Ishmael and Hagar ended up wandering in the desert of Beersheba, dying of thirst and crying. Ishmael cried from thirst; Hagar cried at the prospect of watching her son die. God heard Ishmael crying and reassured Hagar that Ishmael would become a great nation. Only then did Hagar spy the well nearby.

On that day, Ishmael became acutely aware of the significance of his name, 'God hears.' It was a constant reminder that God could hear him anywhere. He marveled that, though he was merely whimpering while his mother was sobbing out loud, God heard *him*. El Roi specifically told Hagar, "God has heard *the boy* crying."[139]

Sitting beside the well which his mother had named Beer Lahai Roi, the well of the Living One who sees me, Ishmael hid his face in his hands and let the tears flow. Being sent away prior to Abraham's death reminded him of being sent away the first time. Both dismissals were for the same reason—to make sure that Isaac was recognized as the son of the Promise. Ishmael had long since reconciled himself to not being considered the firstborn son, but being denied any place in Abraham's family hurt him deeply. He loved Yahweh. He had been circumcised. Unlike Isaac, who had been circumcised eight days after birth, Ishmael's circumcision was his own choice, not a choice of his father's.

While Ishmael sat grieving, he felt a light touch on his shoulder. He looked up to see Isaac, who also looked sad.

"Father died two days ago," Isaac said gently, "but we haven't buried him yet. We wrapped his body in spices and left him in his tent. Would you like to help me place his body in the tomb with my mother?"

---

[139] Genesis 21:17

Ishmael was grateful for the opportunity to pay his last respects to his father. On the journey back to Hebron the half-brothers dealt with their grief by reminiscing about Abraham. Isaac shared with Ishmael Abraham's focus in his latter days about being gathered to his people.

"I know I am not the son of the Promise," Ishmael responded, "but I am Abraham's people. I am Yahweh's people. I willingly chose to be circumcised. I know I am not the easiest man to get along with, but I love Yahweh. When I die, I will be gathered to your people and mine."[140]

In Hebron the two gently laid Abraham's body to rest beside his beloved Sarah in the cave of Machpelah near Mamre in the field of Ephron son of Zohar the Hittite, the field Abraham had bought from the Hittites. Together they rolled a giant stone over the mouth of the cave.

For seven days Isaac and Ishmael sat shoeless in ash-covered clothes in Abraham's tent receiving condolences from friends and neighbors. Neither of them washed or shaved for the entire week. The visitors sat in silence until they numbered at least ten men. Then Isaac would stand and address them. Following that, the visitors would share memories of Abraham.

"He was a great man," was a common refrain. "He died at a good old age, an old man and full of years," said others. "He taught me to love Yahweh," said many. But the epitaph which gave Isaac the most satisfaction to hear was: "He was God's friend."[141]

---

[140] See Genesis 25:17
[141] See James 2:23

25

Friction Over the Firstborn

Following Abraham's death, Ishmael bade farewell to Isaac. Both knew there would be no lasting peace between them. Ishmael respected Abraham's wishes by moving close to the border of Egypt. Yahweh's prophecy concerning Ishmael had come true. He was a wild donkey of a man. He couldn't get along with anybody for long. His hand was against everyone and everyone's hand was against him.

Hagar, like Sarah, had only one son. Ishmael had no full brothers. Having been the concubine of the legendary Abraham, Hagar would consider no suitor of lesser status. Having once been the heir apparent of Abraham, Ishmael couldn't get along with any of his half-brothers. Not with Isaac. Not with any of Keturah's sons. And Ishmael's own sons did no better—they lived in hostility toward all their brothers.

Isaac wanted no part in the quarreling and hostility in Ishmael's family. He hated quarreling. He even had difficulty resolving disagreements with his wife. Isaac also pretended that there was no rivalry between his own two sons.

Jacob, however, knew differently. The rivalry between him and his brother Esau had been there as far back as he could remember. Weren't brothers supposed to have a special bond of friendship? Not in this family.

Maybe it was because they were twins. Or maybe it was because their parents disagreed about who would have the birthright. That was more likely it, thought Jacob.

The firstborn was always treated with special affection by his parents. He would enjoy special rights and privileges during his lifetime, and upon his father's death he would receive a double portion of his father's estate.

But with the privileges came double responsibility. Men postponed marriage until they were well enough established to support a wife and family, but women were married off almost as soon as they reached puberty. That way their husbands could be sure they were marrying a virgin. As a result, most wives were significantly younger than their husbands, and the wife usually survived her husband. When the father died, the firstborn stepped into the patriarchal role. Not only must the firstborn take care of his mother until her death, he must also care and provide for any unmarried sisters. That is why parents insisted from early childhood that siblings respect the firstborn almost as much as they would respect their father.

Besides the responsibility of caretaker, the firstborn also had the spiritual responsibility of carrying on the family religion. Therefore the firstborn was groomed in religious duties. This was not unique to followers of Yahweh. One had only to look around to his neighbors to see anyone who was serious about his religion diligently teaching the eldest son the fine points of practicing that religion.

"That's Esau's problem," Jacob thought. "He has no quarrel with the caretaker responsibilities, it's the spiritual responsibilities that rub him the wrong way."

Isaac was a traditionalist. Esau was the firstborn; by virtue of that fact, he had the birthright. Jacob had missed the birthright by a matter of seconds. He came out grasping Esau's heel. But the birthright could not be shared. No tie for twins!

Rebekah was not so bound by tradition as her husband Isaac.

"Exceptions prove the rule," Rebekah argued, "and Yahweh made an exception to the rule right from the start. Cain was Adam's firstborn and should have had the birthright, but he forfeited his birthright by murdering his brother Abel. With Abel dead and Cain disqualified, someone else had to be chosen to inherit the birthright. The choice had to be made very carefully. A hundred and thirty years had passed since God introduced Eve to Adam. They had many children. How else could Cain have married and built a city? But none of Adam's living sons could hold a candle to Abel when it came to following Yahweh. It wasn't until Seth was born that God found someone who could be trusted with the birthright. Seth followed Yahweh with all his heart; therefore Seth's name was recorded in the godly line.

"Seth was the polar opposite of Cain," Rebekah continued explaining to Isaac. "Cain openly deserted the beliefs of his father Adam. Seth just as openly declared himself on Yahweh's side. He started public, formalized assemblies of worship and proclaimed the name of Yahweh.[142] As a result, men began calling themselves by the name of Yahweh.[143] Those who followed Cain's example called themselves 'sons of men.' Those who followed Seth's example called themselves 'sons of Yahweh.' Through Seth's line came Noah, the one Yahweh chose when he decided to destroy the earth with the Flood and start over again with righteous people."

"So how does that fit our sons' situation?" Isaac asked.

"Open your eyes," Rebekah said. "Don't you see? Look at Esau. He is just like Cain. No, he hasn't murdered his brother—yet. But what was the argument about in Cain and Abel's case? It was over how to worship Yahweh. That's why I want you to transfer the birthright to Jacob. Yahweh told me before the twins were born that the older will serve the younger. Don't you think that means that Jacob will inherit the promises given to Abraham? Don't you think Yahweh foresaw that Jacob would love him more than Esau would? Don't you think we, as the boys' parents, should stand by Yahweh's will?"

"How can you compare Esau to Cain?" Isaac retorted angrily. "He hasn't done anything to disqualify himself from Yahweh's favor."

---

[142] Consider Genesis 4:26, YLT: ". . . then a beginning was made of preaching in the name of Jehovah."

[143] See margin, Genesis 4:26, NASB

"Yet," said Rebekah under her breath so quietly that Isaac didn't hear.

Isaac was not willing to concede to Rebekah that the birthright should be transferred from Esau to Jacob. He determined to redouble his efforts to teach his sons, especially Esau, the ways of Yahweh. Isaac spent many evenings telling and retelling the stories that he had learned from his father Abraham. Stories Abraham had learned from his forefathers. Stories that had been passed down from generation to generation through the godly line from Adam to Noah. Stories that Noah continued to tell to his descendants for 350 years after the Great Flood.

When Esau and Jacob sat side by side listening to these stories, it was increasingly obvious who was more interested, not just in the stories, but in issues of faith and practice. Jacob was fascinated by the names of God, just like Isaac himself. Jacob wanted to know as much as possible about Yahweh's promises to Abraham. Esau learned just enough to keep his father from exploding in frustration. Esau was content to learn how to perform the Sabbath rituals; Jacob wanted to explore the meanings behind them.

From time to time in conversations with Isaac, Rebekah raised the issue of Jacob's interest and Esau's indifference.

"Noah discerned that his second son Shem was more interested in Yahweh than his two brothers," she argued, "so Noah spent more time with him, teaching him the ways of Yahweh. In each succeeding generation, the first son to demonstrate a determination to follow Yahweh with all his heart received the most careful instruction from his father. Sometimes that was the firstborn; sometimes it wasn't. The ways of Yahweh are too important to be treated casually."

"You mean that the Covenant promises are too important to be entrusted to Esau," Isaac said, putting into words what Rebekah had been careful not to say.

"Exactly," replied Rebekah brightly, hoping that Isaac was about to agree.

"You still want me to transfer the birthright and the blessing of the firstborn to Jacob."

"Yes."

"I'll do it if Yahweh tells me to," Isaac replied. "He still hasn't said anything to me about my sons."

"You're still upset that Yahweh spoke to me and not to you," said Rebekah.

"No, I'm upset that you won't let go of the silly notion that Yahweh spoke to you," Isaac shot back.

Rebekah's shoulders drooped. What would it take to convince Isaac? she wondered.

One evening when the family was relaxing together, Jacob raised a question.

"We've heard over and over again the story of Grandma Sarah. That she was barren. That she finally gave birth at the age of ninety," said Jacob. "It seems as if the whole world knows that story. But Grandpa Abraham told me something before he died that I wasn't aware of. He said that you were barren, too, Mother. Is that true?"

Rebekah was glad that Jacob had raised the question. Isaac didn't like to discuss details around the birth of his sons. It only opened the door for Rebekah to tell people that she believed Yahweh had spoken to her. Now she had the chance to say something.

"Yes, but your father prayed for me, and Yahweh answered his prayer—with not one son, but two!"

Rebekah was about to say more when her husband caught her eye, gave her a stern look of warning, and immediately changed the subject. Jacob noticed the tension between his parents and decided to bring up the topic with his mother in private.

Knowing how much his father Isaac longed to hear Yahweh's voice, Jacob was open-mouthed to learn that Yahweh had spoken to his mother. He was even more surprised at what Yahweh had said to her.

"You mean that Yahweh wants *me* to have the Covenant promises and not Esau?" he asked incredulously.

Rebekah nodded.

"Why haven't you and Father said so before?"

"Your Father doesn't believe me. He doesn't believe Yahweh spoke to me."

"Then you have to convince him."

"I've tried. Believe me, I've tried. Ever since before you were born."

Jacob was stunned both to learn what Yahweh had said and to learn that his father didn't believe it. For a long while he was silent as the truth sank in. Finally he spoke.

"So the birthright belongs to me—or should belong to me."

Rebekah nodded.

"And Yahweh wants me to have the blessing of the firstborn."

Rebekah nodded.

"But Father won't give it to me."

She nodded again.

"What can we do? Father won't give it to me, and I can't see Esau giving it to me." Jacob thought for a moment. "Maybe I can buy it from him."

Jacob and Rebekah discussed what might be an acceptable price and hoped that Esau's seeming indifference to spiritual things might result in his agreeing to a price Jacob could afford. They agreed not to mention any negotiations to Isaac. Jacob wanted to go immediately and find out what price might be acceptable to Esau, but Rebekah stopped him.

"You can't say anything to Esau now," Rebekah said.

"Why not?"

"You aren't of age," she replied. "Any sale you make will be overruled by your father. Only when you are fully adult—when you are thirty—will you be able to make a binding purchase of something as valuable as a birthright."

Jacob was disappointed to learn he would have to wait. Then he smiled. He would have many years to plan his strategy carefully. It would be a foolproof strategy.

26

Signs of Rebellion

Esau picked up his bow and slung his quiver of arrows over his shoulder.

"Where do you think you are you going?" asked his father Isaac.

"Out to hunt wild game," Esau replied.

"Oh, no. Not today you don't," said Isaac.

"Why not?"

"The sun will have set before you return."

"So? Dusk and dawn are the best times for hunting."

"But the Sabbath begins at sundown. You know better than to go hunting on the Sabbath."

Esau grimaced. "I forgot," he said with a pout. He hated the inactivity of the Sabbath. Isaac was pretty sure Esau hadn't forgotten, but he let the issue pass. He didn't like to get into arguments with his son.

"Besides," said Isaac, "I want you to lead the Sabbath worship for the family today. I have showed you many times what to do and how to do it. Being the firstborn son means more than getting the best portions of meat to eat. You also have the responsibility of passing on the ways of Yahweh to the next generation. You start by practicing on your brother and your parents while I am still around to watch and teach and correct you."

Esau put his bow and arrows back in their place, walking past his twin brother Jacob as he did so.

"I despise this Yahweh crap," he muttered under his breath.

"What did you say?" Isaac asked.

"Nothing."

Isaac looked inquiringly at Jacob, who shrugged his shoulders as if he hadn't heard.

Jacob had heard, but he said nothing. A few years ago he would have tattled on his brother, but not any more. He knew Esau would look for opportunities to get back at him later. It wasn't worth it.

"Esau, go out to the flock and select a sheep for the evening sacrifice," Isaac said.

"Why can't Jacob do it?" Esau asked.

"Yes, Father, please give me a turn." Jacob looked pleadingly at his father. "Please. I enjoy going through the flock. You know I have an eye for selecting the strongest and best."

"Yes, Jacob, I know you are good at it. My flocks are increasing rapidly and getting stronger and better under your care. But this is for the Sabbath. Esau is the firstborn, and it is his responsibility."

Both young men were disappointed, but they resigned themselves to their father's wishes. Esau walked out of the tent. He knew there was no point arguing.

"And Esau, while you are selecting the sheep, prepare some thoughts on Cain and Abel for our worship time."

Esau scowled, but he didn't dare to outwardly disobey his father. Selecting a sheep gave him something to do, but it was nothing like the thrill of hunting.

"Your brother had better bring a good sheep," Isaac said to Jacob. "Last time he brought a diseased one."

Rebekah entered the tent just in time to hear.

"Remember the time he brought a crippled one?" she said. "'It had to be put down anyway,' Esau said, 'and there's nothing wrong with the meat. It's perfectly good to eat.'"

Rebekah continued, "Esau sees this as just culling the flock so the best remain to breed. 'Killing two birds with one stone,' Esau once said."

Isaac sighed. "I have done my best to teach him that Yahweh deserves our best, but he doesn't seem to care."

"I remember," Jacob added, "when Esau brought an antelope which he had just caught for the Sabbath. 'It's a clean animal,' Esau said when you objected. 'It has cloven hooves and chews the cud.'"

Isaac sighed again. "Yes, but it didn't belong to him. It had cost him nothing. Yahweh requires that we bring a sacrifice from our own possessions—from our own flocks and herds."

At the sound of a sheep bleating just outside the tent, Isaac looked up in surprise.

"That didn't take long."

Isaac got up to look outside. Jacob and Rebekah joined him.

"Esau," Isaac said, "Are you sure you got the best?"

Before Esau could reply, Isaac's surprise turned to horror.

"Esau!" Isaac spoke in an uncustomarily loud voice. "How could you?"

"What?" Esau pretended to be surprised at his father's reaction. "It's a sound healthy one."

Isaac was apoplectic. His mouth opened and closed wordlessly several times. Finally he was able to speak.

"It's blind!" he thundered. "You can't sacrifice a blind animal! You know that you can't offer a blemished animal to God Almighty!"

Esau looked around at his family with a smirk on his face.

"It was a joke," he said lamely. His eyes rested on his brother, hoping he would share the joke, but Jacob was as horrified as his parents. "Besides, it's only blind in one eye."

"A joke!" Isaac shouted. "A joke? Yahweh is no joking matter!"

Esau had never seen his mild-mannered father so angry. With uncharacteristic submission Esau turned around without a word, leading the sheep behind him.

"Esau, wait! I'll come with you."

Jacob ran to catch up. For once Esau looked happy for his brother's company.

"I don't get what Father was so upset about," Esau complained to Jacob as soon as they were out of earshot of their parents. "We don't eat the eyes. We don't even burn them on the altar as an offering to God. They get discarded and burned on the garbage heap along with the head and the intestines."

"That's not the point," said Jacob. "Before the animal is slaughtered, we put our hands on its head. In doing so, it becomes our substitute. A flawed sheep is no better than a flawed human being. It is no substitute. Such an offering does not prepare us to meet at Yahweh's table."

"I find all the rules and regulations associated with Yahweh's table ridiculous," Esau blurted out defiantly. "Utterly absurd! Contemptible!" Jacob had never heard Esau express his contempt for the things of Yahweh so openly, but he wasn't exactly surprised. He had often noticed Esau's facial expression and heard him mutter things under his breath when his father was trying to teach him the finer points of following Yahweh.

Isaac shook his head slowly as he watched his sons disappear in the direction of the flock. He sat down cross-legged on the ground. Rebekah remained standing.

"They are approaching thirty—the age at which most young men marry and leave home," Isaac said thoughtfully.

"Thirty," Rebekah repeated, settling down beside him. "The age of maturity. The age of responsibility." She paused. "But Esau isn't mature."

"The townspeople think he is," Isaac countered. "They see him as mature and successful. He is certainly a skillful hunter. And he makes a good living selling wild game. The meat commands a good price in the marketplace, and artisans outbid each other for the horns of exotic animals."

"Yes," Rebekah said slowly, "Esau has matured outwardly, but . . . ." Her voice trailed off.

"I know what you are going to say," said Isaac. "But . . . he is not mature spiritually." They had had this conversation before. "He is not yet responsible enough to pass on the ways of Yahweh to the next generation. Maybe it is a good thing that he has not married yet."

"Is it merely immaturity?" Rebekah prodded, "Or is it something deeper than that?"

"What do you mean?" asked Isaac.

Rebekah didn't answer immediately. She knew from experience that Isaac was not open to criticism of Esau, their firstborn.

"What do you mean?" Isaac pressed her.

"Sometimes," Rebekah started slowly, "sometimes I think it's a deep-seated rebellion."

Rebekah braced herself for Isaac's denial and defense of his firstborn, but their conversation was cut short as they saw their sons returning.

When the young men reached their parents' tent, Isaac rose to inspect the sheep Esau was leading. He bent over to examine it thoroughly, then straightened with satisfaction.

"Good work, Esau," he said. "You have picked a flawless sheep."

"Thanks," Esau muttered. He glanced briefly at his father, then looked back at the sheep but not at his brother.

Jacob spoke, almost proudly. "I'll bet you couldn't find a better sheep if you picked it yourself, Father."

Jacob looked at his father, then at his mother. Rebekah's gaze held his as if trying to discern more than Jacob was saying. Was he praising his brother, or was he telling her that he himself had picked the sheep?

"Continue with your Sabbath preparations, Esau," Isaac said. "I'll watch."

"Whose tent are we meeting in for the Sabbath?" Esau asked. "Yours or mine?"

"Seeing you are leading the Sabbath preparations, let's meet in your tent," said Isaac.

"Alright, Father."

There were three tents pitched close together—one tent for Isaac and Rebekah, and one each for Esau and Jacob. To the right of the three tents was a well, and a hundred yards beyond that stood an altar.

Isaac had built the altar when he first moved to this place near Beer Lahai Roi. The altar was made of rough stones carefully selected and skillfully arranged together without mortar to make a relatively flat top. Over the years the ashes of many sacrifices had filled in the spaces between the rocks, making the altar even more stable.

The town of Beer Lahai Roi had sprung up around a spring which created an oasis in the desert. Isaac's well drew water from the same source as Beer Lahai Roi, only underground.

Beyond the altar and on the opposite side of the well from Isaac's family's three tents were many more tents. All of their inhabitants worked for Isaac as sheep and cattle herders and domestic servants. They, together with their families, formed a tent town almost as big as the town of Beer Lahai Roi.

Rebekah rose to her feet, then she and the three men walked to the entrance of Esau's tent. First Isaac, then Rebekah and Jacob stretched out their right hands and placed them on the head of the sheep. Esau glanced around at his family, then slowly did the same.

Remembering Rebekah's recent comment about rebellion, Isaac noticed Esau's hesitation. Was there reluctance on Esau's part, Isaac wondered, to admit he was a sinner? Did he fail to surrender his heart to God?

Isaac raised his head to the sky while holding his hand on the sheep's head.

"Yahweh, God of my father Abraham," he prayed, "we recognize that You are holy and we are sinners. We recognize that we deserve to die for our sins. By placing our hands on this animal, we transfer our sins to it in faith that you accept its death in our place. This sheep is now our substitute. Amen."

"Amen," Rebekah and Jacob echoed in unison. Esau shuffled his feet, then turned and led the sheep past the well and toward the altar a hundred yards away.

Isaac and Jacob followed Esau and watched. Esau pulled his hunting knife from the sheath hanging from his belt. His knife was his most valued possession. He kept it razor sharp. Expertly Esau slit the sheep's throat so that it died quickly and painlessly. He arranged the animal's body carefully so that its blood would drain completely and not pool anywhere within the carcass.

Isaac nodded his approval.

"You did that well, son."

"Thank you, Father."

This part of the ceremony was no different than killing a gazelle or any other wild animal, Esau thought.

The men said little as they waited for the blood to drain into a large bowl. Each had his own thoughts. Jacob wished that he could make the sabbatical preparations for once. Esau took his mind off the Sabbath by pretending he was working with a gazelle.

Isaac's mind wandered back to his recent interrupted conversation with his wife. Esau didn't appear to be rebelling. He seemed quite content at the moment. The skills he had developed in hunting were quite evident, and stood him in good stead for these Sabbatical duties.

Isaac watched as Esau sprinkled the blood on all four sides of the altar. He started a small fire on the altar and then added larger pieces of wood. As the fire started to burn, Esau skinned the sheep and passed the hide to a servant to be attended to later. He butchered the animal expertly, separating it into three distinct categories—to be sacrificed on the altar, to be prepared as food, and to be discarded. The head of the sheep, the intestines and most of the internal organs were removed and taken by a servant to be burned in a garbage area away from the tents. Esau then washed the abdominal cavity and the legs with water before proceeding to cut the animal into pieces. He placed the kidneys and the liver on the fire along with the fat surrounding them.

As the smell of burning fat permeated the air, Esau cut the meat into smaller pieces. He selected the best cut of meat and lifted it up to the sky. Then he picked up a second piece and waved it briefly to and fro above the flames. This meat would be his because it was his turn to make the offering. He was entitled to two portions because he was the firstborn. This was one regulation that he did not object to!

Isaac was watching his firstborn with approval. He interpreted Esau's actions as cheerfully giving his portion of the sacrifice up to God for his acceptance. Lifting it up signified his acknowledgment of Yahweh as the God of heaven. Waving it to and fro signified acknowledging Yahweh as Lord of the whole earth. Isaac saw in Esau, not rebellion, but a desire to honor Yahweh. Suddenly Isaac's reverie was cut short. "Aren't you going to cut away the rest of the fat, son?" asked Isaac with concern. He was sure that he had taught his sons to do so.

"That's the best part," Esau objected. "That's what gives the meat flavor."

"That belongs to Yahweh," Isaac said sternly. "All the fat is Yahweh's. Burning it sends a pleasing aroma up to him. Anyone who eats fat from an animal sacrificed by fire to Yahweh must be excluded from our people.[144] I've told you that many times."

"I forgot," Esau said lamely.

"Yeah, right," Jacob said just loud enough for his brother to hear. Esau gave his brother a dirty look. Quickly and skillfully Esau cut out the fat around the tail, near the backbone, and around the inner parts, and deposited all the fat on the altar. Outwardly Esau was compliant; inwardly he was upset that his father had noticed.

As the family waited for their meal to cook over a fire separate from the altar, they took turns expressing their gratitude for Yahweh's blessings to them. Esau didn't feel very thankful at the moment. He wanted a little fat with his meat, but he managed to think of something.

When everyone was comfortably full, Isaac turned to Esau.

"What thoughts have you prepared for our worship time, Son? I asked you to share something about Cain and Abel."

Esau was ready. He had heard the story of Cain and Abel so often that he could recite it by heart. After the recitation, Esau was expected to express his thoughts on the story; then the whole family would participate in discussing it. Isaac listened proudly as Esau recited word for word the story his grandfather Abraham had learned verbatim from his father and forefathers. Then Esau added his own interpretation.

"Cain means 'acquisition'," Esau began. "When he was born, his mother Eve said, 'I have gotten a man from God.'"

Jacob noticed Esau's slight misquote, but said nothing. Esau usually substituted 'God' for 'Yahweh' whenever he thought he could get away with it. His parents seemed not to notice. Esau continued.

"Children are God's gifts. Jacob and I are God's gifts to you," Esau said looking at his parents, who smiled in agreement. "Cain and Abel were not brought up in idleness. God had given their father, Adam,

---

[144] This restriction was later formalized in the Law given by Moses. See Leviticus 7:25.

work to do in the Garden of Eden, so he taught his sons to work hard. Cain worked the soil and Abel kept flocks. It's the will of God that every one of us should have something to do in this world. That's why Jacob tends sheep."

"Just like Abel," Jacob interrupted.

"I tend sheep *and* hunt," Esau shot back quickly. The rivalry between her sons was not lost on Rebekah.

Esau continued. "At the end of a set period of time—maybe on the Sabbath, which is at the end of the week, or at the end of the growing season when they kept their feast of ingathering—Cain and Abel each brought before Adam, as the priest of the family, an offering to God. I think it must have been an occasion much like ours today. Adam was teaching his sons how to worship God, just like you are teaching us, Father."

Isaac was impressed with Esau's insight. Esau knew how to impress his father, if not his mother.

"So Cain and Abel brought their offerings according to their employments," Esau continued. "We should every one of us honor God with what we have, according as he has prospered us. And Cain was the first to do so. He brought an offering from his garden. Then along came Abel with a lamb from his flock. For some strange reason that I fail to understand, God approved Abel's offering, but not Cain's. It appears to me like just plain favoritism. Cain was the firstborn, but God liked Abel better. So, understandably, Cain got into a fight with his brother, and Abel got the worst of it."

"Hold it, Son," Isaac interrupted. "That's not how it happened."

"I know what happened," Jacob volunteered. He was eager to show off his knowledge and understanding of the story. "Abel brought a blood sacrifice and Cain didn't. Abel was righteous and Cain wasn't."

"Abel was a goody-goody. Yahweh's pet! Just like you are mother's pet," Esau sneered. "Cain offered the best from his labor. Why wasn't that good enough?"

"Sin can only be atoned for with a blood sacrifice," Isaac replied, purposely ignoring the friction between the brothers. "Yahweh made that clear to Adam and Eve. When they sinned, they became aware of their nakedness, and they knew even before Yahweh talked to them that they deserved to die. That's why they hid. Abel brought a lamb from his flock and sacrificed it as per Yahweh's instructions. Cain didn't follow instructions. He brought an offering from his garden, and Yahweh wasn't pleased."

"Maybe it's more than that," Rebekah said thoughtfully. "Maybe if Cain's heart had been right, Yahweh would have accepted his offering. Adam seems to have accepted them both. But Yahweh doesn't see the way man sees. Yahweh looks at the heart. Perhaps, to a bystander, both the sacrifices of Cain and Abel would have seemed good and equally acceptable, but God saw their hearts. Abel, as we all know, was a righteous man; Cain obviously was not. If Cain had been righteous, either Yahweh would have accepted his offering or Cain would have brought a different offering—a blood sacrifice, a sacrifice of atonement."

"Abel brought the firstlings of his flock—the first and the best," Jacob said. "And . . .," here he shot a meaningful look at his brother, *"and the fat thereof."*[145] His sacrifice was an aroma pleasing to Yahweh."

Esau stuck his tongue out at his brother when his parents weren't looking.

"Cain was so angry when Yahweh didn't accept his offering that he killed his brother," said Isaac. "He couldn't take it out on Yahweh, so he murdered his brother instead. Cain's reaction is further proof that he was not a good man."

"Cain should have been angry at *himself* for not bringing an acceptable sacrifice," Jacob observed. "Instead, he got angry at Yahweh. Though his brother had done nothing to insult him or provoke him," Jacob said sweetly, glancing over at Esau, "Cain envied his brother and looked upon him as a rival and as an enemy."

Esau knew that Jacob was trying to send a message to him, but he didn't dare say so in front of his parents.

"It's not uncommon for those who have lost favor with Yahweh due to their own actions to be indignant at those whom he has favored," commented Rebekah.

---

[145] Genesis 4:4, KJV

"Cain didn't have to react as he did when Yahweh found his offering unacceptable," Isaac said. "Yahweh gave him a second chance to bring an acceptable sacrifice, but he didn't take it. Though we have offended Yahweh, if we repent and return to him, we will find mercy. Cain didn't repent; instead, he hardened his heart and murdered his brother. So he ended up doubly cursed by God. He was robbed of his occupation—the earth would no longer yield crops for him—and he was condemned to wander the earth for the rest of his life, condemned to perpetual disgrace, fearing for his life."

"I think God's sentence upon Cain was too harsh," said Esau.

"Cain said so himself. He said, 'My punishment is greater than I can bear.'"[146]

"Cain was more concerned about his suffering than about his sin," Rebekah observed. "He felt wronged by his punishment instead of acknowledging God's justice. He quarreled with the sentence instead of repenting of his sin. That shows clearly how hard his heart was."

"He went out from the presence of Yahweh," Jacob added. "That seems to indicate that he renounced all that his father Adam had taught him. He cast off all pretense of fearing Yahweh and never associated with God's people again."

"How could he?" Esau replied. "They would have murdered him!"

"Killed, not murdered," Jacob corrected. "The murder of Abel deserved the death penalty. Justice is not murder."

"But Cain didn't end up as a restless wanderer," Rebekah pointed out. "He would have been a wanderer if he had stayed anywhere close to godly people. Instead he moved east of Eden, far distant from Adam and his religious family. He built a city in defiance of God's sentence upon him."

"Yet Cain *did* end up a restless wanderer," Isaac corrected her. "Outwardly he may have appeared to be settled in his city, but to him it was 'the land of Nod,' the land of shaking and trembling. He could move away from godly people, but he could not move away from the

---

[146] Genesis 4:13, KJV

Spirit of God. Cain lived with the perpetual uneasiness of his own spirit. He never rested this side of the grave."

"Wandering isn't so bad," commented Esau. "Grandfather Abraham wandered in Canaan for a hundred years, and he was happy. He preferred the nomadic lifestyle to life in a city."

"Good point, Son," Isaac replied. "Maybe if Cain had submitted to Yahweh's sentence and wandered as a nomad, his curse might have been turned into a blessing. Abraham certainly was blessed. Abraham obeyed God's command to wander while on earth and found peace and rest in the heavenly city. Cain rejected that city and built himself one on earth. Having gone against Yahweh's instruction, he never found peace."

The family settled into silence, lost in memories of Abraham.

Finally Isaac summed up the discussion.

"Abel and Cain. Saints and sinners. The godly and the wicked. Children of God and children of the wicked one. It seems to me that all mankind are represented in one or the other. Each of us makes a choice to be like one or the other. Like Cain or like Abel."

27

Jacob Buys the Birthright

As the twins approached their thirtieth birthday, Jacob became more and more obsessed with the thought of buying the birthright from his brother Esau. He didn't discuss it with his father because he knew Isaac would disapprove. He didn't discuss it with Esau for fear that if Esau knew how much he wanted the birthright, he might raise the price beyond Jacob's reach.

Only occasionally did Jacob raise the issue with his mother. He was never sure who might overhear their conversation and report it to either his father or his brother. Jacob's main concern in such conversations was to learn how to make a transaction that would be binding. He had already been told that if he bought the birthright while he was under age, his father could overrule the sale.

The purchase of a birthright, like the purchase of a piece of land, had to be done in the presence of at least ten witnesses. Jacob had heard many times the story of his grandfather Abraham's purchase of the burial site for Sarah. He had gone to Kiriath Arba to negotiate the purchase and have it properly witnessed. Just outside the main gate of every city was a raised platform and throne on which the king sat, a stone bench long enough for ten elders to sit and a canopy over the throne and elders' bench to protect them from sun or rain. Land transactions were routinely done at the city gate with a scribe to record the duly witnessed purchases.

Isaac excused both Esau and Jacob from working with the flocks and herds on their thirtieth birthday, but they didn't spend the day together. Esau wanted to indulge his favorite pastime, hunting, so he went off into the open country with a few friends.

Jacob was happy to spend the day close to home. He built a fire and filled a big pot with his favorite recipe for lentil stew. As it simmered, he wandered in and out among the tents of his people, chatting with friends and neighbors, watching the women busy with their chores, listening to the happy laughter of children at play, and enjoying the peace and tranquility of it all. At regular intervals he came back to stir the pot, taste the stew and make sure it was seasoned to perfection with tomatoes and red peppers. When the stew was almost done, he baked a batch of flat bread over the open fire.

Late in the afternoon, as Jacob was about to sit down for his meal, he heard a commotion in the camp. Esau was returning from his day in the open country. He and his friends looked dejected. They hadn't caught a thing—not even a rabbit!

Esau was more than hungry after a long day. He was famished! Then he caught a whiff of Jacob's stew.

"How about sharing some of your stew, brother," Esau said to Jacob. "Quick! Let me have some! I'm famished!"

Now would be a good time to negotiate with Esau, Jacob thought. *Esau is distracted by his hunger. This is the perfect opportunity to buy the birthright at a price I can afford!*

In his wildest dreams Jacob hadn't dared to think he could negotiate a price so soon. With his heart pounding, he broached the subject.

"First sell me your birthright."

It came out more forcefully than Jacob had planned. He was surprised by his own boldness.

"Look, I'm about to die," Esau said impatiently. "What good is the birthright to me?"[147]

---

[147] See Genesis 25:32

Jacob couldn't believe his ears. Was Esau going to let him name his price? He knew how impulsive Esau could be, but this was truly rash. Jacob was about to make an opening offer, when another thought struck him. If he treated the matter lightly, Esau might give him a good deal.

Jacob ladled out a bowlful of stew and waved it under Esau's nose, taunting him.

"I'll sell you some stew for the birthright!" Jacob said playfully.

Esau took a deep breath, savoring the mouth-watering aroma. Jacob held his breath for the answer. He didn't expect it to be this easy.

"Like I said," Esau repeated, "I'm about to die. What good is the birthright to me when I'm dead?"

Was Esau really willing to sell his birthright for some *stew*?! Never in his wildest dreams had Jacob imagined Esau would take him seriously. Jacob couldn't believe his brother would sell such a priceless heritage for so little. But Jacob wasn't about to let such an opportunity slip past him.

"Swear to me first!" he said.

Jacob made a quick count of Esau's friends, both those who had hunted with him and those who had gathered around after the hunt. There were exactly ten! He could buy the birthright and make it legal.

"Do you, Esau, swear to sell me your birthright for this stew?" Jacob asked, raising his voice so all could hear.

"I do," Esau replied impatiently. "Now give me some stew."

Jacob was in no hurry. This had to be done right. Turning to Esau's friends, he asked, "Do you bear witness to the fact that I have purchased Esau's birthright for a bowl of stew?"

Esau's friends were in good humor and enjoying the exchange between the brothers. None of them cared two figs what Esau did with his birthright.

"We do," they replied in unison in a mock-solemn tone.

Jacob was about to run into his tent to get some parchment, ink and a quill to record the purchase, but he was afraid that if he gave his brother time to think, he would change his mind. He dared not presume too much upon Esau's weakness. But he needed some proof of purchase. How could he have proof of an oath without a written record?

Then he had an idea. If someone in the marketplace wanted to make a purchase but didn't have payment with him, he would leave his staff with the vendor until he could return with payment. A staff was something its owner would never part with lightly. It was often uniquely carved with his name or symbol. Jacob would ask for something that all would recognize as belonging to Esau. He couldn't ask for Esau's bow; he would never part with it.

"Give me one of your sandals," Jacob said to Esau. It was the only thing Esau had in his possession that he could readily part with.

"What?" Esau asked.

"Give me one of your sandals," Jacob repeated.

"What for?"

"As a token of your oath," Jacob explained, again waving the bowl of stew under Esau's nose. "If you or any of your friends try to deny this oath, I will have your sandal as proof."

By this time all Esau could think of was that tantalizing stew. He took off a sandal and handed it to his brother.

Jacob invited his brother to sit down, then handed him the bowl of stew and some bread. Esau sopped the bread in the stew and devoured it hungrily. Then Jacob served a little stew to each of Esau's friends. As they ate, the friends watched Esau in amusement. He ate so hungrily that stew dripped onto his beard.

"Hey, Esau," one said. "Your beard is red. Red from the red stew."

Esau didn't care.

"That reminds me of something I heard about you," said another. "Weren't you red all over when you were born? I heard that your father wanted to call you Edom, red, but your mother objected."

The men laughed. Jacob brought some wine in a wineskin, and the men passed it around for a drink.

Then someone chanted, "Edom! Edom!"

Soon all the men took up the chant for their friend. "Edom! Edom! Edom!"

Esau reached for the wineskin and drank deeply. When he had eaten his fill, he belched, patted his stomach contentedly, got up and walked away. His friends watched and laughed. They weren't sure whether

Esau's unsteady gait was due to too much wine or to walking with only one shoe.

The name Edom stuck. First Esau's friends called him Edom. Whenever anyone asked why, the story was told of the red stew that Jacob sold to his brother in exchange for the birthright. Esau was embarrassed at the laughter directed at him.

When Isaac found out that Jacob had purchased Esau's birthright, he was furious. But he could do nothing about it. The whole world seemed to know that Esau had sold his birthright for some red stew and now everybody was calling him Edom.

When Isaac remonstrated with Esau for selling his birthright, Esau tried to deflect his father's anger by putting the blame on his brother.

"Jacob deceived me!"

"I did not!" Jacob retorted. "You sold your birthright with your eyes wide open."

"You deceived me," Esau accused. "You're just like your name. A deceiver!"

"You just don't want to admit that you despise the birthright," Jacob replied. "It means no more to you than a bowl of stew. You care more about your stomach than about the Covenant promises. But I do care about the birthright. I want it. And now I have it! And you will never get it back! I would die before selling it back to you!"

"Stop quarrelling!" said Isaac in a voice louder than usual.

The twins were so startled to hear their father raise his voice that they stopped. After a moment of silence they walked away in opposite directions.

Isaac turned and entered his tent, but he dreaded the conversation with his wife. He knew she would approve of this turn of events. He sat down and let out a big sigh.

Rebekah allowed the silence to linger between them. Finally Isaac broke the silence.

"I suppose now you're happy. Go ahead and say it: 'I told you so!'"

"Oh, Isaac," Rebekah said sadly, "I never wanted it to happen this way. Yahweh said that the older will serve the younger, but I didn't anticipate the pain of it happening like this. Maybe if we had agreed with Yahweh and given the birthright to Jacob, there wouldn't be the rift between the brothers that exists now. If *you* had given it to Jacob, Esau wouldn't have minded. He doesn't really care about the birthright. But having his brother get it this way . . . ."

Her voice trailed off.

"So it's all *my* fault!" exploded Isaac.

Rebekah had never heard her husband so angry with her.

"No! . . . Yes . . . . Oh, I don't know," she finished lamely. "How can we know how Yahweh planned to bring it about?"

"So you still believe that Yahweh spoke to you," said Isaac, "that all of this is his will. What next? Am I supposed to give Jacob the firstborn's blessing, too?"

Rebekah didn't say anything. *When will Isaac believe that Yahweh spoke to me?* she wondered.

28

Isaac Hears God's Voice

Early in their marriage, when Isaac and Rebekah had learned that she was barren, they had resolved to walk in Abraham's footsteps of faith and learn from his lapses in faith without repeating his mistakes. They didn't want to fall into the same traps that Abraham had fallen into.

Isaac and Rebekah started well, not resorting to a surrogate wife to provide the child of promise. But the fact that Yahweh spoke to Rebekah without speaking to Isaac raised a barrier between them and seemed to stall their spiritual growth. After Esau sold his birthright to Jacob, Isaac in particular experienced a low point in his relationship with God.

Isaac spent most of his life in southern Canaan. He seldom moved his flocks and herds much north of Hebron. From Hebron he rotated his flocks annually southward into the Negev desert, going as far south as Beer Lahai Roi, before swinging westward toward the coast of the Great Sea. The Philistines lived in a narrow strip along the coast and would quite readily attack anyone they felt was encroaching on their territory. Consequently, Isaac routinely turned northward when he reached the Shephelah, a lush low valley which runs parallel to the coast, before circling back to Hebron.

Isaac enjoyed the desert, a place to be quiet and away from crowds. He looked forward to the time each year when his household tended their flocks and herds near Beer Lahai Roi. He loved to sit quietly in the evening by the well where Yahweh had spoken to Hagar and meditate on El Roi, the God who sees me. Just as Hagar had taken her troubles to Yahweh here, so Isaac poured out his troubles—especially his family troubles.

When his sons didn't get along, Isaac told Yahweh. When he argued with his wife, he told Yahweh. By talking everything out with El Roi, the God who sees it all, he could leave his troubles there at the well and present a serene front to his family and his neighbors. Isaac never heard an audible voice from Yahweh, but he always left with the distinct impression that Yahweh had heard and understood, and most of the time that satisfied Isaac. Rebekah could always tell when her husband had spent quiet time at the well.

The year following Jacob's purchase of Esau's birthright was unusually dry, so Isaac had to move his livestock more often. As his flocks restlessly searched for food, Isaac just as restlessly searched for answers.

Was Jacob's purchase of the birthright man's will or Yahweh's will? Esau's indifference to spiritual things had grown to thinly disguised contempt. Isaac had been increasingly aware of it but refused to admit it. Rebekah had tried to convince Isaac to transfer the birthright to Jacob. Jacob had rebelled against the rule which declared that the birthright should belong to Esau, and had found a way to break the rule.

Had Rebekah been right? Could it possibly be that she had heard Yahweh's voice? Why had God never spoken to *him*, the man of the household? Now, with the drought added to his personal problems, Isaac needed more than ever to hear Yahweh's voice.

As Isaac moved his livestock up through the Shephelah, he was faced with a dilemma. The land north and east was too dry to support his flocks. That left two options—Egypt to the south, or Philistia to the west. Philistine territory was closer, so Isaac decided to try there first. To secure permission from the king to live in Philistia, Isaac would have to go to Gerar.

The day before Isaac arrived there, he received the surprise of his life. He was out working with his flocks when a stranger approached.

He looked like an ordinary man, but as soon as he opened his mouth, Isaac knew it was no stranger. There was no mistaking that voice! Isaac had heard it as a thirteen-year-old when he was bound hand and foot on an altar on the top of Mount Moriah. Though many decades had passed since, he had never forgotten the sound of that voice. It was Yahweh!

"Don't go to Egypt," Yahweh said. *"Stay where I tell you. Live here in this land for a while, and I will be with you and bless you. I will give all these lands to you and your descendants. I will fulfill the oath that I solemnly promised to your father Abraham. I will make your descendants as numerous as the stars in the sky and give all these lands to your descendants. Through your seed all the nations of the earth will be blessed. And why? Because Abraham obeyed My voice and did everything I required of him, keeping my commands, my decrees and my instructions."*[148]

The stranger disappeared as quickly as he had appeared. As soon as the man left, Isaac ran to tell Rebekah. Jacob, watching from a distance, had never seen his father move so fast. He followed his father to find out what the excitement was all about.

"Rebekah!" Isaac called as he neared their tent. "Yahweh spoke to me! I heard Yahweh's voice! I heard his voice!" Isaac grabbed his wife and danced her around the tent. She laughed in happy surprise.

"What did he say?" she asked.

Isaac carefully repeated Yahweh's message word for word. He would savor these words until the day he died.

"It's so much like what he said to my father Abraham. *'I will make your descendants as numerous as the stars in the sky.'* Remember how many times we said that while waiting for a son? As the stars in the sky."

"As the sand on the seashore," Rebekah chimed in.

"Like the dust of the earth," Jacob quoted, *"so that if anyone could count the dust, then your seed could be counted."*

Isaac turned to Jacob with new appreciation.

"Well said, Son."

Maybe it's a good thing that Jacob has the birthright, Isaac thought. *He certainly values the Covenant promises.*

---

[148] See Genesis 26:2-5

"'*I will bless you*,'" Jacob continued. "'*I will give all these lands to you and your descendants. Through your seed all the nations of the earth will be blessed.*' All those were things promised to Grandfather Abraham."

"Yahweh hasn't spoken to our family for many decades, but He hasn't forgotten us," Isaac said with a happy sigh.

Rebekah didn't want to disturb her husband's happiness so she didn't say what she was thinking. *It hasn't been as many decades as Isaac likes to think. The last time Yahweh spoke to Abraham was almost 80 years ago, but it was only a little more than 30 years since He spoke to me!*

"All these promises come to us because of Grandfather," Jacob observed. "He obeyed Yahweh's voice and left Ur. Then he left the rest of his people in Haran and came to Canaan. He did everything Yahweh required of him, keeping His commands, His decrees and His instructions—even sacrificing you, Father, on Mount Moriah."

"You're right, Son," Isaac replied. "You are starting to remind me of myself and my interest in the Covenant promises."

Jacob smiled. This was the first positive reaction he had had from his father since the day he bought the birthright.

"Does that mean that one day you will give me the firstborn blessing?" Jacob asked hopefully. "That's part of the birthright, you know."

Isaac scowled. "Don't count on it, Son." He almost said, "Not a chance!" but thought it better not to shatter the new rapport that was building between him and Jacob. Rebekah brought both of them back to the present.

"Well, now we know where *not* to go," she said. "If we can't go to Egypt, our only choice is to stay right here in Philistia."

"What we have to do now is get permission from King Abimelech," Isaac said.

"If it's Yahweh's will, he will say yes," asserted Jacob.

Isaac nodded. "I'll talk to him tomorrow."

Reference to Yahweh's will reminded Isaac that Jacob had bought the birthright. Was that Yahweh's will? Isaac was still too ambivalent about the issue to say more. He walked outside to end the conversation.

29

Isaac's Failure of Faith

Much to Isaac's relief, Abimelech, king of the Philistines, received him kindly. When Isaac was ushered into Abimelech's palace, the king did not have any advisors or military officials at his side, which was a sign of peace. So Isaac stayed in Gerar.

It wasn't long until the Philistine men noticed his beautiful wife Rebekah. When one of the men enquired who she was, fear gripped Isaac's heart.

"She's my sister," he said, almost without thinking. He was afraid that these powerful people, who were quick to take up arms against those who offended them, might kill him if he stood between them and a woman they wanted.

When the men enquired as to Rebekah's age, rather than say she was "over sixty," as was the custom, Isaac said that she was "over seventy." Isaac quieted his conscience about that lie by rationalizing that it was close enough. Better for the men to think that she was a few years older than a few years younger, just in case that made a difference.

It didn't occur to Isaac that most men looking for a wife would not consider Rebekah potential marriage material. Philistia was not Egypt, and Abimelech was not Pharaoh, who made a showy display of his power by parading his harem of beautiful women down the Nile River on barges. Abimelech would not take a woman into his harem simply because she was beautiful. She must also be of child-bearing age.

Word spread throughout Gerar that the beautiful woman in Isaac's camp was his sister, but nobody made any advances toward her. One man spoke for the others when he commented that she didn't look her age. They appreciated her beauty as that of an older woman.

"Imagine what she looked like 40 or 50 years ago!" one man commented. "I would have killed for a wife like that!"

But in Isaac's eyes, Rebekah was as beautiful as the day he first saw her. He was still madly in love with her and had eyes for no other.

Though Isaac was ashamed of himself, he didn't have the courage to confess the lie and tell the truth. He didn't even have the courage to admit to Rebekah what he had done. In the days and weeks that followed, Isaac was miserable. His conscience bothered him for telling a lie. Hadn't he and his wife resolved to avoid the mistakes that his father Abraham had made and walk only in his footsteps of faith? Yahweh had promised to bless him, not to harm him and his family. Why did he lack faith to believe that?

Rebekah interpreted Isaac's glum face as depression over Esau's selling his birthright. She had no idea that it was due to a guilty conscience. She feared that to probe would only make matters worse. After all, Isaac could do nothing to restore the birthright without Jacob's consent. And Jacob would never sell what he had dreamed about for years.

Rebekah would have liked to discuss with Isaac whether what Jacob did was Yahweh's plan or whether Yahweh had some other way of bringing Jacob into the Promise. But that subject was taboo. That would require Isaac to admit that Yahweh had spoken to her. That would require Isaac to believe God for the unconventional and the non-traditional—both with regard to His speaking to a woman and with regard to giving the birthright to someone other than the firstborn.

Isaac had always objected when Rebekah had treated Jacob as the firstborn. She said it was her way of showing her faith in what Yahweh had said to her before the twins were born. Isaac called it favoritism.

When Rebekah called Isaac's treatment of Esau favoritism, he said he was merely treating *Esau* as the firstborn.

Isaac's lie caught up with him one day when Abimelech looked down from a window and saw Isaac caressing his wife. Abimelech immediately summoned Isaac and confronted him.

"Quite obviously she is your *wife*!" he shouted. "How could you say, 'She's my *sister*'?"

"Because I thought I might get killed by someone who wanted her," Isaac answered weakly.

"But think of what you might have done to *us*!" Abimelech exclaimed. "Given a little more time, one of my men might have slept with your wife; then you would have been responsible for bringing guilt down on *us*."

"You remind me of someone in my grandfather's time," Abimelech continued. "A man by the name of Abraham pulled the same stunt. My grandfather Abimelech was afraid of Abraham because he was powerful. Even more than that, he served a very powerful god—a god he called Yahweh, who was not at all like the gods of the nations around us. This god rained down fire and brimstone on Sodom and Gomorrah and completely destroyed those cities because of their wicked ways. You may have heard about it."

Isaac nodded but said nothing, his face beginning to turn red. Abimelech kept talking.

"So Grandfather Abimelech took Abraham's wife into his harem, thinking that would guarantee peace between him and Abraham. Grandfather had been told by both Abraham and his wife that she was Abraham's sister. Soon things went terribly wrong. One of Grandfather's wives gave birth to a stillborn child; another had a miscarriage. One by one, all the women in our city who were pregnant either had miscarriages or gave birth to stillborn children. None of those who wanted to get pregnant could do so . . . ."

Abimelech's voice trailed off. He noticed that Isaac was blushing and beginning to squirm.

"What's the matter?" Abimelech asked. Then the truth dawned on him. "You aren't related to this Abraham, are you?"

"Yes. He was my father," Isaac admitted in a quiet voice.

"How could you do this to us?" Abimelech thundered.

Isaac bowed his head in shame. Fear showed on Abimelech's face. "So you are the miracle son born to a ninety-year-old woman?"

Isaac nodded without looking up.

"Your god can rain down fire and brimstone on us? Your god can put powerful armies to flight? Your god can turn people to salt?"

Isaac nodded again.

Abimelech jumped into action. He called for Phicol, his commander-in-chief, to come as quickly as possible. Then he announced, "Anyone who touches this man or his wife will be put to death! Issue a public proclamation. Spread the word quickly! Make sure everyone knows."

Abimelech would gladly have chased Isaac out of his country, but he didn't dare incur the ire of his god. A very chastened Isaac hurried out of the king's presence and back to his flocks.

When Rebekah heard by way of the grape vine what Isaac had done, she was embarrassed for her husband, but she didn't say anything. She waited for him to tell her his story.

After confessing his sin to Yahweh and asking for forgiveness, Isaac stumblingly told his wife what he had done and asked for her forgiveness. She gave it freely, knowing that he was deeply sorry both for telling a lie and for repeating his father Abraham's mistake. Then they settled down to every day living, raising cattle and sheep and goats, and planting crops.

In the same year that Isaac had so foolishly and faithlessly told a lie to save his skin, he reaped a hundredfold harvest. Thus Yahweh showed to Isaac that He had freely forgiven him and that He would be faithful to His own promise to bless him.

Isaac became a very rich man, and his wealth continued to grow. He acquired so many flocks of sheep and goats, herds of cattle, and servants that the Philistines began to envy him. They wanted to get rid of Isaac, but dared not resort to warfare because of Abimelech's orders not to molest him. So they resorted to more subtle persuasion. They filled up all of Isaac's wells—the wells that had been dug during his father Abraham's lifetime—with dirt and debris.

Finally, Abimelech ordered Isaac to leave the country. "Go somewhere else," he said, "You've become more powerful than we are."[149]

Isaac could have stood up for his rights to the wells his father had dug, but he didn't. He knew the land on which he stood would belong to his people some day, but now was not the time. He simply moved away from Gerar into the nearby valley and settled there. Scattered throughout the valley were wells that his father had dug and that the Philistines had plugged up with dirt. Isaac quietly instructed his servants to reopen the wells, giving each one the same name Abraham had given them.

Abraham's old wells did not provide enough water for Isaac's rapidly multiplying flocks and herds, so Isaac's servants dug a new well. No sooner did they discover fresh water than the herdsmen from Gerar claimed it was theirs. Rather than quarrel, Isaac moved on and dug another well. The Philistines claimed that one, too.

Isaac moved further away and had his servants dig a third well. This time no one quarreled over it. Isaac named it Rehoboth, which means 'room', saying, "Now Yahweh has given us room and we will flourish in the land."

But no patch of land could sustain Isaac's livestock for long. He moved on again, ending up in what he would later discover to be Beersheba. That very night Yahweh appeared to Isaac in the same form as he had earlier. He could easily have been mistaken for an ordinary man—expect for something mysterious and very compelling about his eyes and his voice. His message was reassuring.

"I am the God of your father Abraham. Don't be afraid, for I am with you. I will bless you and will multiply your offspring because of my promise to Abraham, my servant."[150]

Yahweh used a verb tense that spoke of the future as if it were already done. Using the word "offspring", literally "seed", reminded

---

[149] Genesis 26:16. Compare GW and NLT.
[150] See Genesis 26:24

Isaac of Yahweh's earliest promises to Abraham. *Like the dust of the earth. Like the stars in the sky. Like the sand on the seashore.* Uncountable!

As Isaac and Rebekah pondered this latest message from Yahweh, they mused about how slowly Yahweh was fulfilling such a big promise. The Son of Promise was not born until Abraham was a hundred years old. That one son, Isaac, had twin boys when he was sixty years old. Those two were now men over thirty, and neither had yet married. So 115 years or more after the original promise, Abraham's descendants consisted of a "great nation" of three!

Uncountable? Hardly!

Yet Isaac and his wife resolved to believe.

"By the time my father Abraham was my age, he had heard Yahweh's voice on five different occasions—once in great detail," Isaac said. "Before he died, Father had heard Yahweh another five times, and some of those were long conversations. I have heard Yahweh's voice twice now in the span of a year, and neither of those times did he say much. I wonder how many more times I will hear his voice."

"How can you measure Yahweh's voice by the number of words?" Rebekah objected. "Look at the magnitude of the promises! And the fact that he is repeating them indicates that all of Abraham's promises are yours."

Isaac quickly admitted that his wife was right.

"It just occurred to me," he added. "On many of the occasions when Yahweh spoke to my father, Abraham built an altar and called on the name of Yahweh. He used the altar as a pulpit from which to preach in the name of Yahweh. I should have built altars long ago. Subconsciously I was waiting for Yahweh to speak to me first. Maybe if I had taken the first step, he would have spoken to me."

"Maybe if you had built an altar and preached in the name of Yahweh, you wouldn't have told Abimelech I was your sister," Rebekah said, surprising herself at her boldness. She quickly put her hand over her mouth, hoping she hadn't spoken too bluntly.

To her relief, Isaac didn't deny the possibility.

"First thing in the morning I will build an altar," Isaac declared. "I can't change the past, but I can make good choices in the future."

So that's what Isaac did. He built an altar, worshiped there, and preached in the name of Yahweh. There he pitched his tent, and there his servants dug another well.[151]

Meanwhile, Abimelech was watching. He saw that no matter what the Philistines did, Isaac prospered. Though Philistine herdsmen drove Isaac's herdsmen away from one well after another, Isaac prospered. Abimelech noticed Isaac's renewed zeal in worshiping and proclaiming Yahweh. Abimelech watched—and he feared Isaac and his god Yahweh.

The king knew that in any armed conflict with Isaac, he would lose even if he had more men in his forces. To avert the possibility of war between the Philistines and Isaac, Abimelech decided to make a treaty with Isaac.

Isaac was surprised when he was approached by Abimelech and two other men, his lawyer and his military commander.

"Why have you come here?" Isaac asked. "You obviously hate me, since you kicked me off your land."

Abimelech, under the advice of his lawyer, was careful how he worded his request.

"We can plainly see that Yahweh is with you. So we want to enter into a sworn treaty with you. Let's make a covenant—a covenant that we maintain friendly relations. Swear that you won't harm us. We have never bothered you in the past; we treated you well and let you leave us in peace. And now look how Yahweh has blessed you!"[152]

Isaac smiled to himself at the implication that Yahweh had blessed him because he had lived on friendly terms with the Philistines. He was amused at the thought that they had "let him leave in peace." Abimelech's version of the past was different from what Isaac remembered. Isaac could have pointed out that Abimelech's people kept plugging up his father Abraham's wells and kept claiming the new wells he dug, but he bit his tongue. He had not been guiltless. The lie he had told about Rebekah being his sister could have resulted in disaster.

Regardless of the reason, Isaac had to admit that Yahweh had blessed him—more because of Abraham than because of anything Isaac

---

[151] See Genesis 26:25
[152] See Genesis 26:28-29

had done. And Isaac did want peace. He hated confrontation—either with family members or with the surrounding nations. So Isaac agreed to formalize peace between his people and the Philistines.

When Isaac was introduced to Abimelech's commander-in-chief, Phicol, Isaac remembered that the name meant "tamarisk." He also noticed a grove of tamarisk trees nearby.

Isaac prepared a covenant feast to celebrate the treaty, and they ate and drank together. Early the next morning, they exchanged oaths not to interfere with each other. Then Isaac sent them on their way, and they left peacefully.

Later that same day, Isaac's servants came to him with news about a new well they had been digging.

"We've found water!" they exclaimed.

Isaac named the well Sheba, Oath; and the town that grew up there became known as Beersheba, Oath-Well.

When Isaac learned that the town by the well had been called Beersheba, it dawned on him that history was repeating itself. When he was a little boy, his father Abraham had dug a well only to have it seized by the Philistines, just like what had happened to him recently. Then and now, Abimelech, king of the Philistines, had been told that a wife was a sister. In Abraham's time the king's commander-in-chief was named Phicol, just like the current commander of Abimelech's forces. Both the Abimelech of Abraham's day and the current Abimelech had requested a peace treaty.

Abraham had killed seven lambs, cut them each in half, and arranged the halves in two rows, bloody side up. Then Abraham and Abimelech had solemnly walked between the rows. Abraham had called the place Beersheba, which can mean "well of seven" or "well of the oath." Around the well where the oath was made, Abraham had planted a grove of tamarisk trees.

It dawned on Isaac that the grove of trees he had noticed when being introduced to Phicol was the very grove that Abraham had planted! The new well Isaac's servants had dug was in the same vicinity as Abraham's well. This town had the same name Isaac's father had given it—Beersheba! This Beersheba was the very same place!

When Jacob learned that his father Isaac had heard Yahweh's voice, he was excited. No one had heard that Voice in Jacob's lifetime! Jacob was also interested to see his father build an altar and use it as a place from which to proclaim the name of Yahweh. Isaac was more excited about Yahweh now than Jacob had ever seen.

His father's renewed spiritual fervor gave Jacob new hope.

"Do you think Father will now give me the firstborn blessing?" Jacob asked his mother one day.

Rebekah shook her head sadly.

"I had hoped so, Son, but your father still won't consider it. I brought up the topic myself, but he still believes that blessing belongs to Esau."

"But I bought the birthright from Esau. The blessing is part of the birthright."

"I know, Son," Rebekah said with a sigh.

"Does Father still refuse to believe that you heard Yahweh's voice?"

"Unfortunately, yes. If Yahweh's message had been more conventional—more in line with the messages he heard, more in line with the messages to Abraham—your father might have been convinced. But Yahweh's message to me—what I *claim* was Yahweh's message to me, your father would say—is too far out."

"I bought Esau's birthright from him in a moment of weakness," Jacob said, "He despised the birthright. He doesn't care about Yahweh. But Father has no such weakness. He lives for Yahweh and the Covenant. He will give me the firstborn's blessing only if he understands that I legitimately own the birthright. So far I don't see that happening."

"Yahweh wants you to have it, Son," Rebekah replied. "I just don't know how He is going to work it out. Only He can change your father's heart and mind."

30

The Rebel

"I overheard Esau and his Hittite friends talking the other day," Jacob said one evening while he and his parents were sitting outside watching the sun set. "The Hittites told a story about someone called Gilgamesh. They swore that the story was true and that Gilgamesh was a historical figure. They said they had read the story in ancient documents—an epic poem of some kind.

"I heard Esau and his friends laughing, so I moved closer to hear what was so funny. The Hittites were telling a story that had lots of wild action and plenty of explicit sex. Apparently Gilgamesh was a vile, filthy, perverted man. I was starting to walk away when the Hittites noticed me. When I said I wasn't interested in their dirty stories, they invited me to stay and learn about their hero, a god-man who had lived shortly after the Flood.

"According to their story, Gilgamesh, the king of Erech in southern Mesopotamia, was the greatest, strongest hero that ever lived. He was a mighty hunter, a great builder and warrior, and very wise. He was also two-thirds god and one-third man. Gilgamesh founded a powerful kingdom—first building the cities of Babylon, Erech, Akkad and Calneh, then building four more cities.

"But there was a threat to his kingdom. Another powerful creature by the name of Huwawa had destroyed Gilgamesh's forefathers by drowning the whole world in a flood. There was a possibility that, having done it once, Huwawa might do it again. All Gilgamesh's people were at risk.

"Gilgamesh had two solutions. He would build a tower too high for the waters to be able to reach, and he would avenge himself on Huwawa for destroying their forefathers! To make sure that Huwawa would not trouble them anymore, Gilgamesh planned to kill him or die trying.

"'If I fall,' Gilgamesh said, 'I will establish a name for myself. "Gilgamesh is fallen," they will say, "in combat with terrible Huwawa." But if I win, they will say, "Gilgamesh, the mighty vanquisher of Huwawa!"'

"Gilgamesh went on a long journey to the Cedar Mountain to find and destroy the monster who had sent the Flood. He vanquished Huwawa and cut off his head. Then Gilgamesh went back to Erech and other cities and told the people not to worry about Huwawa anymore.

"'Huwawa is dead,' Gilgamesh told them. 'He won't trouble you any more. I killed him over in the Lebanon mountains. So just live however you like, I will be your king and take care of you.'

"What do you think of that story?" Jacob asked his parents. "It sounds like a myth, but the Hittites swore Gilgamesh was a historical figure. If that is so, why haven't I heard of him before?"

"You have heard of him, Son," Isaac replied, "but not by that name. The Hittites, Philistines and Babylonians call him Gilgamesh, which is his real name; but our people refuse to honor him by calling him by that name. We refuse to treat him as a hero. We call him Nimrod."

"Nimrod!" Jacob exclaimed. "Do you mean Nimrod, 'the mighty hunter before Yahweh'?"[153]

"Not before Yahweh in the sense that your grandfather Abraham walked before Yahweh," Isaac explained patiently. "Nimrod was before Yahweh in the sense of being *in Yahweh's face*. He was *against* Yahweh, in defiance of Him. Nimrod was not at all reverent or submissive to

---

[153] See Genesis 10:9

Yahweh. The Hittite story uses the derisive name Huwawa for Yahweh. We use the derisive name Nimrod—The Rebel—for Gilgamesh.

"The part about his building all those cities is true. But Nimrod was no hero. Nimrod saw himself as a mighty prince, a great conqueror, even as a god; but in God's sight he was nothing more than a mighty hunter.

"Nimrod started out by using his hunting skills to do good, ridding his country of wild beasts; but his motive was not altruistic. His ambition was power. Under the pretence of hunting, he gathered men under his command in pursuit of other game—*humans*—people whom he could master and bring in subjection to him. He was a mighty hunter, alright—a hunter of *men*. So he insinuated himself into the affections of those around him. They saw him as their benefactor and made him their prince.

"This put Nimrod in a position to build great cities. He began his kingdom by building Babylon. From there he aspired to make his rule universal. By the time he had built four cities, Yahweh decided to stop him. Yahweh confused people's tongues at Babylon and turned it into Babel. But even that didn't stop Nimrod. His ambition was boundless. He simply went further afield and built four more cities, one of which was Nineveh.

"Nimrod was the first person to blatantly declare that Yahweh is dead, but I doubt that he will be the last," observed Isaac. "Nimrod, a descendant of Noah and of Ham, rebelled against the religion of Noah and set up a new religion. In rebellion against the Creator, the one true God, he built a ziggurat (Assyrian for 'mountaintop'), a multi-tiered structure with a temple at its top. We call that the Tower of Babel. Nimrod built it to worship the host of heaven, with himself as the greatest of all the gods.

"Just as, before the Flood, Cain had influenced people to oppose Yahweh, so, after the Flood, Nimrod also influenced people against Yahweh. Nimrod persuaded people that any good which came their way was due to him and not to God. He turned people from dependence upon God to dependence upon himself. Nimrod turned people's reverential fear of Yahweh into a craven fear that 'Huwawa', as he called him, would attempt to drown the world again. But not to worry!

Nimrod would save them by building towers too high for the waters to reach! Nimrod would kill Huwawa so they need never fear him again. He built ziggurats or temple towers in each of his cities, dedicating them to various strange gods of his creation—a sun god or a fish god or a winged bull with a human head—Nimrod himself!

"The name 'Nimrod' comes from a word meaning, 'We will revolt.' And that's exactly what Nimrod intended to do—to lead everybody in revolt against Yahweh. He established idolatry in all his cities. Yahweh calls idolatry 'harlotry,' and believe me, Babel was the mother of all harlots!"

"Why do people like Nimrod continue to conspire against Yahweh?" Rebekah asked. "They will never win. Yet kings of the earth routinely gather together against Yahweh, and say, 'Let's break his chains and throw off his fetters.' Their rebellion is futile. The One enthroned in heaven merely laughs. Yahweh scoffs at them. Some day He will dash them to pieces like pottery."[154]

"I had often wondered about Nimrod," mused Jacob. "I know that the cities he founded ended up being very wicked, but I wasn't sure about Nimrod himself. He seemed like a good man according to some who told his story. They stressed that he was a mighty hunter before Yahweh. But when you explain it, I understand. Nimrod saw himself on top of the world—the head of a world empire, but in Yahweh's eyes the best that could be said about Nimrod was that he was a mighty hunter. Considering what he hunted, even that is not a compliment."

"Whether Nimrod was good or evil depends on who is telling the story, Son," Isaac said. "The Babylonians and Hittites talk of him as if he were a hero, but your grandfather Abraham told the story very differently."

"That reminds me of something else," said Jacob. "I overheard one of our people referring to Esau as a 'nimrod'. At first I thought it was a compliment because Esau is such a good hunter, but the way he said it sounded like an insult. Now that I have a better understanding of Nimrod, I suspect that it *was* an insult."

---

[154] See Psalm 2:3-4, 9

Isaac's face darkened. He didn't like to be reminded of Esau's rebellion, but it seemed harder and harder to deny it as time went on.

"I just wish he wouldn't spend so much time with his Hittite friends," Rebekah responded with a deep sigh. "They are such a bad influence."

"They're birds of a feather," Jacob thought to himself, but he didn't say it in front of his father.

31

Esau Shows His True Colors

After Esau sold his birthright, the brothers grew even further apart. Esau's appetite had gone awry. He hungered for a simple bowl of stew, "a mess of pottage" as Isaac called it in disgust, and as a result he traded away an irreplaceable heritage—his status as firstborn, and all the privileges that went with it.

Privately, Esau was relieved to be rid of the birthright. Now he could stop pretending that it mattered to him. Now he didn't have to lead the family in Sabbath worship. Now he didn't have to spend hours listening to his father talking about Yahweh and the Covenant promises.

Esau rarely saw his parents and threw away all pretense of following Yahweh. He was openly hostile toward his brother Jacob. Though Esau didn't want the birthright, he resented the way Jacob had gotten it from him. If his father had taken it away, Esau wouldn't have cared; he would have been relieved of the burden. But Jacob had turned him into a laughingstock. Being called Edom reminded him of it, and his resentment grew to hatred.

One day Esau was returning from an unsuccessful hunting trip when he crossed paths with Jacob. Noticing that his brother was empty-handed, Jacob made a snide remark about Esau's hunting ability. That raised Esau's ire. He was disappointed enough without having his brother rub it in. Being tired made him more short-tempered than usual. Quick as a flash, Esau dropped his bow and pulled out his knife. Noticing that Jacob was unarmed, some bystanders intervened. As they pulled the brothers apart, Esau spat at Jacob.

"If I ever see you again, I'll kill you!" Esau said through clenched teeth.

Jacob walked away shaken. Thankfully, Esau had been stopped before he could do too much damage. Jacob's wounds were only superficial. But Esau's violence scared Jacob. He resolved to avoid his brother in the future. He knew Esau meant it when he said he would kill him.

Jacob need not have worried. Esau moved far enough away from his father's tents so that he could live his life as he pleased but stayed close enough that he could be summoned quickly when his father Isaac decided it was time to bestow the firstborn blessing. Esau knew that Jacob wanted the blessing even more than he did. He did not want to be bested by his brother again.

Esau spent just enough time with his parents that his father would view him as taking his position as elder son seriously. But he spent more and more time with his Hittite friends and less and less time with those his father Isaac referred to as "his people." He hungered for all the wrong things.

Esau preferred the Hittites, who openly abandoned all sexual inhibitions.

"My parents are too straight-laced," Esau told his Hittite friends. "I have much more fun when I'm with you."

Esau was careful not to tell his parents too much about what he and his Hittite friends did. He knew that what he called 'fun', they would call 'sexual perversion' and 'promiscuity.'

"Those Hittites!" Isaac exclaimed one day. "I wouldn't be surprised if some day Yahweh does to them what he did to Sodom and Gomorrah."

Esau's Hittite friends introduced him to two women whom he found particularly interesting. He was attracted to Basemath for her physical beauty, which she flaunted by the way she dressed. Esau often caught himself staring—not so much at her face, which was exceptionally beautiful, but at her body and the provocative way she moved. Basemath noticed Esau's attention and often brushed against him to excite him even further.

The other woman that caught Esau's attention was Judith. He was attracted to her because she was so wild and daring. She stirred thoughts and emotions in him that he didn't know existed.

Judith made no secret of the fact that she worshiped Canaanite gods. At first this repelled Esau. He had enough of religion and wanted nothing to do with gods of any kind. But Judith was different. She mixed religion with sexuality.

"If you think religion is dull and boring," Judith told Esau, "you have the wrong religion. I'll show you how to worship Asherah!"

Judith took Esau by the hand and pulled him toward her tent. Knowing what she had in mind, Esau's male friends laughed as they watched the two disappear. Inside the tent, Esau saw a carving of a voluptuous nude woman bestride a lion with a lily in one hand and a serpent in the other.

"That's Asherah," Judith said as she started to undress seductively. "Use your imagination, Edom. I'll be Asherah and you be the lion."

She pulled a lily out of a bouquet which sat on a nearby table and drew it alluringly across his lips. Noticing a slight hesitation from Esau, Judith knew just what to say to overcome his reticence.

"I'll bet your parents taught you that holiness consists of sexual abstinence until marriage," Judith said. "Don't believe it. Holiness is consecrating your whole body, not just your spirit, to the one you worship. Try it. You'll like it!"

Esau didn't need much persuasion. He stilled the voice of his conscience and yielded to his passions.

* * *

Esau often found himself coming back to Judith's tent for more. But Judith soon became bored.

"I noticed that Basemath is interested in you, Edom," Judith said coquettishly one day. "I also notice that you are attracted to her. Why don't we make it a threesome and worship Asherah together?"

Basemath did not need much coaxing to join the party. Esau had no objections either.

* * *

One day Esau arrived in Judith's tent to find the walls lined with idols of every description.

"What are these?" he asked.

"Marduk and an assortment of lesser gods from Babylon," Judith said, pointing to each one, evidently very pleased with herself. "Ishtar from Nineveh, and a grand medley of deities from Egypt, Syria and Asia Minor," she added with a sweep of her arm.

Initially Esau wasn't impressed.

"Why do we need all these? Isn't one god enough?" he asked.

"We need a little more excitement," Judith explained. "Last night I got an idea. Why don't we invite all our friends to join us and worship whatever gods they prefer?"

Esau wasn't crazy about the idols, but he was open to anything that included sex. The free-for-all left him excited but not deeply satisfied. He and Judith and Basemath came up with increasingly bizarre ideas to satisfy their depraved appetites.

* * *

After the twins, Esau and Jacob, turned forty, Isaac spoke to his wife about something that had been on his mind for some time.

"Esau needs a wife," Isaac said to Rebekah. "His wife has to be very special to be the mother of those who will inherit the Covenant promises."

"Esau sold his birthright. Remember?" Rebekah responded. "It's Jacob who has to be extra careful in selecting a wife."

"I know Jacob thinks he bought the birthright," Isaac replied, "but I don't accept that."

"He waited until he was a man in the eyes of the law," Rebekah reminded him, "and he has Esau's sandal as proof of purchase."

"His sandal!" Isaac snorted. "He should have drawn up a proper bill of sale."

"Jacob had the required number of witnesses," Rebekah countered. "They won't deny the sale. They have called Esau 'Edom' ever since."

"I cringe whenever I hear someone referring to him as Edom," Isaac responded. "But I have something that Jacob didn't think of. I can't undo what Jacob did, but I can still stop the sale. The deal isn't final until I speak a special blessing over him."

Rebekah's eyes widened. She hadn't thought of that. Could Isaac really undo the sale? *Would* he? Would he ignore what Yahweh had told her and pass the birthright to Esau? Could Isaac not see what a disaster that would be?

When Isaac summoned Esau for a serious talk, Rebekah was present, but she didn't say much. Esau knew that his mother sided with Jacob when it came to matters of the birthright.

"I was just your age, forty, when my father Abraham decided it was time for me to get married," Isaac said to Esau, putting his arm lovingly around Rebekah. "He sent his most trusted servant to Aram Naharaim, where our relatives live, to select a wife for me. Father wanted to be sure that I would find a mate who would support me fully in my faith journey in the land promised by Yahweh to him and his descendants. Now that you are forty, I think we should do the same for you. As our firstborn son, you need to take the utmost care in selecting your wife. You need to marry someone who will be like-minded in your love for Yahweh."

Esau was horrified at the thought.

"I don't want to marry a stranger," he objected. "Why can't I marry someone closer to home?"

"Yahweh will go before you to make sure you find the right one, Son. He directed Eliezer straight to Rebekah. Look how well that turned out! I couldn't have made a better choice myself."

"Yes, but I want to make my *own* choice," Esau insisted.

"Do you have anyone in mind, Son?" Isaac asked.

"Give me a little time," Esau hedged. "Let me introduce you to some of my acquaintances and see if you approve."

Esau hurried back to his Hittite friends. Judith and Basemath immediately noticed that something was bothering him.

"What's the matter, Edom?" Judith asked. "You are usually so ready to take part in whatever we suggest, but tonight you seem subdued."

"My folks want me to get married," he told them.

"Married!" Basemath exclaimed. "Why get married?"

"My inheritance depends on it. If I get my father angry, he won't give me the firstborn blessing."

"I thought you didn't care about the blessing," Judith said. "What does it matter whether or not your father speaks a few silly words over you? You don't care about his god. Huwawa was killed by Gilgamesh. Remember?"

"I remember your story," Esau replied impatiently, "but as firstborn *I* should get the double portion of the inheritance."

"Why quibble?" asked Basemath. "Your father is so rich that you won't notice the difference between getting one third or two thirds of his estate. You'll be rich either way."

"It's the principle of the thing," Esau explained. "I can't let my brother get the better of me. He has been grasping at my heel ever since the day we were born. He was rightly named. 'Deceiver!' He tricked me into selling my birthright, but I can get it back if Father blesses me."

Judith rolled her eyes. "The principle of the thing! Since when were you so principled, Edom? You sold your principles for a bowl of stew. Delicious red stew. 'A mess of pottage,' I hear your father calls it. And everybody knows Jacob didn't deceive you. You agreed to the deal with your eyes wide open!"

"I think Jacob got the raw end of the deal," Basemath joked. "He lost a whole bowl of very good stew."

Judith and Basemath both cackled mirthlessly. Esau did not enjoy being the butt of the joke.

"Okay, we'll be serious," Basemath said when she noticed the look on Esau's face. "What do you want us to do?"

"My parents wanted me to marry a complete stranger of their choice from among my relatives in Aram Naharaim," Esau said, "but I talked them into letting me marry someone I already know. Let me introduce you to my parents. Let them decide which of you I should marry. And for heaven's sake, don't call me Edom in front of my parents. That would really tick them off!"

Esau decided to introduce Basemath first.

"Be careful how you dress," he warned her. "Do you have anything modest in your wardrobe?"

"Don't worry," she assured him, patting his hand patronizingly. "I know how to impress the older generation. I will be on my best behavior."

Esau kept the introduction as short as he dared. His parents were struck by her beauty.

"I can see why Esau is attracted to her," Isaac commented to his wife afterwards. "Too bad she's a Hittite. She *is* beautiful. But she doesn't hold a candle to you."

"You're prejudiced," Rebekah responded, blushing. "I like her name. Basemath. 'Fragrant.' Very fitting, since she was wearing a lovely perfume. I hope she is fragrant in character as well."

A short while later Esau introduced Judith to his parents.

"Judith," Isaac commented. "That's a wonderful name. It's the feminine version of Judah, meaning 'praise.'"

"*God* be praised," Judith corrected Isaac with a smile. "My name means 'God be praised.'"

Esau tried to hide his surprise. Judith really knew how to impress his folks! Isaac and Rebekah were eager to learn more about Judith's background.

"My grandfather Zibeon lived much like you do," Judith told them. "He was a Hivite, meaning that he and his people lived in a tent village. But my father Anah preferred a more settled life. He became a Horite, a cave dweller. He hollowed out a cave high up in the mountains of Seir.

There he felt secure and safe. A tent doesn't provide much protection from enemy attacks."

"Esau, you told us Judith's father is Beeri the Hittite," said Rebekah, turning to her son.

"He is," Judith was quick to explain. "While feeding his father's donkeys in the desert, he discovered warm springs. He dug a series of wells—more like pools actually—for the water to flow into, so that people can bathe in them. The pools are wonderful to relax in, especially in cold weather. After his discovery, people started calling my father 'Beeri', man of the wells."

"That explains 'Beeri'," said Rebekah, "but what about Hittite?"

Esau rolled his eyes at his mother's ignorance.

"The term Hittite means 'descendant of Heth, which my father is,'" Judith explained patiently. "The terms 'Hivite' and 'Horite' indicate a lifestyle, not a family line."[155]

Before his parents could ask too many more questions, Esau made an excuse to leave with Judith.

"Now what?" asked Judith when they were out of earshot from Esau's parents. "Are you going to marry me and abandon Basemath, or vice versa? And what about the wedding? Will your folks come to a Hittite wedding? That would kill all the fun."

Esau smiled.

"I have it all worked out. I will let my folks think that they are in control. I will marry whomever they choose. We'll get married in the hill country of Seir. That's too far away and too arduous a journey for my aging parents. Father is a hundred years old."

"If your parents choose Basemath, what will happen to me?" Judith asked petulantly.

"Don't worry. I won't abandon either of you. We will have two weddings in a row and live happily ever after!"

"Edom! I do declare!" said Judith, pretending to be shocked. "What a deliciously decadent idea!"

---

[155] Judith (Genesis 26:34) is called Oholibamah in Genesis 36:2,4,14,18,25,41

"I even know what new names I will give you during the ceremony," Esau said coyly.

"What are you going to call me?" asked Judith eagerly.

"I'm not telling. It's a secret until the wedding."

Judith pouted, hoping that would convince him to spill his secret. "Don't worry, my dear," said Esau with a wicked grin. "I guarantee you'll like it."

Isaac and Rebekah decided that if the choice came down to Judith or Basemath, they preferred Judith. They sent Esau away to be married in Seir with their blessing in spite of some reservations.

All the wedding guests eagerly awaited the moment when Esau, or Edom as everyone at the wedding called him, would rename his bride.

Beeri the Hittite in Genesis 26:34 is called Anah the Horite in Genesis 36:2, 20-24.

"Oholibamah!" Edom announced. "Tent of the high place!"[156]

The weddings guests all caught the significance and exploded with approval. They laughed and whistled, hooted and hollered, stamping their feet and clapping their hands, making a racket that could be heard down the valley. They all knew the bride's reputation for mixing idolatry and sex. No need to go to one of the high places where idols were worshiped. Judith, now Ohilobamah, had everything necessary for idol worship right inside her tent.

Following the ceremony, the guests took part in an orgy of gluttony, drunkenness and sex that lasted a whole week. Edom had planned to marry Basemath the following week, but postponed the celebration for another week so that he and the guests would have time to recover.

"What are you going to call Basemath?" the guests called out during the second ceremony.

Edom milked the moment when he was the centre of attention. He eyed his second bride slowly from head to toe several times until even Basemath began to blush.

---

[156] Basemath (Genesis 26:34) is called Adah in Genesis 36:2,4,10,12,15

"'Fragrant' is too tame a name for this beauty," he said. "I rename you Adah! Ornament. Beauty. *Pleasure!*"[157]

Not to be outdone, Oholibamah jumped to her feet and strode toward the bride and groom. She rubbed her hands dramatically over Edom's hairy arms and hands. Then she drew her hands along the back of his hairy neck. When she pulled open his tunic to expose his hairy chest, she had the crowd's full attention. Finally, Oholibamah turned to face Edom.

"Basemath, I mean Adah, and I have a new name for you," she said, massaging his hairy chest. "Some may call you Edom, but to us you are 'Seir.' Hairy!"[158]

Again the guests caught the double meaning, literal and sexual, and expressed their wild approval. Again they plunged into another week of hedonistic pleasure.

When Isaac and Rebekah heard a short while later that their son had married *both* the Hittite women, they were horrified. From time to time they received reports of Esau and his wives, reports which made them weep. To say that they were a source of grief to Isaac and Rebekah is the mother of all understatements.

Adah gave Isaac and Rebekah their first grandchild, Eliphaz, but he was no joy to them either. He grew up to indulge in idolatry and took a mistress rather than marrying a respectable woman.

"How could a son who was raised to know and love Yahweh have ended up in such a predicament?" Isaac asked his wife. "Poor Esau! His wives hold so much sway over him!"

"We did our best, but we can't make choices for him," Rebekah replied, shaking her head sadly. "Esau is as much to blame as his Hittite wives. He chose not to love the truth. He chose to find pleasure in unrighteousness."

---

[157] The terms 'Edom' and 'land of Seir' are interchangeable. See Genesis 36:8. It is unclear whether the chief of the Horites took his name from the country of Seir or gave his name to it (Genesis 36:20-21).

[158]

32

By Faith Isaac

Isaac wanted to speak the firstborn blessing over his son Esau, but didn't want to do it while Esau was still living a decadent lifestyle. Year after year he waited, hoping to hear good news about his eldest son. Year after year the only stories that drifted back to him from the land of Seir were horror stories about the exploits of 'Edom', as he was known in Seir, and his Hittite wives.

Finally the day came when Isaac felt he could postpone his patriarchal duty no longer. Thirty years had gone by since Esau had married his two wives. Isaac was blind, but still remarkably healthy for being 130 years old. He had no idea how long he would live, but at his age he couldn't gamble on his future. He decided that it was time to bless Esau and hope that in time, maybe even after Isaac's death, Esau would return to the faith of his father Isaac and his grandfather Abraham.

Isaac sent a messenger to summon Esau. A few days later Esau appeared at his father's tent. Curious as to why Esau had come, Rebekah listened in on the conversation from the next room.

"I'm an old man," she heard Isaac say to Esau, "and I don't know when I'm going to die. Do me a favor, please: Take your bow and a quiver full of arrows and go out in the country and hunt some wild game for me. Prepare my favorite dish just the way I like it and bring it here for me to eat so that my soul may bless you before I die."[159]

Esau, pleased that his father was about to bless him, promptly went hunting.

Rebekah, however, was horrified at the thought of Esau getting the firstborn blessing. She also cringed at her husband's choice of words— "so that my *soul* may bless you." *The Covenant blessing is far too important to leave to the soul or the emotions,* she thought. *It must come from the spirit which is in tune with God.*

Rebekah began to panic. Then she looked up to the sky and prayed, "O Sovereign Lord, how can I prevent this disaster? I have tried to reason with my husband for seventy years, but he refuses to listen to me. How can he be persuaded that You want Jacob to be treated as the firstborn?"

Almost immediately Rebekah had an idea.

Jacob was nearby, but he hadn't seen his brother coming and going. Rebekah ran out to tell him what had just transpired.

"Listen," she said to Jacob, "I just overheard your father talking with your brother Esau. He said, 'Bring me some wild game and prepare me some tasty food to eat. Then I will bless you in the presence of Yahweh before I die.'"

"Father is going to bless Esau?" Jacob asked incredulously.

Rebekah nodded.

"With the firstborn blessing?"

She nodded. Jacob was stunned.

"With the *Covenant* blessing??"

Rebekah nodded again, then quickly explained her plan to her son.

"Now, Son, listen carefully and do exactly what I tell you: Go out to the flock and get me two young goats. Pick the best. I'll use them to prepare your father's favorite dish, just the way he likes it. Then take it to your father so he can eat it and bless you before he dies."[160]

Jacob wasn't so sure about his mother's plan.

---

[159] See Genesis 27:2-4
[160] See Genesis 27:8-10

"But my brother Esau is a hairy man," he objected. "I have smooth skin. What if my father touches me? He'll know that I'm trying to trick him, and then he'll curse me instead of blessing me."

His mother dismissed his objections.

"Then let the curse fall on me, Son! Just do what I say. Go and get the goats!"

Still somewhat dubious, but determined to get his father's blessing, Jacob went out and got the young goats for his mother. Rebekah took them and prepared a delicious meal, just the way Isaac liked it. Then she took Esau's favorite clothes, which were there in the tent, and gave them to her younger son Jacob. She covered his hands and the smooth part of his neck with the skin of the young goats. Then she gave Jacob the savory meal, including freshly baked bread.

With not a little trepidation Jacob took the food to his father. Quietly he called out, "Father?" Jacob hoped that if he spoke softly, his father would not notice he wasn't Esau.

"Yes, my son," he answered. "Who is it—Esau or Jacob?"

"I'm Esau your firstborn," Jacob replied. "I have done as you told me. Please sit up and eat some of my game, so that your soul may give me your blessing."[161] Rebekah hadn't used the word 'soul' when talking to Jacob, but he knew how his brother would phrase things. He also knew his father was not in tune with Yahweh on this matter.

Isaac was surprised to see his son so soon.

"How did you find it so quickly, my son?"

Again Jacob was careful to word his reply as his brother Esau would have.

"Yahweh your God gave me success," he answered. Esau would never have said Yahweh was his own God. But Jacob's answer didn't allay Isaac's suspicions.

"Come near and let me touch you, Son. Are you really my son Esau?"

Jacob approached his father. He held his breath as Isaac reached out and felt his hands and neck. The goat skins felt so much like Esau's hairy skin that they fooled the old man.

---

[161] See Genesis 27:19

"The voice is Jacob's," Isaac said, leaning back on his cushion, "but the hands are Esau's." Satisfied that it really was Esau, Isaac prepared to bless his son.

Jacob was just about to serve his father when Isaac hesitated. For the second time he asked, "Are you *really* my son Esau?"

"I am," Jacob answered, stifling his conscience at the lie.

Much to Jacob's relief, Isaac's sense of smell overpowered his sense of hearing. Isaac took a deep breath and his mouth began to water at the delicious smell of the food. His soul won over his spirit. Hungry and impatient, he said, "Bring me some of your game to eat, Son. Then my soul will bless you."

Relieved that he had passed the test, Jacob put the food before his father and Isaac ate. He also drank the wine that Jacob served him. Then Isaac said to Jacob, "Come here and give me a kiss, Son."

So Jacob went over and gave him a kiss. When Isaac caught the smell of his clothes, he was thoroughly convinced it was Esau, so he blessed his son.

"Ah! The smell of my son is like the smell of the great outdoors, which Yahweh has blessed!"[162]

Then Isaac proceeded to pronounce a blessing that would be appropriate not just for his firstborn son, but also for his son's descendants. He even incorporated part of Yahweh's original blessing to Abraham, a Covenant promise to Abraham and his descendants. Isaac had been preparing the blessing in his mind for years.

> "May God give you of heaven's dew
> > and of earth's richness—
> > abundant harvests of grain and new wine.
> May nations serve you
> > and peoples bow down to you.
> May you be the master over your brothers,
> > and may the sons of your mother bow down to you.
> May those who curse you be cursed

---

[162] Genesis 27:27

and those who bless you be blessed."[163]

Jacob drank in the words of the blessing he had longed to hear from as far back as he could remember. He wanted to ask his father to repeat it, but he didn't dare speak. He wanted to hug his father, but that was too risky. Reluctantly he stood up, then left his father's tent without saying a word.

Jacob had scarcely left his father's presence when Esau returned from hunting and busied himself with preparing his father's favorite dish. When it was ready, he strode cheerily into his father's tent.

"I'm back, Father," he announced. "I have the wild game you wanted prepared just the way you like it. Sit up and eat so that your soul may bless me."

Esau wasn't prepared for his father's response.

"Who are you?" Isaac asked in a tremulous voice.

"I'm your son. Your firstborn. Esau."

Jacob was eavesdropping, peeking through the tent flap. He wondered what his father would do when he learned that he had inadvertently blessed his younger son. Would he retract the firstborn blessing?

Isaac didn't answer Esau immediately. He started to shake. Violently. Jacob had never seen such fear. The picture of his father's reaction, of his father trembling uncontrollably, would be seared into Jacob's brain forever.

"Who . . . ?" Isaac stammered querulously. "Who was it, then, who just served me wild game? I have already eaten it, and I blessed him just before you came."

Then Isaac's expression changed. It was as if scales fell off his eyes. The trembling stopped as fear was replaced with faith and resolution. By faith Isaac would stand by what he could now see was God's doing.

"I blessed him," Isaac said firmly, "and indeed he will be blessed!"[164]

---

[163] See Genesis 27:28-29
[164] Genesis 27:33

Jacob felt someone squeeze his shoulder. He turned to see that his mother had joined him. First she smiled, then she appeared about to cry. When Esau heard his father's words, he burst out with a loud and bitter cry.

"Bless me—me too, O my father!" Esau begged.

Isaac's reply was so matter-of-fact, almost cold, that he surprised even himself.

"Your brother was here. He tricked me and took your blessing."

Isaac didn't sound sorry for being tricked. Esau's temper flared. "Isn't he rightly named Jacob? Heel!" Esau wanted to say, "Deceiver," but something about his father's bearing stopped him. "He has cheated me twice. First, he took away my birthright. Now he's stolen my blessing."[165]

Esau paused, expecting his father to say something. His father had always sided with him in any issue related to the Covenant. Now his father remained stoic.

If Isaac had said anything, it would not have been to side with Esau. Isaac could have corrected his son. They both knew that there was no deception when Jacob purchased the birthright from Esau. Jacob had merely seized a golden opportunity. Isaac held his tongue.

"Haven't you reserved any blessing for me?" Esau demanded.

"I've made Jacob your master," Isaac informed Esau, "and have declared that all his brothers will be his servants. I have guaranteed him an abundance of grain and wine. I've given it all away. So what can I possibly do for you, Son?"

Isaac's reply left no room for negotiation, but Esau tried anyway.

"Do you have only *one* blessing, Father? Bless *me*. Bless me too, Father!" Esau pleaded. Then he wept aloud.

For the first time since the twins were born, Isaac could see Esau for what he really was, not for what Isaac wanted him to be.

"Esau," Isaac said gently, "Yahweh's blessing is for those who follow him with all their heart and soul." Isaac wanted to reprimand his son for his godless living, but he didn't know where to begin. He also knew it was too late to say what he should have said decades ago.

---

[165] See Genesis 27:36

Esau only wept louder. Isaac saw his tears as the tears of a child who couldn't get his own way. Crocodile tears. Manipulative tears, not tears of repentance.

Isaac prayed a quick prayer to Yahweh. He really wanted to bless his son. What could he in good conscience say as a blessing for Esau?

"Without faith it is impossible to please me," Isaac heard a quiet whisper to his spirit. "Open your mouth and believe that I will fill it."

Obediently, by faith, Isaac opened his mouth and spoke the words that came to him.

> "You will live far from Earth's bounty,
>   remote from Heaven's dew.
> You will live by your sword,
>   and you will serve your brother.
> But eventually you will gain your freedom
>   and shake his yoke from your neck."[166]

It wasn't much of a blessing, but Esau knew it was the best he would get.

---

[166] See Genesis 27:39-40

33

The Fear of Isaac

Later that evening, Rebekah pretended that she had not overheard Isaac blessing his sons.

"I saw Esau leaving in a foul mood today, Isaac. What was that all about?"

Isaac again began to shake so violently that for several moments he couldn't speak.

"I came so close to ruining everything," he said as if to himself. "I thought that the only reason Ishmael was not the Son of Promise was because he had been born to Hagar, who was not my father Abraham's first wife. But now I see that was not the only reason. Ishmael is a wild donkey of a man. He can't get along with anybody. As Yahweh foretold to Hagar, his hand is against everyone and everyone's hand is against him. His twelve sons are just as bad as their father. They also live in hostility toward everyone—even their own brothers!"

Isaac turned to face his wife.

"Can you imagine what a disaster it would have been if Ishmael had been the Son of Promise? Can you imagine how Yahweh could possibly bless all peoples on earth through Ishmael and the hostile sons he fathered? Look down the road a few decades—a few centuries.

Considering the direction they are headed, how could they end up being a blessing to everyone?"

Rebekah didn't interrupt his train of thinking. She had been thinking along those lines for years.

"All my life I have been conscious of my responsibility as the Son of Promise. All my life I have sought to walk in the faith footsteps of my father Abraham. I determined that I would learn every lesson of faith that he ever learned."

As Isaac talked of faith, his trembling ceased.

"Yahweh has the future of all mankind, all peoples on earth, invested in *me*! He sees me as the only son of Abraham. My father had to raise me right. He couldn't indulge me just because I was a miracle child. If he spoiled me, he would have spoiled the future of all mankind. Either that, or God would have had to scrap his plans for Abraham and start from scratch with someone else."

"God couldn't do that," Rebekah replied. "His promises are eternal. Everlasting. Unchangeable."

"I'm just starting to see that Yahweh keeps his promises in spite of how short we fall of God's glory," Isaac reflected. "In spite of desiring to please God and place my full trust in him, I failed. I was so intent on hearing Yahweh's voice that I missed the obvious. He *did* speak to me—through *you*! I rejected his message because I was jealous that he hadn't spoken to me. All my life I longed to hear his voice, and to whom did he speak? To you! My wife. A woman! I was insulted that he had bypassed the man of the house."

Rebekah smiled. Now that Isaac confessed his unbelief, she did not feel threatened when he put it so bluntly.

"Don't be so hard on yourself, dear," Rebekah said gently. "As far as I know, Yahweh hasn't spoken directly to any woman since he kicked Adam and Eve out of the Garden of Eden. Some of our forefathers assumed that Yahweh would not speak to women again until he restores Paradise. After all, Eve was the one who first ate of the forbidden fruit."

"That doesn't excuse me," Isaac replied. "Eve was deceived, but Adam ate of the fruit with his eyes wide open.[167] He didn't want to live forever unless Eve did too. Adam didn't simply disobey; he worshiped the creature, Eve, rather than the Creator. Eve was more important to him than Yahweh.

"As for me," Isaac continued, "I want to be worthy of Yahweh's promise to make Abraham into a great nation. I thought I had learned all the faith lessons of the faith giants of the past.

"Like Abel, I believe Yahweh wants me to walk before him and be perfect. I believe that missing the mark of absolute perfection brings the penalty of death. But Yahweh is good, merciful and just at the same time. He promised to provide a perfect substitute to die in my place. Until Yahweh's perfect substitute is revealed, I sacrifice a lamb and Yahweh is satisfied when he sees the blood. Like Abel did, I express my faith that Yahweh will provide a perfect substitute by shedding the blood of a lamb.

"Like Enoch, I believe that following Yahweh is the only way to truly live. His laws and instructions provide the road map to a fulfilling life and perfect happiness. I don't fool myself that I have followed Yahweh as successfully as Enoch did, but wouldn't it be great to bypass the valley of death?"

"Amen!" Rebekah agreed.

"Like Noah, I believe in the coming judgment," Isaac continued. "People since Noah are just as sinful as those who were wiped out by the Flood, maybe worse. Yahweh will again bring universal judgment on the earth, but not by a flood, as the rainbow reminds us.

"From my parents I learned the value of trusting God for a child in the face of a barren wife. You were barren, Rebekah, yet Yahweh blessed us with, not one, but two sons. Like my father Abraham, I have lived in tents, living in the Promised Land like a stranger in a foreign country. Like my father, I too look forward to the City with Foundations, whose architect and builder is God himself.

---

[167] See 1 Timothy 2:14

"By faith my father Abraham lived with the contradictory—he sacrificed the one whom God had promised to make into a great nation. We both believed that God could raise me from the dead. I also lived with the contradictory. Wells were my symbol of ownership of the Promised Land, but the Philistines kept plugging them up. So I gave them to God. In a way, I sacrificed them. When the Philistines plugged up one well after another, I simply dug more.

"I thought I had learned all the faith lessons there were to learn," observed Isaac, "but obviously I was wrong. I have learned—after seventy years of resisting the lesson—that Yahweh is not as predictable as I would like to think he is. He surprised me by speaking through a woman. Who knows who or what he will speak through next?"

"A donkey?"[168] suggested Rebekah.

Isaac and his wife both laughed.

"Don't be silly! But I guarantee he will surprise us."

"Jacob and I were watching when Esau came in for his blessing," Rebekah admitted. "I have never seen such fear on your face. Or on anyone's face, for that matter. You shook so hard we could feel the earth tremble!"

Isaac started to shake again, simply remembering.

"Oh, Rebekah! Can you imagine what a disaster it would be if Esau were the Son of Promise? Not just for our family, but for the whole world! Yahweh promised that all peoples on earth will be blessed through my father Abraham, but that blessing would be a curse in Esau's hands! I waited decade after decade for him to change, but he never did. He just got worse and worse. You saw Esau clearly, but I was blind. How ironic, now that I am physically blind, that I can finally see the truth!"

"I love Esau as much as you do, Isaac, but I have been aware since Esau was a teenager that he did not love Yahweh as much as Jacob did. Over the years the difference became more pronounced. Esau not only rejected Yahweh's teachings, he loathed them. He refused to keep his commands. That made him seek companionship from his pagan

---

[168] Centuries later the Lord did exactly that. See the story of Balaam and his donkey in Numbers 22:21-35.

neighbors rather than from his own people. His Hittite wives fed him lies about false gods and Esau did not object, even though he knew they were lies. I wonder when Yahweh will run out of patience with him. He can't put up with Esau's sins forever. I hate to say it, but Esau is on dead-end road leading to destruction." Isaac was still trembling.

"What would Yahweh have done to me if I had blessed Esau and made him the Son of Promise? Would He have turned me to a pillar of salt, as he did to Lot's wife? Would he have destroyed me as he destroyed Sodom and Gomorrah? I fear to displease him. All my life I wanted to hear his voice. For the rest of my life I will fear to do anything that might jeopardize Yahweh's Covenant promises."

34

Jacob Leaves Home

After losing out on the firstborn blessing, Esau went out and got drunk, then he staggered home and beat up his wives. He woke up the next day with a pounding headache.

When he could think clearly enough to remember why he had gotten so drunk, he raged with anger. His wives were used to his fits of temper, but this was different. His anger raged continually; his fury flamed unchecked; his meanness never took a timeout.

Esau shook his fist at God. He shed big tears begging for the blessing that should have been his, but God didn't answer. God was listening for a change of heart, but there was no room in Esau's heart for repentance.

Not only was Esau angry at God, he was angry at his father for being so stupid and gullible as to be duped by Jacob. He was angry at his mother for colluding with Jacob to deceive his father.

But most of all, Esau was angry at his brother Jacob. He held a grudge and breathed murderous threats against his brother. He swore to himself, "Just wait till my father dies! It won't be long now. Then I'll kill my brother Jacob." Esau was especially vocal when he was drunk.

People overheard Esau muttering to himself, and word of his threats got back to his mother Rebekah. She, in turn, warned Jacob.

"Watch out for your brother Esau! He's plotting to kill you, Son. Listen to me. Get out of here. Run for your life! Go to Haran, to my brother Laban, and stay with him until your brother cools down. When his fury subsides and he forgets what you did to him, I'll send for you to come back."[169]

Rebekah worried that she would lose both her sons in one day. She knew that if Esau killed Jacob, he would never return to his parents' home again.

The people who warned Rebekah about Esau's threats also brought back wild tales of the exploits of 'Edom' and his wives. Rebekah reported the stories to Isaac with disgust.

"I'm sick to death of these local Hittite women! I would rather die than see Jacob marry one of them."

Isaac started trembling violently again. The thought of Jacob following in his brother's footsteps gave him nightmares! He feared missing Yahweh's plan to use his descendants, in particular his son Jacob, to bring blessing to the whole world. He sent an urgent message for Jacob to come to him.

Jacob was in the middle of packing to go to Haran when he received the summons. It sounded like an emergency.

"Is Father dying?" he asked.

"No, but the matter is of utmost importance," the messenger said.

When Jacob arrived, his father seemed to be fine.

"What's wrong, Father?" Jacob asked. "I thought you were dying."

"Nothing's wrong, Son," Isaac assured him. "I want to bless you."

Jacob knew he would have to wait to discover what was on his father's mind. He had grown up in this culture where the most important issues of life are never rushed. He had seen his grandfather Abraham serve food and pour multiple cups of coffee before discussing weighty matters. Jacob knew that the longer it took for his father to get to the point, the more important the matter was.

Slowly Isaac rose from his seat, motioned Jacob to come closer, and placed his hand on Jacob's shoulder.

---

[169] See Genesis 27:42-45

"May God Almighty bless you, and make you fruitful and give you many children. May your descendants multiply and become many nations!" Isaac intoned. "May God pass on to you and your descendants the blessings he promised to Abraham, so that you may take possession of the land where you are now living as a foreigner, this land God gave Abraham."[170]

Jacob closed his eyes as he soaked in the blessing. It was a restatement of the Covenant promise and blessing. He could never hear it often enough. He didn't even care whether his father got around to discussing any other issues.

Jacob's eyes were still closed when he was startled to hear Isaac command him in a loud voice:

"Don't you dare marry a Canaanite woman! Don't even think of it!"

Jacob opened his eyes to see his father shaking as he had done when Esau showed up expecting a blessing. Isaac fell backward onto his chair. The fear in his sightless eyes was evident. Before Jacob could reply, Isaac continued.

"Leave at once! Go to Paddan Aram to the family of your mother's father, Bethuel. Marry one of your uncle Laban's daughters."

Jacob was glued to the spot, fascinated by his father's fear.

"Go!" Isaac shouted, pointing to the door.

Jacob embraced Isaac and, with tears running down his face, kissed his father on both cheeks. He knew he might never see his father again.

Rebekah accompanied her son to his own tent.

"May I help you pack?" she asked.

"Thanks, Mother, but I won't be taking much with me," Jacob replied. "I must travel light if I am to escape unnoticed and get a safe distance from here before Esau knows I have gone."

"What about your tent, Son?"

"Someone else is welcome to use it until I return. *If* I return," he added, his voice trailing off.

"Not if. When," his mother corrected him firmly. "Yahweh promised this land to your grandfather and to your father—and to you, the heir of the Covenant promises."

---

[170] See Genesis 28:3-4

Jacob paused in the midst of his packing.

"Yahweh," he said, turning toward his mother. "I have been thinking recently about the names of Yahweh. *El Roi*, the God who sees me. *El Shaddai*, God Almighty. *El Elyon*, God Most High. And many others. But the events of the last few days have given me another name for Yahweh."

"What is that, Son?"

"The Fear of Isaac."[171]

Rebekah didn't reply immediately. She knew what Jacob was referring to. Both of them had seen Isaac tremble violently when Esau came for the firstborn blessing. Both of them noticed how Isaac trembled since then whenever he thought about what might have been.

"It's a strange name, Son, and it strikes me as being strangely appropriate, though I'm not sure I can explain it. Yahweh has certainly put the fear of God into your father."

"I'm not quite sure what the name means either. The phrase just popped into my head. I think Yahweh put it there. I will ponder what it means as I journey to Uncle Laban's place in Haran."

Jacob gave his mother a hug and a kiss.

"I'll tell your father about your new name for Yahweh, Son. I have a feeling he will approve of the name. I suspect it will give us lots to talk about."

"Goodbye, Mother. I love you."

Jacob fought back tears as he hurried away.

"I'll send for you as soon as it is safe," Rebekah called after him. "I love you!"

Jacob turned and waved one last time before turning a corner out of sight. His brother Esau had a long memory. His mother would probably be dead before Esau let go of his hatred for his brother.

Jacob's thoughts turned to Yahweh. Maybe learning to understand him as the Fear of Isaac would overwhelm his lesser fears—of the road ahead, of Esau, of the unknown.

---

[171] See Genesis 31:42, 53

35

Esau Takes a Third Wife

Esau was so intent on killing his brother that he sent a servant to bring back news of his father's health.

"Is the old man dead yet?" Esau asked upon the servant's return.

"No, and from what I hear he won't die any time soon," the servant replied. "He may be blind, but there isn't much else wrong with him. I wouldn't be surprised if he lives longer than his father Abraham. You may have to wait 45 or 50 years to get revenge on your brother."

Esau scowled and swore.

"Maybe I'll have to make Jacob's death look like an accident."

"You'll have to find him first, Edom. He left the country."

Esau looked up in surprise.

"Your father blessed him before he went," the servant continued, knowing he could deliver the news with impunity. He didn't like his master Edom, who was often cruel to him. He knew this news would bother Esau, and he enjoyed being the messenger.

"That's old news," Esau replied. "Father blessed Jacob a few weeks ago."

"No," the servant insisted. "Isaac blessed him again. Just before Jacob left. Your father repeated the Covenant blessing, asking God Almighty to give your brother many children, multiplied descendants, and the land they are living in—everything Yahweh promised to Abraham."

"Not Yahweh. Huwawa," Esau said with a frown.

"You may call him Huwawa, Edom, but don't you dare let your father hear you call him that!"

Esau sniffed.

"What would Father do? Nothing! He has never interfered with what I want to do."

"Your father is a different man lately. Everybody in his camp is talking about it. Your mild mannered father shouted—shouted at Jacob loud enough to be heard several tents away. 'Don't you dare marry a Canaanite woman!' he thundered at Jacob. 'Don't even think of it!'"

Esau's mouth dropped open.

"My father said that?"

"Yes, your father. He is so afraid of displeasing Yahweh that all his other fears pale in comparison. His fear of God overwhelms all other fears."

Esau didn't know what to say, so he changed the subject.

"Where did Jacob go?"

"To Paddan Aram. To your uncle Laban," the servant replied.

"Why there?" Esau asked.

"To get a wife. That's where your father got his wife Rebekah."

"Oh," Esau said. As soon as he heard the answer, Esau knew he shouldn't have had to ask. Quickly he dismissed the servant. He needed to think.

Esau knew his mother didn't approve of Judith and Basemath. She refused to let their new names, Oholibamah and Adah, cross her lips. Rebekah often complained that her life was not worth living because of them. But his mother had always favored Jacob over Esau, so he discounted his mother's objections.

Now, for the first time in his life, Esau realized how displeasing his wives were to his father Isaac. Esau had always enjoyed the favor of his father. Now it dawned on Esau that he was in jeopardy of being totally disinherited.

Even worse than losing his inheritance was the prospect of losing face before his wives, his in-laws and the people of Seir. Esau had worked hard to establish himself as a chieftain in the country of Seir. His descendants and followers called themselves Edomites in honor of him. But they had deep respect for Abraham, even though they didn't honor the God of Abraham. To be disinherited by Abraham's son would be a blow Esau could not live down.

What could Esau do to reinstate himself in his father's good graces?

When Esau posed the question to his wives, they feared he would divorce them.

"Don't be silly," he told them. "I wouldn't do anything that drastic! But what if I took a third wife?"

Oholibamah's and Adah's eyes brightened. This opened up all sorts of kinky possibilities!

"But she can't be from Canaan," Esau said, reading their minds. "She would have to be respectable. Someone that my father would approve."

"Are you going to follow your brother to Paddan Aram and take a wife from your relatives there?" asked Adah. "If so, count me out. I couldn't live with a Huwawa-lover. She would spoil all our fun."

"I would leave too, Edom," Oholibamah threatened.

"Paddan Aram isn't the only place I have relatives," responded Esau. "My father had a half-brother, Ishmael, born to Grandmother Sarah's Egyptian handmaid. Ishmael died a few years ago, but he fathered twelve sons. If he doesn't have any daughters, surely he must have some granddaughters. Maybe one of them will be suitable."

"Where would you find Ishmael's descendants?" asked Adah.

"Uncle Ishmael lived southwest of here, between here and Egypt, in the Desert of Paran," Esau replied. "His descendants must still live in the vicinity."

Esau wasted no time leaving for Paran. When he made inquiries as to where he could find the sons of Ishmael, he received strange looks.

"Why would you want anything to do with them?" people asked Esau. "They are nothing but trouble. They can't get along with anybody—not even each other!"

Esau didn't admit he was looking for a wife; he just continued his search. He learned that the oldest son of Ishmael, the one he would have to negotiate with for a wife, was named Nebaioth, a name which suggested something about high places. Esau found this encouraging. It inferred that Nebaioth and Esau's wife Oholibamah had interests in common.

At last Esau found Nebaioth, introduced himself and was invited to stay a while. Nebaioth served coffee while his wife prepared a meal of wild game for their guest. After everyone was satisfied, the host turned to his guest.

"So, Edom, what has brought you so far from home? You didn't come merely to make my acquaintance. What do you want from me?"

"I'm looking for a wife, Cousin Nebaioth," Esau replied, getting to the point quickly. "Does Uncle Ishmael have any daughters or granddaughters that would be suitable for me?"

"Aha!" Nebaioth exclaimed. "I suspected that was the only thing that would bring a member of your family here. First describe your situation to me, so I can make a wise choice. If you treat her badly, word will get back to me. I'll send my brothers after you, and you'll regret the day you came here. My brothers may not be able to get along with each other, but they will certainly unite to revenge injustice to a family member."

Esau realized that he had met his match. Hiding the truth would bring trouble down on his head—more trouble than he already faced. While still painting himself in a favorable light, he described his two wives and his lifestyle.

When Esau was finished, Nebaioth leaned back in his chair.

"Finding you a suitable wife is a tall order, Cousin," he began. "The young, pretty ones that you are ogling won't do. They don't want to marry a 70-year-old. You need someone that will fit in quietly without complaining. My daughters and my nieces would never be happy in your situation."

Nebaioth noticed Esau's disappointment, and a slow smile crossed his face.

"Your journey is not wasted, Cousin. I have an unmarried sister whom I, as the firstborn son, have been burdened with. She was traumatized by the continual bickering and hostility of her many brothers, and withdrew into a shell."

Fearing he had painted too depressing a picture, Nebaioth hurried on. "But she's not bad looking. Her name is Mahalath, meaning 'mild.'"

"It also means 'sickness,'" Esau observed, not too happy at the prospect of this sister of Nebaioth.

"Give her a chance, Edom. She is frail and susceptible to catching whatever sickness is making the rounds, but her mild manner will enable her to blend in to the circumstances in your home. She really is sweet. And she loves Yahweh. That should make her acceptable to your parents. And she is still young enough to give you a child—if you marry without delay. Let me introduce you. You don't have to decide tonight."

Esau was charming and Mahalath was shy at their first meeting. Esau told Mahalath only those things which she wanted to hear. Mahalath was pleased at the prospect of marrying into her Uncle Isaac's side of the family. She expected it to be an improvement over her present circumstances, living as an old maid amongst quarrelsome brothers.

Esau decided to get married before Mahalath was disillusioned. During the wedding ceremony, he changed Mahalath's name to Basemath, meaning 'fragrant.'[172] She was pleased at her new name because she had never liked her old one. Esau didn't tell her that he had an ulterior motive for choosing that name. It would force his parents to accept the name change of his second wife and call her Adah. Esau couldn't have two wives named Basemath!

Isaac and Rebekah were pleased with Esau's third wife, who soon gave them a grandson. Basemath named him Reuel, 'God is a friend.'

---

[172] Mahalath (Genesis 28:9) was renamed Basemath (Genesis 36:3).

36

Faith That Fears

Life was quiet for Isaac and Rebekah after Jacob left. They hadn't seen much of Esau in the thirty years since he married Hittite wives. Jacob had loved to spend time with his parents and with the hundreds of members of their camp. Jacob knew them all by name, even the little ones. He was good with children, and they often came asking for him on Sabbath days, when he wasn't busy with the livestock.

"I miss Jacob," Rebekah said to Isaac one evening. "And I miss the children coming around to ask for him. I liked to imagine they were my grandchildren."

"I miss them both," Isaac said, referring to his sons. "But I especially miss our discussions with Jacob about Yahweh. For all his faults, he really does love Yahweh. He often asked me to repeat stories in which Abraham learned new names for God."

"Speaking of names of God," Rebekah said, "I meant to tell you that Jacob came up with a new name for Yahweh."

"What was it?" Isaac asked with interest.

"The Fear of Isaac."

Rebekah watched for her husband's reaction.

"The Fear of Isaac," she repeated when Isaac said nothing. "What do you think that means?"

Isaac was slow to reply. When he did, he chose his words thoughtfully, not answering the question immediately.

"I didn't know what fear was for many years," he began. "Being the son of Abraham kept me from many of the fears that others experience. Father was more than strong physically. He was powerful. He put the Babylonian armies to flight with a few hundred men trained in his own household—318 men, plus God! Because Almighty God, *El Shaddai*, was with him, he was invincible. Kings like Pharaoh and Abimelech feared him.

"Growing up, when I was with my father, I didn't fear anything or anyone. Even when Father raised his knife to kill me on Mount Moriah, I was not afraid. I knew he was obeying Yahweh, so God would raise me from the dead.

"When Mother died, I felt alone; but Father sent Eliezer to Aram Naharaim and he came back with you, my wonderful beautiful wife. When we discovered that you were barren, I looked at my father and remembered that he had gone through the same thing. Every difficulty I faced, he had faced before me. So I didn't fear.

"But then Father died.

"For the first time in 75 years I felt really, really alone—even more alone than when my mother died. Even you, my dear wife, and our precious sons could not fill that void. And I felt afraid.

"That's why I told Abimelech that you were my sister. Yet Yahweh blessed me in spite of my fears, and that helped to restore my confidence. As I prospered, the Philistines pushed back by plugging my wells. I feared the Philistines would attack me, so I moved on and dug another well. When they plugged that one, I moved on and dug another. And another.

"Then Yahweh appeared to me. 'I am the God of your father Abraham,' He said. 'Don't be afraid, for I am with you. I will bless you and multiply your descendants for the sake of my servant Abraham.'

"That was the beginning of the end of my fear. I didn't need to be afraid because Yahweh was with me. I didn't need my father at my side. The God of Abraham was at my side. He is more powerful than my father Abraham ever was. It was because Yahweh was at my father's side that he was powerful. Now that same God is at my side. With *me*! All I have to do is believe it.

"That understanding took care of my fears of physical enemies. I built an altar and preached Yahweh boldly. Abimelech noticed and became afraid of *me*! That's why he insisted on making a treaty with me.

"But I had a spiritual enemy—unbelief! I refused to believe that Yahweh had spoken to you, that he had told you that the older would serve the younger. I refused to treat Jacob as the firstborn in obedience to God's revelation to you. I refused to admit that Esau was not fully devoted to Yahweh. Even when Jacob bought the birthright from Esau, I refused to see Yahweh's hand in the background overruling my unbelief.

"Jacob wouldn't have had to buy the birthright if I had declared that the birthright and the accompanying Covenant promises would go to him rather than Esau. And you, my sweet conniving wife, wouldn't have had to collude with Jacob to deceive me to get the blessing if I had believed Yahweh's message to you.

"If it had been up to me, I would have blessed Esau and overturned Jacob's purchase. In fact, I thought I *was* blessing Esau. I spoke over Jacob the Covenant blessing I had been composing mentally for a long time, thinking I was speaking it over Esau. It was only when Esau came in asking for the blessing that I realized that Almighty God had overruled again. He had allowed Jacob to purchase the birthright, and He had allowed Jacob to steal the blessing by deceit.

"Have you ever missed danger by a hair's breadth and realized it only after you were safe?"

Rebekah nodded. "When you realize how close you came to mortal danger, you shake like a leaf."

"That's exactly what happened to me," Isaac agreed. "When Esau came for his blessing, I realized I had escaped disaster by the skin of my teeth. Yahweh had intervened and protected me from passing the Covenant promises to the wrong person. That realization shook me to the core of my being."

"I know," Rebekah replied. "Jacob and I both watched you tremble violently."

"Since then I realized that fear is not always a bad thing," Isaac said thoughtfully. "Yahweh designed fear in us for our own protection. We are right to fear danger. Fear keeps us from getting too close to a fire or to the edge of a cliff.

"I like Jacob's name for Yahweh. The Fear of Isaac. The right kind of fear. I want Yahweh to be my Fear. I want to fear the things he wants me to fear.

"Sometimes I wonder if my physical blindness is a result of my spiritual blindness," Isaac mused. "My father Abraham had good vision right to the end of his 175 years. I'm blind at 130. If I could see, Jacob couldn't have deceived me. Yahweh knew that, so He made me blind. Now that I am blind, I see some things more clearly then I ever did before."

"I would be slow to blame your blindness on your lack of faith, dear," Rebekah replied gently. "We live in a fallen world with all its consequences."

"I know," Isaac said, "Yahweh is gracious and doesn't treat us as we deserve, but I can't help but feel that there is a connection."

"I can't change how you feel, dear," Rebekah replied, "but be assured that I will never throw your blindness in your face. I don't believe your blindness is a direct consequence of not believing Yahweh spoke to me."

Both were silent for a while, then Isaac spoke again.

"With Yahweh as my Fear, I don't need to be afraid of anything except displeasing him. Fear of missing Yahweh's plan for me and my descendants overwhelms all my other fears. It enables me to prioritize the things I naturally fear. Yahweh, my Fear, fills me with awe and wonder. Fear of Him frees me to trust Him completely."

Sounds of laughter drifted in from the children playing outside their tent.

"I miss the sound of laughter," Isaac mused. "I remember how much my parents used to laugh. They used to laugh just watching me play. When I asked them what was funny, they said they were laughing for joy. For the joy of having a child in their old age. For the joy of Yahweh's promise fulfilled.

"They even laughed for unfulfilled promises. They used to kick up the dust as they were walking along the path. One would say, 'Like the dust of the earth,' and the other would answer, 'So shall your offspring be.' Then they would laugh out loud. They used to laugh at the sight of stars in the sky and say, 'Like the stars in the sky.' When they were at the seashore, they would dig their toes into the sand and giggle. Then they would look at each other and say in unison, 'Like the sand on the seashore,' and burst into laughter. Others wondered what was so funny. Yahweh's promises were so ridiculously impossible, yet they were true."

"You have told me the story many times," Rebekah responded. "I know that's why you were named Isaac, 'laughter.' But I was thinking the other day how seldom I see or hear you laugh. When Eliezer came to my home in Aram Naharaim and told me my future husband's name was Isaac, I thought you would be laughing all the time. But for the most part you are very serious."

"I suppose it has to do with having the weight of the Covenant promises on my shoulders," Isaac replied.

"But that is exactly what is wrong with you," Rebekah said gently. "It is not up to you to fulfill the Covenant promises. That's Yahweh's responsibility. You need to laugh more. Like your parents did. Your parents could laugh because they could see themselves as others see them—as a ridiculously old couple, with a baby! Their ability to laugh at themselves brought elasticity into their lives. It stretched them to the point where they could do what was necessary to raise a child in their old age.

"But you are so focused on getting things right, that you aren't free to laugh. You are so bound by fixed ideas of how things should be that you have become rigid. Your rigidity even put Yahweh in a box. According to you, Yahweh couldn't speak to a woman. Sometimes I hoped that you would laugh at the idea rather than dismissing it outright. Laughter allows you to react without committing yourself one way or the other. You could be laughing in faith or laughing in disbelief. Only God knows. I hoped that if you laughed at the idea that Yahweh spoke to me, you might some day believe it."

Isaac was about to object when he stopped short. Maybe there was some truth to what his wife was saying. Wasn't that what had happened with his parents?

"Come to think of it, my parents—both of them at separate times—laughed when Yahweh spoke. They both laughed at the prospect of having a child in their old age. Yet Yahweh didn't rebuke either of them for laughing. He just restated his promise that I would be born. Given time, they believed the promise. Maybe their initial laughter was faith in embryo."

"Faith in embryo," Rebekah repeated thoughtfully. "I like that idea. It suggests that laughter may not be outright unbelief. If you can't make the leap from unbelief, anxiety or worry to full blown faith or trust—laugh! Use laughter to bridge the river that separates faith and fear, or faith and unbelief. Laugh at the absurdity of the impossible. Laugh at the unlikelihood that God will do the impossible. Giggle when little things happen to indicate that God may indeed give you the desire of your heart. Laugh out loud when you look back at the stepping stones that laughter provided to enable you to cross the river from doubt to full blown faith."

"Wow!" exclaimed Isaac. "I believe I married a preacher!"

37

Faith That Rests

Years passed as Isaac and Rebekah waited for Esau to forgive his brother and for Jacob to return home. Rebekah's fear of losing both her sons was realized. She very seldom saw Esau, and news from his camp was always distressing. Jacob was busy working for Rebekah's brother Laban far away in Paddan Aram. From time to time, word about Jacob and his two wives drifted back from Paddan Aram. It seemed that every message from Jacob brought news of the birth of another son. Rebekah longed to watch her grandchildren grow up and be part of their lives, but that was not to be.

Rebekah died without seeing Jacob and his children and without seeing a positive change in Esau. Isaac buried her in Hebron in the cave where Abraham and Sarah were buried, in the field Abraham had purchased as a burial place for his family. Isaac grieved alone with neither of his sons present to share his grief.

Having passed the Covenant blessing to Jacob and having officially recognized Jacob's purchase of the birthright as both legal and ordained of God, Isaac began to relax. He honored his wife's memory by taking her advice and laughing a lot more.

Isaac prayed for the opportunity to make up for the lost years he had poured into Esau rather than Jacob. God graciously answered his prayer. After twenty years working for his Uncle Laban and ten years living in Shechem, Jacob returned to Hebron where Isaac was living. There God gave Isaac almost twenty years to spend with Jacob and his family. Isaac used that time to pour into his family all the wisdom he had accumulated over his lifetime.

As Isaac observed Jacob and the love he had for Yahweh, he thanked God over and over for overruling his own lack of faith and bestowing the Covenant promises on Jacob.

"Thank you, Lord," Isaac prayed, "for twisting my arm and giving me the faith to believe the promise you made to my wife Rebekah. 'Two nations are in your womb . . . The older will serve the younger.' Thank you that Jacob, not Esau, will lead your chosen people into the future.

"You promised my father Abraham, 'I will make you into a great nation.' Jacob's family now numbers thirteen—twelve sons and a daughter. That is a good start. Some of them are married and have children of their own, so my descendants are well on their way to becoming like the dust of the earth, like the stars of the sky, like the sand on the seashore—uncountable!

"You promised my father Abraham, 'All peoples on earth will be blessed through you.' Laban was blessed through Jacob. Even Esau was blessed when Jacob gave him hundreds of sheep and goats and camels and donkeys. I have no idea how people in the future will be blessed through my descendants, but I believe Your promise.

"As to Esau's future, even that is in your hands. I commit him to you. Have mercy on him, Lord."

* * *

Isaac lived a hundred and eighty years.
Then he breathed his last and died and was
gathered to his people, old and full of years.
And his sons Esau and Jacob buried him.

Genesis 35:28-29

Study Guide

These questions are included for your personal study and reflection and/or for small-group discussion. In many cases there are no right or wrong answers; such questions are designed simply to stimulate your thinking and to encourage you to examine your heart. Some questions are answered in the story, *By Faith Isaac*.

Introduction: Faith Hall of Fame

> "By faith Isaac blessed Jacob and Esau in regard
> to their future" (Hebrews 11:20).

1. What was the big deal about Isaac blessing his sons? Why did it require faith?
2. What are the implications for you today?
3. Do you need faith to bless your family members?

Author's Comment:
The fact that this verse shows up in Hebrews chapter 11 indicates that the blessing was a "big deal." This book will explore exactly what it was that required faith.

Chapter 1: Abram Hears God's Voice

1. Compare Genesis 11:31-2:1 with Acts 7:2-4. Do these verses describe the same event? If not, what are the differences?
2. How did God use Abram's father Terah to get Abram going?
3. Scan the genealogies in Genesis 5 and Genesis 11. What do you notice about the numbers? What effect would this have on people's knowledge of God and the past?

4. Why did God confuse the languages at Babel?
5. What was Noah's occupation (Genesis 9:20)? Does this surprise you?
6. Note the prophecy in Genesis 9:25-27. How has this been fulfilled?
7. Compare Genesis 6:5 and 8:21. What was the condition of man's heart before and after the flood?

Chapter 2: Abram Leaves Haran
Genesis 12:1-9

1. Note Genesis 11:26. Then compare Genesis 11:32 and 12:4. How old was Terah when Abram was born?
2. Abram had already left his home in Ur. Why do you think God asked him to move from Haran?
3. Discuss ways in which God can reveal His will to us.
4. Discuss the witness Abram was providing by example.

Author's Comment:
Terah was not 70 when Abram was born. Nor was Terah the father of triplets. Terah was 70 years old when he became a father for the first time. Compare Terah with Noah.

The Bible says, "After Terah had lived 70 years, he became the father of Abram, Nahor and Haran" (Gen. 11:26). It also says, "After Noah was 500 years old, he became the father of Shem, Ham and Japheth" (Gen. 5:32). We know from Genesis 10:21 and 11:10 that Japheth was older than Shem by two years. Japheth was born 100 years before the Flood.

The Bible often lists names in order of importance to the Redemption story. For example, Genesis 10:1 gives the account of "Shem, Ham and Japheth" (descending order of importance). Then it reverses the order, recording the least important genealogy first (Japheth, vs. 2-4), followed by the second least important (Ham, vs. 6-20), ending up with the most important (Shem, vs. 21-31). Their birth order was none of the above. Their birth order was Japheth, Shem and Ham.

In Abraham's case, putting the clues from Genesis 11:32 and 12:4 together with Genesis 11:26, we deduce that Abraham was certainly not the eldest son, and very likely the youngest.

Abram witnessed both in word and in deed. "There he built an altar to the Lord and *called on* the name of the Lord" (Genesis 12:8, NIV) is rendered ". . . and *preacheth in* the name of Jehovah" in Young's Literal Translation.

Chapter 3: Detour to Egypt
Genesis 12:10-20

1. Hagar is first mentioned in the Bible in Genesis 16:1. Where did Sarai likely find her maidservant?
2. Discuss how we deceive others without outright telling a lie. Is this wrong? Read Leviticus 19:11.

Chapter 4: Abram Separates from Lot
Genesis 13and 14

1. When it became necessary to part company, why did Abram give Lot first choice?
2. What does that tell us about his faith?
3. How did God confirm to Abram that He approved of Abram's actions?

Author's Comment:
The label 'Hebrew' appears first in Genesis 14:13.

Chapter 5: Abram Rescues Lot
Genesis 14

1. Lot got into trouble for not paying taxes to Babylonia. After rescuing Lot, why would Abram turn around and give a tithe/tax to Melchizedek?
2. What was Abram's oath (14:22-24)? How or what can we learn from his attitude?
3. How did Bela king of Sodom behave like Satan? What indication do we have that Abram anticipated his 'bribe'?

4. Bela offered Abram more than the normal spoils of war. What would accepting that bribe imply? Compare Bela's offer to Satan's temptation of Jesus (Matthew 4:8-9).
5. Bela's offer to Abram in the Hebrew language was, "Give me the <u>souls</u> and keep the goods for yourself." Discuss the implications of this.

Chapter 6: The Covenant Promise
Genesis 15

1. In light of what transpired in chapter 14, discuss the impact of God identifying Himself as Abram's shield and very great reward.
2. Whom had Abram chosen as heir to his estate? Why?
3. Immediately after being told that Abram's faith was credited to him for righteousness (v. 6), Abram questioned God (v.8). What hope does this give you for your failures of faith?
4. Which is more important—to have great faith, or to have some faith in a great God?

Chapter 7: "Helping Yahweh"
Genesis 16

1. Life gets messy when we try to "help" God fulfill His promises. What messes arose in Abram and Sarai's situation?
2. Whom does Sarai blame for her woes?
3. Ishmael means "God hears." What had God heard in Hagar's case?
4. What clues do we have in the prophecy about Ishmael that he was not the child of promise? Compare this prophecy with the earlier one to Abram in 12:2-3.

Chapter 8: The Covenant Sign
Genesis 17

1. In this chapter God introduces Himself using a new name. What is it?

2. Why is this name important to Abraham's situation?
3. Share how it is important for you to know God as *El Shaddai* or God Almighty in your current circumstances.
4. Why do you think God named Abraham's son Isaac—'he laughs'? Who was laughing and why?

Chapter 9: Sarah Laughs in Unbelief
Genesis 18:1-15

"Is anything too hard for the Lord?" (v.14)

Share a situation past or present in which you found (or find) it difficult to believe that God is able.

Chapter 10: Bold Enough to Bargain
Genesis 18:16-33

1. Why did God reveal to Abraham His plan for destroying Sodom? (v.17-19)
2. "Will not the Judge of all the earth do right?" (v.25) What do we learn from this story about the balance between God's justice and His mercy?
3. When is it appropriate to bargain with God?
4. What part do Christ-followers play in delaying God's judgment?
5. The book of Job teaches us that being righteous is no guarantee that we will escape suffering and calamity. What does the story of Lot (as well as the story of Noah) tell us about the fate of the righteous when God's final judgment falls? See Luke 17:24-29 and 2 Peter 2:4-10.

Chapter 11: Another Faith Detour
Genesis 20

1. Abraham failed twice over the same issue. Why do you think the Bible includes details of Abraham's failures of faith?

2. What did Abraham have the most difficulty believing God for? (See Gen. 12:10-13.)

Chapter 12: Living Water

In North America we tend to take the availability of water for granted. Only when water is scarce do we understand how vital a resource water is. Ancient civilizations developed proverbs based on the value of water.

- Discuss the appropriateness of the following:
- Proverbs 9:17, KJV. Adultery is likened to stolen waters. Also Proverbs 5:15-18.
- 2 Samuel 14:14, NIV. Death is likened to spilled water.
- Proverbs 18:4; Proverbs 20:5. Wisdom is likened to deep waters.

Chapter 13: Child of Promise
Genesis 21:1-7

The passage says twice that Sarah bore Abraham a son "in <u>his</u> old age" with no reference to hers. Is this focus on Abraham a tribute to his faith, or is it a touch of humor?

Chapter 14: Ishmael and Isaac—Sibling Rivalry or More?
Genesis 21:8-21

"Sarah saw that the son whom Hagar the Egyptian had borne to Abraham was mocking, and she said to Abraham, "Get rid of that slave woman and her son, for that slave woman's son will never share in the inheritance with my son Isaac" (Genesis 21:9-10).

1. Was Sarah justified in sending Hagar and her young son out to the desert where they might die?
2. Was Ishmael's treatment of Isaac typical sibling rivalry?

Author's Comment:

There is never any justification for cruelty or bad behavior, but there is justification for sending Ishmael away. Ishmael's mocking was much more than typical sibling rivalry, and God knew it would only escalate.

If you do the math, you will discover that "Ishmael's mocking" was the beginning of the descendants of Abraham being "enslaved and mistreated four hundred years" (Gen. 15:13).

The Exodus occurred 430 years to the very day from when Abraham set foot in Canaan. "Now the length of time the Israelite people lived in Egypt and Canaan [see Septuagint or margin if your translation mentions only Egypt] was 430 years. At the end of the 430 years, to the very day, all the Lord's divisions left Egypt" (Exodus 12:40-41). Galatians 3:16-17 also tells us that it was 430 years from the Promise to the Law: "The promises were spoken to Abraham and to his seed . . . .

The law, introduced 430 years later [at Sinai] . . . ." The Promise was given in Genesis 12:2-3 when Abraham was 75 years old (v.4) and had arrived in Canaan (v.5).

The mistreatment, which escalated to slavery in Egypt, ended with the Exodus, so it must have started 400 years earlier, when Abraham was 105 years old and Isaac was 5. Galatians throws further light on the subject by saying that Ishmael "persecuted" Isaac. "At that time the son born in the ordinary way persecuted the son born by the power of the Spirit" (Galatians 4:29).

We will never know how God would have sent Ishmael away if Sarah behaved herself, but it would have happened. God would have found a way to ensure that "the slave woman's son will never share in the inheritance with the free woman's son" (Galatians 4:30).

Sarah is just another example that God can use even our failures for His purposes.

Chapter 15: Abimelech and Beersheba
Genesis 21:22-31

Abraham never explained to Abimelech why he gave <u>seven</u> lambs as a witness to the treaty between them. What do you think is the significance of the seven?

Chapter 16: Planting a Faith Garden
Genesis 21:32-34

Why would Abraham, a nomad, plant a tree?

Chapter 17: Son of the Commandment
Genesis 22

1. Discuss how this event was as much a test of Isaac's faith as it was of Abraham's.
2. Discuss the elements in this story that point to Jesus' death on the cross.

Chapter 18: Heaven
Genesis 23

The story, *By Faith Isaac*, has Abraham talking about his permanent home being in Heaven. Clearly Abraham expected to see God face to face after his death, but "Heaven"?

1. What did Old Testament characters know about Heaven? Isn't Heaven a New Testament concept?
2. Is it legitimate to use NT words and concepts to explain OT events?

Author's Comment:
Hebrews 11:10 tells us that Abraham was "looking forward to the city with foundations, whose architect and builder is God." That sounds to me as though Abraham had a pretty good handle on Heaven. I am not

aware of any earthly city whose architect and builder is God. Our cities would be much better planned and built if that were true!

The KJV Old Testament and the Hebrew language use the same word for both the firmament of heaven and the dwelling place of God. This forces us to use the context to discern which kind of heaven is implied. If the Bible used a capital H for God's dwelling, it would be much easier for us to understand! NIV differentiates for us by using the word 'sky' for the atmosphere and space. This reduces KJV's 313 uses of the word 'heaven' to 174 in NIV.

In the NIV, Abraham, Isaac and Jacob used the word 'heaven' ten times. I will use a capital H to clarify.

Abraham knew God as the Creator of Heaven and earth (Gen. 14:19, 22). The angel of God called to Hagar from Heaven (Gen. 21:17). Similarly, the angel of the Lord called to Abraham from Heaven (Gen. 22:11, 15) when Abraham was about to sacrifice Isaac. And when instructing his servant to get a wife for Isaac, Abraham asked him to swear by "the God of Heaven" (Gen. 24:3,7). Isaac blessed (if you can call it that!) Esau with the words, "Your dwelling will be away from the earth's richness, away from the dew of Heaven above" (Gen. 27:39), which told Esau that he didn't live under God's blessing. The final references to Heaven in Genesis are in the story of Jacob's dream of a ladder reaching to Heaven (Gen. 28:12,17).

I think we don't give Old Testament saints enough credit for what they knew about the Good News. They didn't know the Messiah by the name Jesus, but those who were closest to God knew plenty—especially Enoch, Abraham and Moses. Gal. 3:8 tells us: "Scripture foresaw that God would justify the Gentiles by faith, and announced the gospel in advance to Abraham: 'All nations will be blessed through you.'" If this message was the gospel, God must have told Abraham much more than is recorded in the Old Testament.

Chapter 19: Lot Pays a Visit
Genesis 22:20-24; Genesis 19:1-29; Genesis 19:30-38

1. What do you think of Lot, based on the Genesis account?
2. What light does the New Testament shed on Lot's character? See 2 Peter 2:7-8. What warning does this present to us?

3. The first Bible references to child sacrifice mention Molech, the god of the Ammonites. See Leviticus 18:21 and 20:2. Discuss the possibility that child sacrifice was invented by Ammon, son/grandson of Lot and that other Canaanite nations learned it from Ammon.

Author's comment:

An internet search reveals that child sacrifice was practiced by the following:

Pre-Columbian cultures:
- Aztec culture (Aztec empire 1325—1521 AD)
- Inca culture (Inca empire 1200—1572 AD)
- Moche culture (100—800 AD)

Ancient Near East:
- In Knossos (Greece) and dating to Minoan Crete (2600-1200 BC).
- Phoenicia (1550 to 300 BC) and Carthage (Carthage founded 9th century BC)

Of these cultures only one, Minoan Crete, started before Moab and Ammon were born. Lot's sons were born around the same time as Isaac (2066 BC). As we don't know when within the 1400 years of the Cretan period Cretans began sacrificing children to their gods, there is plenty of room to speculate that the Ammonites and Moabites invented child sacrifice.

Chapter 20: Lessons from Lot
Genesis 19:1-29; Genesis 19:30-38

Abraham and Lot had much in common. They came from the same family and their lives followed parallel tracks for many years.

1. What experiences and character traits did Abraham and Lot have in common?

2. In what ways did Abraham and Lot differ in choices and deeds?
3. What was the fork in the road for Lot? What motivated his choices?
4. What can we learn from the differences between Abraham and Lot?

Chapter 21: A Wife for Isaac
Genesis 24

1. What can we learn from Abraham's servant about discerning the Lord's will?
2. What do you find remarkable about Rebekah?
3. What do we learn in this chapter about Isaac's personality and his relationship with God? (vs. 62-67)

Chapter 22: Yahweh Speaks to Rebekah
Genesis 25:19-23

This is the first record in the Bible since Adam and Eve that God spoke to a woman. Why do you think the Lord spoke to Rebekah and not to Isaac?

Chapter 23: Twins!
Genesis 25:24-28

1. Malachi 1:2-3 and Romans 9:13 tell us that the Lord loved Jacob and hated Esau. We know that the Lord loves everyone in the world (John 3:16) and is not willing that any should perish, so what are the verses in Malachi and Romans telling us?
2. How do these verses impact your view of Isaac's and Rebekah's attitudes toward their sons in Genesis 25:28?

Author's comment:
Isaac and Rebekah have received a lot of bad press for "loving" one son over the other. Before judging them in the light of our culture, consider that this may be the Bible's way of saying that Isaac treated Esau as the firstborn while Rebekah treated Jacob as the firstborn.

Chapter 24: The Death of Abraham
Genesis 25:1-18

1. Abraham "was gathered to his people" (25:8). This expression is used of what other people? See Genesis 25:17; 35:29; 49:33; Numbers 20:24,26; Numbers 27:13; 31:2; Deut. 32:50.
2. What does this tell us about Ishmael?

Author's comment:
A concubine in Bible times could refer (1) to a mistress or (2) to a wife who didn't require a bride price. A slave woman or a prostitute or a woman who was not a virgin at the time of marriage did not require a bride price. Such a woman would be a second-class wife, not as highly esteemed as a woman who was a virgin at the time of marriage.

Abraham's concubines (v.6) were Hagar and Ketura. Ketura is also called Abraham's wife (v.1), so Abraham had married her without having to pay a bride price. Abraham never married Hagar.

Chapter 25: Friction Over the Firstborn

1. In ancient times was the firstborn son always given special privileges?
2. Under what circumstances might the firstborn forfeit his birthright?

Chapter 26: Signs of Rebellion: Esau's Character
Malachi 1—3

1. What kind of character was Esau?
2. See what the Bible says about him in Hebrews 12:16 and Genesis 25:34. See also Obadiah 1:8-10.
3. What was God's attitude toward Esau? (Malachi 1:2-4) Was that attitude justified?
4. Study the book of Malachi for clues to the actions and attitudes of Esau, and later of the priests, which brought the Lord's displeasure.

Author's Comment:
The clearest picture of the sins of Esau comes from the book of Malachi, in which the Lord denounces the priests of Judah for behaving like Esau. Studying their actions gives us insight into what Esau did wrong.

First, they did not give the Lord Almighty the respect due to Him (Malachi 1:6). Then they showed contempt for His name by offering defiled food on His altar (1:6,7). They offered blind, injured, lame and diseased animals as sacrifices (1:8, 13). They switched acceptable animals for blemished ones (1:14).

They profaned the Lord's name by proclaiming that the food at His table was contemptible and their duties burdensome (1:12, 13).

Neither Esau nor the priests of Judah honored the Lord or His name (2:1-2). The Lord was determined that the covenant He made with Abraham be carried on by someone who would revere Him and stand in awe of His name (2:4-5).

"A detestable thing has been committed in Israel and in Jerusalem: Judah has desecrated the sanctuary the Lord loves by marrying women who worship a foreign god. As for the man who does this, whoever he may be, <u>may the Lord remove him from the tents of Jacob</u>—even though he brings an offering to the Lord Almighty" (2:11-12). What the Lord said of Judah in the book of Malachi was certainly true of Esau.

The next verses suggest that Esau was not faithful to his wives (2:14-16). This would fit with the declaration in Hebrews that Esau was sexually immoral.

Malachi 2:13 evokes memories of Esau's tears when he learned Isaac had blessed Jacob. "Another thing you do: You flood the Lord's altar with tears. You weep and wail because he no longer looks with favor on your offerings or accepts them with pleasure from your hands."

Malachi 2:17 sounds like something Esau would say about Jacob. "All who do evil are good in the eyes of the Lord, and he is pleased with them" or "Where is the God of justice?"

Yes, Jacob did wrong to use deception. Leviticus 19:11 says, "Do not deceive one another." But Esau's complaint that God is unjust to choose Jacob simply makes the Lord weary (Malachi 2:17).

No wonder the Lord Almighty, foreseeing Esau's attitude and actions, chose Jacob over Esau to perpetuate Abraham's line!

Chapter 27: Jacob Buys the Birthright
Genesis 25:29-34

1. Why did Esau sell his birthright for so little? See Genesis 25:34.
2. Esau later accused Jacob of deceiving him to get the birthright (Genesis 27:36). Is that accusation true?

Chapter 28: Isaac Hears God's Voice
Genesis 26:1-6

1. Finally, when Isaac was over 90 years old, God spoke to him.
2. What did God say to him that He had already said to Abraham?
3. What did He say that was new?

Chapter 29: Isaac's Failure of Faith
Genesis 26:7-33

1. Compare Isaac's failure of faith (26:7-11) with Abraham's (20:1-17). What are the similarities?
2. What similarities do you see in the events that followed? Compare 21:22-33 with 26:12-33. What differences?
3. What indication did God give Isaac that He had forgiven him? (26:12-14)

Chapter 30: The Rebel
Genesis 10:8-12, 25; 11:1-9

1. Do you recognize the names of any of the cities Nimrod founded? What do you know about those cities whose names you recognize? What does this tell you about Nimrod?
2. What is God's reaction to people like Nimrod? See Psalm 2:1-6, 9.
3. What does Genesis 10:25 indicate regarding the timing of the story of the Tower of Babel?

Author's Comment:
Some Jewish traditions portray Nimrod as living and ruling at the time Abraham was born and later feeling threatened by Abraham's belief in one true God. I cannot accept these traditions as credible. By the time God confused man's language at the Tower of Babel, man's lifespan had shrunk to about 200 years. One tradition says Nimrod lived 215 years. Abram was born 251 years after Peleg. This would mean that if Nimrod was alive when Peleg was born, he would have died before Abraham was born.

Chapter 31: Esau Shows His Colors
Genesis 26:34-35; Genesis 36; Hebrews 12:16

1. What light does the New Testament throw on Esau's character in Hebrews 12:16?
2. What is suggested by the fact that the name Judith (praise) was changed to Oholibamah (tent of the high places)? Compare Gen. 26:34 with 36:2, 24-25.
3. What did Isaac and Rebekah think of Esau's wives? Genesis 26:35; 27:46; 28:1,6
4. Consider the circumstances under which Esau took a third wife. What does this tell us? Genesis 28:6-9.
5. What light does Malachi 2:11-12 throw on the subject?

Author's Comment:
Research into Canaanite religious practices suggests that there was a lot of sexual immorality involved.

Esau seems to have married Ishmael's daughter simply to appease his parents and deflect his father's anger, rather than out of love. ("Oops! Dad is really angry. I better choose a wife he will approve of.") I also see his choice as a compromise between his more religious relatives in the north and his relatives through Hagar.

God's ideal for marriage has always been one man, one woman. Of the three patriarchs, Isaac was the only one to adhere to that.

Chapter 32: By Faith Isaac
Genesis 27:1-40

1. Whose idea was it to obtain the Covenant blessing by deception? Why do you think history has blamed Jacob?
2. Isaac could have retracted his blessing of Jacob, but he didn't. Why not?
3. Compare the two blessings spoken by Isaac. What contrasts do you see? What are the positive aspects of Esau's blessing?

Chapter 33: The Fear of Isaac
Genesis 31:42, 53

1. What name of God resulted from Isaac's blessing of Jacob?
2. What do you understand from this name?

Chapter 34: Jacob Leaves Home
Genesis 27:41—28:5

1. How did Esau react to Jacob's receiving the Covenant blessing? (Genesis 27:41)
2. Why did Isaac send Jacob to Paddan Aram? (Genesis 28:1-5)

Chapter 35: Esau Takes a Third Wife
Genesis 28:6-9

1. What motivated Esau to take a third wife?
2. Who was she, and why did Esau choose her?

Chapter 37: Faith That Rests
Hebrews 11:20

In what way was Isaac's act of blessing his sons an act of faith? What did he need to believe?

Bibliography

Abarim Publications' Biblical Name Vault, http://www.abarim-publications.com

Curry, Rex, "Yarek Oath, Circumcision, God's Inner Thigh, Kneeling and Praying Hands", http://rexcurry.net/yarek-oath-praying-hands-kneeling-inner-thigh-circumcision.html

Josephus, Flavius, "Antiquities of the Jews, Book 1", in *The Works of Flavius Josephus* in three volumes, translated by William Whiston, Oxford, 1839.

Livingston, Dr. David P., Associates for Biblical Research, "Nimrod: Who was he? Was he godly or evil?" originally published in ABR's BIBLE AND SPADE 14.3 (2001), pp. 67-72.

Mindel, Nissan, "Abraham's Early Life", http://www.chabad.org/library/article_cdo/aid/112063/jewish/Abrahams-Early-Life.htm

Matthew Henry Commentary on the Whole Bible (Complete), Genesis 10, originally written in 1706.

Rachel's Tomb, http://en.wikipedia.org/wiki/Rachel's_Tomb

Spangler, Ann, *Praying the Names of God*, Zondervan, Grand Rapids, Michigan, 2004.

Steinberg, David, "Where is Your Heart? Some Body Part Metaphors and Euphemisms in Biblical Hebrew", http://www.houseofdavid.ca

Unger, Merrill F., *Unger's Bible Dictionary*, Chicago: Moody Press, third edition, 1966, reprinted 1969.

Vine, W.E., Merrill F. Unger, William White, Jr., *Vine's Complete Expository Dictionary of Old and New Testament Words*, Nashville: Thomas Nelson Publishers, 1985.

Wight, Fred H., Manners and Customs of Bible Lands, Chicago: Moody Press, 1980.

Young, Robert, *Analytical Concordance to the Holy Bible*, London: Lutterworth Press, eighth edition, 1939, reprinted 1967.

Young, Robert, *Young's Literal Translation of the Bible*, Grand Rapids: Baker Book House, revised edition, 1898.

____, Methuselah, www.christiananswers.net/dictionary/methuselah.html, and http://www.christconnections.com/Word/Methuselah.pdf

www.ingramcontent.com/pod-product-compliance
Lightning Source LLC
LaVergne TN
LVHW091701070526
838199LV00050B/2236